Never Understood

Never Understood

The Jesus and Mary Chain

William and Jim Reid

(with the assistance of Ben Thompson)

 hachette
BOOKS

New York

Hachette Books

Hachette Book Group

1290 Avenue of the Americas

New York, NY 10104

HachetteBooks.com

Twitter.com/HachetteBooks

Instagram.com/HachetteBooks

First US Edition: September 2024

Originally published in Great Britain by White Rabbit, an imprint of The Orion Publishing Group Ltd

Published by Hachette Books, an imprint of Hachette Book Group, Inc. The Hachette Books name and logo is a trademark of the Hachette Book Group.

The Hachette Speakers Bureau provides a wide range of authors for speaking events. To fi nd out more, go to hachettespeakersbureau.com or email HachetteSpeakers@hbgusa.com.

Books by Hachette Books may be purchased in bulk for business, educational, or promotional use. For information, please contact your local bookseller or Hachette Book Group Special Markets Department at: special.markets@hbgusa.com.

The publisher is not responsible for websites (or their content) that are not owned by the publisher.

Typeset by Input Data Services Ltd, Bridgwater, Somerset

Library of Congress Cataloging-in-Publication Data has been applied for.

ISBNs: 9780306835513 (hardcover); 9780306835537 (ebook)

Printed in Canada

MRQ-T

Printing 1, 2024

William:
To my beauty, Bernadette

Jim:
To those who said we wouldn't last a year – we're alive and we thrive. To Simone and Candice for the good things I thought I'd never have. And to Rachel, my love, you kept me breathing. X Also immeasurable love to Linda aka Sister Vanilla – the Mary Chain's UN. She is a sister in a million.

Contents

Part 1
Glasgow (1958–66)

William

Being poor is like a real cold bath – nobody wants it, but in some ways it's good for you. It brings all of your senses together.

I grew up sharing a bathroom with three other families. If that doesn't teach you respect for other people's personal space, then nothing will. To this day I can never feel that I wouldn't say thanks if someone opens the door for me. If I'm in a hotel in LA and someone just walks through a door someone else has held open for them without saying anything, I'll be like 'What the fuck, dude?'

Imagine if you've got to do a shit and lots of people can hear you just walking down the stairs to the communal toilet. You can't stay in there too long, because you don't want your next-door neighbour knocking on the door asking 'Are you finished?' What do you do? Especially if you had a nasty situation going on digestively, which was quite likely, because our diet wasn't great – we were eating just what my ma and da ate, which was meat and potatoes, chips almost every night, then in the summer chips with some cold ham and some lettuce and tomato. That was the summers in Scotland. This might be why in later life I've been drawn to live in the wide open spaces of Arizona – because in all the American films I watched in my teens, I never saw anybody sharing a toilet.

My earliest memories of Glasgow are from 1961, when Jim was born. I was three at the time, and what I remember is my granda telling me that I was still his favourite – I think he was the only one who noticed that I was at all upset. It wasn't that I was threatened by the new arrival, it was just a big change.

My granda was a bit of a character. He was a street bookie, which meant what he did was stand on the corner and give better odds than William Hill. I say he was a bookie, but in truth he was a bookie's runner, because if he was an actual bookie I would've been brought up in a giant house in Paisley or Rutherglen, instead of a tenement in Parkhead, about half a minute from Celtic Park.

We lived so close to the stadium that we could hear it when somebody scored a goal. If Celtic went one up, my house reverberated with the sound of the enemy. I shouldn't say 'the enemy', except that's exactly what they were, because I was born to be in the Rangers version of Islamic State. I was the young idealist who just believed in everything they told me. If someone had said 'Strap this bomb to your chest for the sake of Rangers' I would definitely have considered it. Growing up in Glasgow in the sixties, the Rangers and Celtic thing was furious, although I should make it clear that for most people – except the idiots who were already violent anyway – it never came to violence. It was mostly just a weird stand-off.

My da was very capable of hurling abuse out of the window at the Celtic fans walking up to the stadium on match days – in fact he did that often – but there was absolutely no feeling that he was going to punch someone who was a Celtic supporter. He might have an argument with them and tell them how shit Celtic are – that was to be expected – but it went no further. Have you ever seen that phenomenon on the internet which shows you two dogs separated by a fence and they're really growling at each other, then they lift the fence and they just look down at the ground, then they lower the fence again and they go right back to growling? Rangers and Celtic was like that. My da was that dog.

Or maybe I was. You know when you walk somewhere with your dog and your dog has to sit outside? I was a bit like that with my da when I was small. Sometimes he would take me to the pub and I'd be left standing outside in the street because children couldn't go in. That was one reason why I loved going to Ibrox so much as a child. It was the greatest thing that was happening because your da would take you and you loved your da, so spending time with him when you were a wee boy was just brilliant. There were so many amazing things going on at the same time. Looking back from an adult perspective, it was like someone had said you had won a million dollars.

It wasn't just about being with your da, it was about meeting his pals. 'Hey Jim, how're you doin?' They would greet him in deep voices, then they'd see you and say 'How you doing, wee man?' You felt special, and they'd sit you up on your da's shoulders, but then you had to go for a pee and when you got back he'd be all depressed because Rangers were losing. It wasn't just because my da liked them that I loved Rangers, it was my da's da and his da before him – it was tribal. And my sense of belonging didn't even depend on them being there. Back then, if you were in the know you would be aware that they opened the gates at half time . . . Also, as a wee boy you could walk up to a man and ask him to lift you into the game and he would illegally flip you over the turnstiles. I should say that this practice was no longer considered socially acceptable once you were in your early twenties.

Jim

I hated football as a kid. William was quite into it and occasionally as a small boy I did go to Ibrox with him and my dad, but I just found it horribly uncomfortable and excruciatingly boring . . . The only thing that grabbed my attention visually was when you walked up the steps to get to the top of the stands and looked down at the colour of the pitch and the strips of the players – that spectacle was amazing, for about a minute, but the excitement soon wore off after an hour and a half standing next to some old man who kept farting in your face.

On the rare occasions when you could actually see any of what was going on down on the pitch, Scottish football was just so fucking boring – it was like a game of pinball. There seemed to be no skill on display. I didn't like it, didn't understand it and didn't want anything to do with it. On top of that, the Scottish weather is not that pleasant and the facilities were as basic as you could imagine . . . It was bad enough if you were a kid – if you were a woman who needed to go to the toilet, forget about it . . .

William

My ma's maiden name was McLeish – which is Jim's middle name. Scottish first names of my generation were all William or James, with Adam and Stuart as outliers. It was quite an entrenched order that you all had to be called the same thing. There were so many Williams and Jameses in my family, I used to think it was the product of a lack of imagination, or even a lack of courage in terms of not wanting to disappoint your da and granda, who were still alive and expected you to name your kids after them. You couldn't be certain because nothing was said, but sometimes if it burns like a fire, it is a fire.

That's why I'm William Reid and my middle name's Adam. I've got two cousins called Adam and an uncle and two cousins called William, which is usually shortened to Bill. In fact I'm the only one who actually allowed myself to be called by my full name because that was the only way to establish a mark of distinction. William was a nerd's name before the category of nerd existed – a name for all the indie-kids-in-waiting who grew up feeling like 'I can't quite agree with anything, I just want to go and watch *Star Trek.*'

Me and Jim would both be into *Star Trek*, though strangely enough I hated *Star Wars* later when that came along, and still do. *Star Trek* felt like it was about grown-up situations, like two women kissing or a white man kissing a black woman. *Star Wars* was just stupid fighting in space. It was amateurish. I never went to see *Star Wars* when it came out, but you take it in by osmosis – I know who Chewbacca is and all that nonsense.

One day in later life I sat down with my son, Keir – who is named after the Scottish socialist and founder of the Labour Party Keir Hardie, so I guess I broke with tradition on that one – and said 'OK son, show me the best *Star Wars*.' He played it to me and I said 'This is garbage, this is the stuff they used to put on Saturday morning picture shows in the fifties.' Only time will tell the damage that exchange did to him, but I had no option but to speak my truth.

In Parkhead we lived on the top floor of the tenement building. Everything had to be blue because of the Celtic and Rangers thing I mentioned before, but my da was colour-blind, so he didn't know that we had a green phone. He couldn't tell the difference but he had his suspicions. 'What colour is that phone?' 'Blue, da, blue.'

My ma and da slept in the living room – there was an alcove where you pulled a curtain across – while me and Jim had the other room, overlooking the Barr's Irn-Bru factory. When I wasn't at school I loved to sit and stare out of the window at what went on in that building. I was fascinated by it. The production line which brought Scotland's favourite soft drink to the world gave off no smell, but the manufacturing and distribution process required endless lorries backing up, loading in these huge pallets and then driving away to make room for the next consignment. It was an efficient industrial machine, which when I realised the nature of the end product – 'That's *Irn-Bru*!' – seemed almost miraculous.

Jim

I have got memories of the big brownstone block we lived in when we were in Glasgow, but not many, because I was only four when we left. In terms of luxuries, there were none. Each flat was two rooms with a not very hygienic toilet on the landing, which was like an outhouse but indoors, with a rough wooden door. You had to time your visits not to coincide with the neighbours', otherwise you'd hear their feet on the landing and warning shouts of 'Get out o' there, son.'

We all lived pushed up against each other, and there was no privacy and no way to get clean. Everybody used to go to the public baths every week – not the swimming bath, an actual bath – but because I was a teeny wee kid I used to get bathed in the sink which was in the living room.

The layout of that place is indelibly stamped on my memory – I could draw you a floor-plan of that flat and it would be absolutely accurate. There was a tiny little hallway, then the living room with the sink and an alcove which was just big enough for a double bed with a curtain you could pull across, which was where me and William slept. I always thought it would've made more sense for my mum and dad to sleep in there but they didn't – they had the one separate bedroom on the far side of the living room. I remember lying there behind that thin curtain listening to the TV and trying to get to sleep. My mum and dad used to watch the sci-fi show *The Outer Limits* which always scared the bejesus out of me.

It was so cramped it was no wonder my parents were eager to move when the opportunity arose. People were flocking out of the city to the relatively wide open spaces of East Kilbride at that time – it was mass overspill. My mother's sister Auntie Matty (her real name was Martha but nobody called her that) was the first one to go and she said it was great. We went out to see her there when we still lived in Parkhead and that was when my parents decided to apply. They were really pleased when we got a council house and the day we left in the furniture van there were people shouting abuse at us from the tenement – 'Away ye go ye snobby bastards' – which seemed to confirm we had made the right decision. It was good training for leaving Creation for Warners eighteen years or so later.

It wasn't ideal in the tenements but there was a sense of community in those places that never seemed to translate into the tower blocks which replaced them. Both my mum's mum and my dad's mum and dad ended up in those blocks, but they never really saw them as home – they felt very disconnected from everyone around them. Especially my granny on my mum's side, who got moved into a tower block in Parkhead which she absolutely hated – she never felt like she belonged there. I used to go up and stay with her at the weekends in the hope of making her feel better about it, but I didn't like it there either.

You had no idea who was living next door to you, there was no feeling of anyone looking out for each other and the only people you ever saw were the little skinheads who hung around at the bottom of the stairs and were probably best avoided. I realise this probably sounds like I'm looking back at the tenements through rose-coloured glasses – and maybe I am a little – but I lived through this as a child and it's a fact. I don't know why, but it felt like the spirit was kind of ripped out of people when they were thrown into those places.

They basically gutted Glasgow in the 1960s and '70s. Those tenements that we lived in had originally been quite grand and beautiful buildings, they'd just been allowed to get incredibly run down. Our flat had high ceilings and the ancient fixtures and fittings looked like they would once have been quite classy, but by the time we got there everything was crumbling and it wasn't very well appointed. If only somebody could've invested a bit of money in those buildings, they would've been well worth saving.

I watched a documentary on BBC2 once where a bunch of Glaswegians got together to refurbish their tenement building. So rather than being shunted out to some horrible newly built ghetto where nobody had any hope and the only activity people had during the day was to knock shit out of each other or wait for the ice cream van, a group of neighbours pooled their resources to get their tenement block totally refurbished with toilets and kitchens. It was a total success story, but why couldn't the councils have figured that one out under their own steam? They were way too quick with the wrecking ball – those buildings just needed a bit of care and attention.

You couldn't just put it down to fashion and modernism and wanting to build cities in sky, because the one we lived in finally came down at the back end of the process, and by that time people were already complaining about the high-rise flats with puddles of piss in lifts that never worked anyway. I think there must've been a lot of backhanders flying around the local council. Someone must've been making money out of knocking up the dumps everyone got shipped out to, because it certainly wasn't being done for the benefit of the unfortunate bastards that were going to live there.

William

I think my da had worked in a bakery before I was born, but by the time I came along he was a hospital porter, because I remember my mother telling me he had to get called from a shift there when she went into labour. Then he worked in a carpet factory called Templeton's for a while. A lot of my uncles on my ma's side worked there too. It used to be that way when a couple got married in Glasgow, the man went with the woman's family, so my da came from Dennistoun but he didn't live there.

My ma and da were in their twenties in the sixties, but they were as likely to go and see The Beatles or the Stones as they were to go to New York and take heroin – there was just no way. When me and Jim were older and starting to get into music, we would ask them 'Why didn't you go and see The Beatles and the Stones? You could've seen them for two and six!' But they'd just say 'That was for teenagers . . .' Nowadays you can be a teenager till you're in your sixties – I'm living proof of that – but it wasn't like that then.

When we were kids, I didn't think Mick Jagger actually existed – how could he? His life was too much like a great story – that he just somehow met this guy called Keith on a train and he was carrying some blues records – and yet it was all true. It was the same with The Beatles. How can you have four geniuses in Liverpool all in the same generation? And fuck you if you're raising an eyebrow – I am calling Ringo a genius because all the drummer friends I have will tell you that he is one.

I'll be honest and say that when I was growing up I thought Charlie Watts was the better drummer. He had this kind of tribal sound – real basic. Reading articles and books throughout my life I learnt that Charlie's secret was that he was really half bored with rock 'n' roll. When he played jazz I'm assuming he was all flamboyant like jazz drummers are, but when he played rock 'n' roll it was really more like 'I'm going to give you what you think of as the basic rock 'n' roll backbeat and I'm not going to do any more.' Which was fine with the Stones because that was all they wanted.

Every time the call came to go out on tour he'd be thinking 'Oh fuck, let's get through this, it's a lot of money – how can I refuse it?' The first tour or two it was 'OK, I'll buy a car,' the next one 'I'll buy a nice little house.' Half a century later, he's on his eightieth car and twelfth house thinking 'Fuck me, how much longer can I do this for?'

There are certain bands that have just been there my whole life. The Stones, The Beach Boys, The Kinks, The Who . . .

shaping my consciousness from my first moments as an aware human being, an immature one maybe, but even though I didn't know it at the time, giving your attention to something was very important when you were young, because you would study the things that interested you with great enthusiasm, and that's how your brain would grow. The Beach Boys were just an engine of sunshine, with so many different colours and variations. My mind opened up like a flower when I listened to them, but most of all it was The Beatles I grew up with.

I went to see *A Hard Day's Night* in Parkhead when I was five. I know that seems young to be going to the cinema, but it was only five minutes' walk away and a bunch of us would go together. At about the same age I also remember walking on my own to a railway bridge with a 100-foot drop and standing on the edge. My whole life I've looked back to that moment and thought 'Why did I do that?' Maybe it's just being young, because being young is mental and brilliant, and that's why most great music – unless you're talking about people like Bob Dylan or Paul McCartney who have seemed to be able to do it forever – is made by brilliant, young, mental people.

You can understand the challenge I face, as at the time of writing I am sixty-four – the actual age Paul McCartney chose to represent the idea of being unimaginably old. I'm always gonna make music, but who is my audience at this point? Should it just be old men and women? Should I be playing in Butlin's? Would the best thing be to just go in the garage, play loud music on the car stereo and leave the engine running?

Jim

Our life in Parkhead was by no means a comfortable existence, but I do have fond memories of those tenements and the streets that tied them together. Even now I often have dreams where I'm back there. I really wish those buildings still existed because in some kind of weird way it felt like part of me was torn down with them. It was some years after we moved away when they finally got demolished – we left in 1966 but we carried on going back to Parkhead regularly because lots of our relatives lived there, so that's where family gatherings would happen – but even when that finally happened around 1973–74, I really felt the loss of them.

The piles of rubble remained for almost a decade as a mute testament to lives left behind. In the early eighties, when my East Kilbride friend Stuart passed his driving test, we sometimes used to drive into Glasgow, and when we drove down our street the road was still there but there was just a pile of dust and stones where the tenements had been. I remember seeing a kerbstone that would've been right outside the entrance to our flat and thinking 'That'll be a nice souvenir – I'll go home and get a chisel,' but somehow we never got around to it.

William

Because I lived the first seven years of my life in Glasgow, that's still where I get my accent from. Like the Jesuits say, give me the boy till he is seven years old and I'll show you the man. Jim's got more of an East Kilbride accent than me. So has my wee sister, Linda, because we'd moved before she was born. She sounds so much more posh than me – almost Edinburgh in a way – whereas I'm the 'Shut the windae' guy. Left to my own devices I won't say 'go home', I'll say 'gay hame'. Jim's lived in England for years so maybe that's the reason his accent has softened, but then again I've lived in America almost as long, and you can't hear a lot of it when I talk . . .

Jim

Me and William had exactly the same accent when we lived in East Kilbride. When we moved to London I found that I got really fucked off with having to repeat everything, so it wasn't a conscious decision to soften my accent, it just happened that way over time. I lived in Fulham for a while when I first got to London. I'd get in a taxi and ask 'Take me to Fulham please' and the driver would say 'You what, mate? You want to see a fillum?' 'No, no, no.' It was that way with everything, I had to repeat everything I said, and over time I learnt to say things in a way where I knew I wouldn't have to repeat it, whereas William is a bit more pig-headed than me and doesn't give a fuck, so he'll say 'Ye bastard ye, take me to Fillum.' The driver would go 'Oh fuck! I'll take you anywhere you want, mate. Could you write that destination down on a piece of paper?'

He lived in LA for years and now he lives in Arizona and he still kind of stumbles around talking like Rab C. Nesbitt. I don't know how he gets by – he says he moderates it with Americans . . .

William

One last thing I remember is that whenever the big teams came to play at Celtic Park, people would have to run the gauntlet of a gathering of baby-faced Glasgow gangsters to park their cars around the stadium. I don't want to incriminate myself too much but surely the statute of limitations will have passed by now on a little bit of juvenile extortion? You would see someone stop their car and approach them with a knowing leer: 'Hey mister, maybe your motor will get scraped if you leave it here, but if you make it worth our while, we can make sure it won't.'

In truth it was the older boys doing the real intimidation. They would do the deal on the basis of all the cruel, evil stuff that might happen while the car owner was away watching the game, then me and my wee pals would offer them a way out by promising in our high voices 'Yeah, we'll watch it' – it was like good cop, bad cop. Of course, if you did actually talk the driver out of some money, you never actually watched the car, 'cos there was no real danger at all. We were like Fox News, exaggerating the threat level for our own material gain.

Part 2
East Kilbride

i. Before Punk

Jim

East Kilbride was by no means luxurious in absolute terms, but compared to where we'd come from, it absolutely was. We got there in 1966 and I didn't go to school till a year or so after, so it was different for William as he was already at primary school in Glasgow and therefore had to change schools. My memory is that we both adjusted to the move quite well, but I can't be sure because we weren't close at that stage. By the time I'd got to East Kilbride I'd figured out that there was no point tagging along with him because William wasn't up for it – the three-year age difference was just too much. Who wants a little brother following them around?

William

In Glasgow I was popular and sociable and had tons of friends, so when we moved to East Kilbride I was confident I was going to fit in, especially as we already had family there – our cousin James had moved there about a year before us, which was how we knew East Kilbride was not just an option, but coming from Glasgow it looked like a paradise. You didn't have to go to the public baths any more, and you could have a shit in your own house. But for some reason it didn't work out that way.

I just felt a bit cut off – like I'd been amputated from Parkhead, and the memory of the place I used to be was left behind as a phantom limb. For reasons I couldn't quite get straight in my head, I struggled to make friends. On the face of it, East Kilbride was a great place to grow up – it was more suburb than concrete jungle, and you were never far away from woods and rivers and trees to climb and fields to play football in – but I found it hard.

I definitely had depression as a child and a teenager, but I don't think anybody in our circles or even wider society in Britain would've called it depression, because I don't think a depressed child existed in the sixties and seventies. How it manifested with me was it would be a beautiful sunny day and I would be upstairs reading comics. A friend would come to the door asking 'Is William coming out to play?' And my response would be 'I don't wanna! I don't wanna see him!'

I liked my friends, and I liked going out to play football in the park, but then there I was sitting in my room alone with my *Batman* comic or *Amazing Stories,* worrying about why I didn't want to go out. It's natural to want to be by yourself sometimes, but when it becomes a reflex you can't get the better of, that's depression. I know this because I've experienced it as an adult as well, and if it happened to one of my kids now, I would take them to a child psychiatrist, but of course my ma and da weren't going to do that because at that stage it wasn't a thing you did. Children were not really human beings yet in terms of being seen and heard.

Even though Jim and I have been very aware of each other's mental states as adults, for some reason the subject of whether he suffered as I did when we were children has never really come up. Maybe that's a hangover from the time when it was something you weren't really supposed to talk about . . .

Jim

I had a feeling of isolation right through my primary school. There were periods where I had some level of normality, but there was a lot of times where I just slunk about on my own and couldn't connect with other kids properly. I never really felt like I fitted in, but in a way that's just me: I didn't want to be the life and soul of the party, or even the centre of attention – I still don't. I realise that's a strange thing for someone who ended up being the frontman of a band to say, but there you go, it's the truth.

There were no thoughts of stardom when I was a kid, no glimpse of the big time at a school talent contest or walk-on part in a nativity play which hinted at something more. There was none of that 'I'm so talented why can nobody see it?' kind of shit. It was pretty much 'Keep your head down and try to get through it.'

William

Because I still wanted to support my team but my da and my uncles only wanted to go to the football a few times a year – they were just as happy watching it on telly on a Saturday night, really – I joined the East Kilbride branch of the Rangers supporters club. The meeting point was in Calderwood Square and I'd get up at five or six in the morning – five if it was Aberdeen, 'cos that would just mean driving all day – to be down there for the pick up. If you think of it from today's perspective, it was quite outrageous. I was only eleven or twelve and I'd be going away hundreds of miles with a bunch of men I didn't even know and my ma and da didn't bat an eyelid. I'd say 'I'm away tomorrow to see Aberdeen,' and they'd say, 'Who are you going with?', 'Rangers supporters club', 'Oh OK.' That was the kind of trust in institutions that people had back then, which is obviously how a lot of bad things ended up happening, but I was lucky that they didn't happen to me. Quite the opposite in fact, as the older guys on the bus would always take care of me. If I never had enough money they would buy me a bridie, which is like a cheese and onion pastie. It can be a nice delicacy but if you buy it at a football stadium it's a cold lump of lard. It still tasted good to me. I had patience for the travelling – I thought to myself 'I'm going here for a reason.' If you're thinking 'That's good preparation for your rock 'n' roll touring lifestyle later on' then you're quite right. Jim wasn't into football – he's not a football guy, little twit that he is. How can you not be into football?

My da used to like going to the pictures more than the football. We'd been in East Kilbride two or three years by the time they opened the cinema. One of the first things that happened was the younger one from *Steptoe and Son* – Harry H. Corbett – came to do a personal appearance. This was written about in the local paper as a major news story and I remembered thinking at the time that if I had the money I would've went to see him.

Jim

Famous people were like distant gods. The idea that somebody famous could be in your eye-line was simply preposterous. One of the most surreal moments of our childhood was when we were just playing out in the street and Lulu came walking down the road and went into our next door neighbour's house. Fucking hell, Lulu! This would've been in the early seventies when she was hanging out with David Bowie. She was like a messenger from another world.

William

One day, when we were adults, Jim said to me, 'You were cruel to me when we were kids' and I did apologise to him, because even though I don't think I was a bully by nature, there were a few times when I definitely mistreated him. I am still embarrassed by this, but let me tell you what I did to him. When I was maybe eight or nine we were in the lift going up to my granny's flat and I told Jim there was a spider on his back, and he went totally nuts. He was screaming and trying to pull his jacket off, but when I told him 'No, it's away', he was instantly quiet and completely calm.

He just accepted it, which was weird to me, because I would've taken longer to adjust. So I did it again – 'Wait a minute, there is a spider!' And he freaked out again, then when I said 'Oh no, my mistake it's not', he calmed down straight away. He was just a little kid at the time but I couldn't understand how he could he go from crazy panic to being completely calm in the blink of an eye, so I might have done it a few more times as a kind of scientific experiment, and he carried on responding in just the same way. Looking back, I suppose you could see this as early training for his later life as a performer.

There was another time when I have to confess for the sake of full disclosure that the two of us were in the bath together – no, we weren't in our late twenties at the time – and I poured hot water over his back and it was too hot and he didn't like it. It's not the worst but I shouldn't have done it and I hope that if Jim's ever seen a therapist about it he remembered to tell them that I said I was sorry.

I feel like once I was a bit older, in my early teens, I didn't bully him but I just thought he was a stupid little idiot because he was my wee brother. I wasn't actually cruel to him, I just didn't like it when he would walk in my space or talk to my friends. But that's what you do with little brothers, isn't it? 'You're there, we're here, we're bigger than you.' It wasn't like it was just the two of us, because the move to East Kilbride was by no means a clean break as far as our extended family was concerned. We left Glasgow but not everyone came with us, so we'd still go back to my granny's flat for New Year parties and other celebrations. In fact, early on it felt like we went back most weekends.

Jim

Those family gatherings when we were little were quite memorable. The kids all seemed to get on pretty well and the adults would amuse us by drinking way too much and getting into all sorts of bother. What we'd now think of as being alcoholism was basically the norm back then. All the adults would drink and smoke themselves senseless and the kids would hide under the table pissing themselves with laughter as the chaos unfolded.

Once a few drinks had been had, the sing-song would begin. Everybody had to do one. The older people would sing Scottish folk songs that nobody could ever remember properly – some shit about a bonnie lass, but it felt like they were making it up as they went along. The younger ones would sing Beatles tunes or whatever was in the charts. In terms of performance levels, it was a real mixed bag. If you remember Vic Reeves's club singer on *Shooting Stars,* that's how all of my uncles used to sound.

A few more drinks would go down the hatch and then family grudges would start to get aired. 'Do you remember that time thirty years ago? Do you remember what you said to me?' As far as we were concerned you couldn't buy this level of entertainment – after all, there were still only three channels on TV at that time – and we'd be rolling around on the floor laughing.

There was never any actual violence but there was a while where it was all 'Ye bastard ye', until about four hours in when they'd all be crying in each other's arms and saying how much they loved each other – 'I love ye, ye bastard.' The next day none of the adults could remember a thing about what had happened and we'd just be thinking 'Ah well, it'll all happen again next year.' This would later be the template for our international touring schedule.

At least some of that extended family atmosphere did transfer to East Kilbride, in that we'd be in and out of my Auntie Matty's house all through the summers. School would shut its doors and William and I could basically spend six weeks over there hanging out with our cousins. There were a bunch of them as Matty and Uncle Rab had five kids, and between the seven us we used to have a bit of a laugh. It was pretty uneventful but also easy-going and I remember being generally quite happy – even though looking back I'm not sure why, as we had fuck all and no real prospects of anything better.

William

The first time we went to Ayr as a family was in 1969. We stayed at Mrs Murphy's B&B. *Carry On Camping* was at the pictures and a man – well, two men – had just walked on the moon. A horse escaped and ran wild through Ayr, but we weren't so lucky . . . Two years later, we came back and stayed at Butlin's.

Jim

We almost never went on holiday because we couldn't afford to, and whenever we did go it was spectacularly unspecial. Ayr is not a bad little seaside town but the Butlin's was horrible. It was like a cross between *Hi-de-Hi!* and *Stalag 17* – the paint was flaky, the food was flaky, the paedophile redcoats were flaky . . . You were told before you arrived that everything would be free, and of course it was, but once you got there you found out that the stuff that was free was stuff you didn't want anyway.

The slightly out-of-focus cinema didn't even have *Carry On Camping*, it was showing films starring Victor Mature. The place hadn't seen a lick of paint in years. The swimming pool that should've been painted blue with the water all crystal clear was just a swamp of green sludge. I remember thinking that for how long it took us to get there – we got the bus and it seemed to take forever – we could have probably gone to Africa, but it was only about forty miles. It was good because it wasn't our day-to-day existence and a change from the norm was welcome, but I remember even as a kid thinking 'Fucking hell, there's got to be more than this.'

William

The worst thing that happened at Butlin's was I sang my ma and my auntie a song some older kids had taught me, thinking it was going to really impress them, but for some reason it didn't. It went to the tune of 'Oom-pah-pah, oom-pah-pah everyone knows' from *Oliver!* And the revised lyrics were 'Bum tit tit, bum tit tit . . . play on my hairy banjo'.

My ma and aunt were totally horrified – 'What the fuck are you singing?' How was I to know that was dirty? Years later I would attempt to heal the scars left by this unhappy event by releasing a B-side called 'Jesus Suck', but the pressing plant weren't having any of that either.

Drinking was pretty big with the men in our family, but the women were more into swearing. I never really heard my father say 'fuck' – or it was a special occasion if he did – and it was the same with my uncles. They were all gentlemen – the women were ladies too, of course, but they swore like troopers. They were always f-ing and cunting, and I grew up with my granny calling us 'skinny cunts' – 'this cunt did this, this cunt did that'. I honestly thought that's the way it was throughout Britain. As I became an adult and met people from different backgrounds, I would ask them: 'Does your mother call ye a cunt?', 'No', 'What about your granny?', 'No', 'OK, fair enough.'

Jim

The beginning of the long musical coming together that William and I had was when the Reid household acquired its first record player. It was one of those old Dansette-style devices in a suitcase, and I thought it was just something we came by as a family until William brought this up recently and I realised it was actually his birthday present which somehow became a family object, so he got screwed out of a gift that should have been his alone.

William

That's what happened – I got robbed. My ma and da ripped me off by giving me a gift that turned out to be for the whole family. It was one of those things that would irritate me for years. A record player was my dream present, but the first red flag was when I was told by my ma and da that I couldn't take it upstairs because it would be 'better in the living room'. Better for them, maybe. Jim had an even worse time than me at birthdays, usually, because he was born four days after Christmas. That was something he was still resentful of to my ma years later – 'Why did I never get a real present?' Because there was never any money left, he'd get a selection box or maybe a couple of Mars Bars – whatever was left over after Christmas. So I suppose he was due a change of luck with the shared record player.

Jim

My mum said 'Jim, go and get a record' – because we had nothing to play on it – so I went round all the neighbours' houses going 'Gissa record' and eventually it was the Willses two doors down who came up with the goods. OK, so the only single they were willing to trust us with was 'Chirpy Chirpy Cheep Cheep' but I ran back with it and played it about fifty times in a row – 'Where's your mama gone?' – thinking 'Fuck, this is amazing.' I have to say I still love that song.

Not long after that, one of my cousins took pity on us because we had no records and lent me and William a bunch of Beatles and Bob Dylan albums – the early solo ones, not the ones with

27

The Band on. William was into both because he was older, but I was only about nine, so when I heard Dylan I just thought 'Who's this old guy singing with a scratchy voice?' The Beatles on the other hand were a revelation. I remember very clearly thinking 'I never realised music could be like this.'

Of course, they had split up by this point. But even though their music was everywhere when I was younger – in fact, my mum had even bought me a little plastic guitar and she used to get me to amuse the relatives by pretending to play it and shouting 'She loves you, yeah yeah yeah' – this was the first time I'd really inhabited the worlds it contained. It didn't matter that The Beatles weren't a band any more, I was into them. And this was the start of music being very important to me – and to William – in a way that gradually began to bring us closer.

William

I know 1971 was the year the record player came into the house, because the first single I got for Christmas was 'Gypsies, Tramps and Thieves' by Cher. I can't remember why – it must've been on the radio and I must've said something about liking it. Next up after that was 'Without You' by Harry Nilsson, who I still think is a fucking genius even though that's not actually his song.

Jim

As well as the record player, the other new arrival around that time was my sister, Linda. I was nine when she was born and I'm pretty certain – and I don't think this will come as news to her either – that Linda was not planned. But I remember that as being a nice period in our lives – everything went relatively smoothly and I used to do quite a lot of babysitting and nappy changing. If I'd been closer to her in age there might have have been more adjusting to do in going from being the young one to not being the young one any more, but, as it happened, there was none of that.

William

One minute you're at primary school where everyone's drawing pictures and telling the teacher 'He was mean to me', then you go to high school and it's a giant place with lots of people and all the kids are smoking – it's like a jungle. I've never been in prison but I'd imagine the experience of arriving there is similar in terms of suddenly feeling at risk of violence. I don't know what it was like for the girls – knowing girls it was probably more psychological torture. I'd have to ask Linda.

Jim

At primary school you're in the same class all through it and you get to know those kids pretty well. There were a couple of nutters in mine but only a couple and it was easy enough to stay out of their way, but going to high school at the age of eleven was more like being drafted to Vietnam. Suddenly you're thinking 'Fucking hell, what's going on?' It was like all innocence had ended. Hunter High in East Kilbride was where childhoods went to die.

William and I were only there a year or two together. Either he'd had a different experience, or he just didn't prepare me for what it was going to be like, but whatever the reason it definitely came as a shock. Maybe I'm just a sap and an utter softy, but I found it quite difficult. You got glimpses of what the world you were going to have to make it in was actually like, and the realities of life started to seek you out.

William

The sectarianism aspect was a part of the reason me and Jim did not have a great time at high school. Most people were Protestant in East Kilbride – there was only one Catholic high school, St Bride's, but there were about four Protestant ones. William Mulhern lived about four doors away from me and one summer we were best friends, then he went to his Catholic school and I went to my Protestant school and that was it – we were done.

There are a lot of awful things about America, especially with all the right-wing stuff over the past few years, but at least you don't get people going to Christian school or Muslim school – they're all thrown in together. Even the English don't seem to care too much. It's just this weird thing we've had in Scotland and Ireland – 'Are you a Protestant or are you a Catholic?' I think it's got much better as the new generations have peeled off old skin – 'Why would I hate a Catholic just because I'm a Protestant?' In my kids' culture it's just weird to be racist, and I'm proud of them for that.

Jim

The worst thing about growing up in Scotland was the sectarian bullshit. It wasn't such a big deal in the new town environment as it probably would've been if we'd stayed in Parkhead, but the Protestant/Catholic divide certainly didn't disappear when people moved out of Glasgow. Obviously it wasn't as bad as growing up in Belfast, but it was crazy that I could've chucked a stone out of my bedroom window and hit my best friend Stuart Cassidy's house (not that I did, of course), but because his family were Catholics he had to go to a different school to me.

Sectarianism was something I never gave much thought to till after I left Scotland. It was only once I got to London in my mid-twenties that I started to look back and realise how fucked up it was. I've lived in England for nearly forty years now, so I don't know what that situation is like in East Kilbride any more, but it's probably just as bad.

Maybe I'm making it out to have been worse than it was – after all, my mum and dad never tried to stop me being friends with Stuart – but there were definitely some parents who were bigoted enough to stop their kids hanging out with children of the other faith. The irony of it was, we weren't actually Protestants in any sense that had any meaning. I was not religious in any way and had never been to church as a kid. If I was anything, I was an atheist. It was supposed to be about religion, but it was really about colours – 'My colour's orange, your colour's green.' The ones who used to knock lumps out of each other, there was no religion in them, really. They said there was, but there wasn't.

William

The other thing about our education besides the sectarianism that completely sucked was the teachers. They just didn't seem to give a shit about anyone who was in any way struggling. It was just the way things were at the time, but that didn't make it any easier to take. I know kids have a terrible time at all kinds of schools, but I think that level of not being encouraged – almost of institutional discouragement – is a specifically working-class experience.

In those days if you told people you thought you were clever but you kept failing exams, they'd just tell you 'No, you're stupid.' The idea of anxiety as something that might cause a child to underachieve had yet to take root. So I would find myself at the bottom of the class or in a low stream when it came to the next year, and think 'Why am I in classes with these guys who light their own farts?' When outside the lesson I'd be friendly with all the kids we thought of as the leading intellectuals of the day. The equivalent of having read Noam Chomsky then was having read or touched or even seen a copy of *Oz*.

I always had a hard time understanding algebra, and was just about keeping my head above water when I got flu and was off school for a week. By the time I got back, everyone in the class had advanced far out of sight of anything I had a handle on. I told the teacher I didn't understand this new thing they'd learnt and he was such a lazy cunt he just said 'Ask around.' Even all these years later I can still remember the pain of knowing there was no point doing that – my classmates didn't care. That was meant to be his job. I always thought if I bumped into Mr Cunningham in adult life I would politely tell him: 'Hey, Mr Cunningham, you weren't that great – your teaching methods hurt people. I was just a little fourteen-year-old who had the flu and got off the algebra train and because you couldn't be bothered to help me, I never got back on it.'

The same thing happened to me in what we called technical drawing. I was so bad at that. I've got this thing where I struggle with practicalities – not uniformly, but certainly with spatial chal-lenges. If I read a book and they describe the inside of a house, it's very hard for me to imagine it unless they say something like 'It looked like the *Psycho* house.' Everybody else seemed to be getting this subject really easily but I couldn't quite figure it out, and instead of trying to explain it, another terrible teacher was shouting and screaming at me every single lesson, to a point where I couldn't handle it and told my ma I wasn't going to go to school any more.

When she found out what had happened, she got my cousin Robert – who went to university so we all think he's an academic titan, and he actually is pretty clever – to come over and help me out. I won't say I was good at technical drawing after that, but I certainly stopped being hopeless.

Jim

There were no support structures, in fact even using an expression like 'support structure' would probably have got you a slap around the face. I remember the woodwork teachers who used to work on building sites would kick the shit out of kids who gave them any lip. If you got mouthy with them they'd ask you to give them a hand in the store-room and then the wee ned concerned would emerge looking dishevelled but a bit more respectful. To think of things like that happening now is just unimaginable really

In general, my school was dreadful. There was just no one there to give you any direction in terms of the possibilities of life – nobody who tried to open up your imagination or foster intellectual curiosity. There was a crushing sense of heading nowhere other than on a conveyor belt towards the factory down the road, which was in fact exactly where I was headed, in the short term at least. It makes me very angry when I think back to it, but I learnt next to nothing at Hunter High beyond basic literacy, and any useful knowledge I did pick up I acquired on my own from going to the library, going out into the world and experiencing things, or just sitting at home watching TV.

For instance, I love history, but the way they taught it made it the most boring subject in the world – you would go into the classroom and look at the blackboard where there would be a whole big jumble of names and dates and the teacher would just say 'Copy that into your jotter' and that would be it. It was just the dullest way to spend a couple of hours, and every subject was like that. You could tell that the teachers didn't give a shit. It wasn't that they would stamp down on signs of individuality – it's not like there were people reading Oscar Wilde in the corner and the teacher was telling them 'No, you mustn't do that' – it was just a complete lack of interest.

I hated it, but I couldn't say that I rebelled. Basically everyone seemed to accept this situation – the teachers were doing a job that they clearly weren't into and the kids were thinking 'This is all we've got, so fuck it.' The best you could hope for was to get from one end of the day to the other without being bullied. There were tough guys there – most of whom had been shipped out from Glasgow like us – and you had to keep an eye out for them. At that time I looked, and probably behaved, much younger than everyone else in my class – when I was fifteen, I looked about ten. It could've made me vulnerable but in a weird way looking younger made me invisible. I wasn't a threat to anyone and that was definitely for the best because I did see some nasty violence. It would come out of nothing – one kid would look the wrong way at another and the next thing you'd know they'd be getting horribly beaten up. You'd see that going on around you and think 'Thank fuck no one at Hunter High's noticed me.'

William

I, on the other hand, was a wee bit of a glam rocker.

Jim

The Beatles I came to kind of after the fact, but glam rock was the first big cultural experience I actually had while it was happening. Me and William were still into slightly different things at that point because of me being younger. I was more into Slade where he was into Bowie. I liked Bowie as well, but to me in 1972–73 Slade was the best band in the world. A lot of people seem to grow out of the first records they buy but I think those records still sound amazing – I love them now as much as I did then. The first single that I really remember making the hairs on the back of my neck stand up was 'Blockbuster' by The Sweet and I still think that sounds great. Yeah it owes a certain debt to 'Jean Genie', but so fucking what.

On Sunday night when we were supposed to be in bed early for school the next day we'd stay up listening to music. As well as the record player we had a little transistor radio, so me and William would be under the covers at night listening to Radio Luxembourg. The reception would drift in and out so you'd be listening to Roxy Music and it would start fading into the distance and you couldn't know if that was on the record or not, but that was part of the magic of it.

Because we shared a room, that was part of the reason we bickered a lot as kids, but with no personal space and people living on top of each other, that's bound to happen. The upside of it was that hearing that music together, in such close proximity, started to forge a bond between us. It wasn't easy to hear great music and it sounded like shit coming out of that little transistor radio, but somehow that just made the shared experience seem more valuable.

Top of the Pops was the only place you could really see the people making the music – even if they were miming – and that's why it was so important and absolutely everybody watched it.

Of course there was *The Old Grey Whistle Test* as well, but the presenters were just like the teachers who made everything incredibly fucking boring. Whispering Bob Harris would say 'And now, it's Head Hands & Feet with a twenty-minute jazz-rock fusion experimental piece' and I'd be thinking 'When are Slade gonna be on?' Why couldn't someone invent punk rock and blow all this shit away?

At this point the only person likely to blow all this shit away was my dad who every now and then would say 'You're not watching this *Top of the Pops* shite – *The Andy Stewart Show*'s on.' And I'd have to walk a mile to my cousin's house to watch it, thinking 'Oh for fuck's sake', but it was worth it to get a glimpse of Marc

Bolan. William had a bit of a social life by this stage and would quite often go out on a Thursday. He was probably trying to make it with some girl by then.

William

Top of the Pops was always in danger – my da would let us watch it so long as it didn't get in the way of what he wanted to see. So you'd see it for ten weeks straight then suddenly something new would come on ITV and we'd have to go to make other arrangements. I would go round to my friend Gordon Smith's house because *Top of the Pops* was really unmissable – if you did miss it everybody would be in school the next day talking about this guy Brian Eno who looked like a Martian and you'd be wondering who he was but they already knew – 'Oh, he played this song with this band' they'd say, not giving too much away like they were in on a secret. It was the same with *Monty Python* – I would beg my ma to let us watch it but in Scotland it wasn't on till about eleven o' clock in case it corrupted the youth.

I used to buy boxes of ten awful cassettes for 99p to tape songs off the top 40 at my friend's house. I don't remember ever worrying about sound quality, I think I was too engrossed with the content. That was how I listened to music for a long time because records were pretty expensive. I'd go down to the Barras sometimes – the market near the Barrowlands – and there were stalls where you could get four or five older records for the price of a new one. I remember buying a Who record, *Mind Games* by John Lennon and a tape by Elton John. At those prices you could take a chance on something you didn't know. I also used to try and acquire *Words* magazine or *Disco 45* so I could get the words to songs and commit them to memory. It's kind of uncool to say it but the thing about certain songs that appeals to you is that they're well structured and effective. I

came across 'Tom Tom Turn Around' by New World on You-
Tube recently, and half a century on I still knew all the lyrics
by heart.

I was trying to write songs of my own from the age of about
fourteen. I took it quite seriously but my early attempts were just
bad versions of songs that existed already. The only one I can
really remember was basically a rip off of a Glitter Band tune and
it was called 'My Name Is Jonathan'. The emotional content was
quite heavy – 'I walked by the park about half past two/Then I
saw Colin McKay walking with you/I began to cry/My name is
Jonathan . . . and it's Jonathan Wrigley to you'. It's a touching
story of loss and betrayal . . .

Jim

I remember 'My Name Is Jonathan'. To be honest it was kind of
a joke between us because William would say 'I've got a song',
then he'd just sing it because we couldn't play any instruments at
that time and I'd say 'That's not a song, that's just shite.'

William was quicker out of the traps than me in fashion terms
as well. He took his affinity for glam rock to a ridiculous level
where he had a giant pair of platform shoes which were about
two storeys high. He would wear them to the Olympia which was
the local dance hall – more or less a disco.

William

There was dancing three nights a week at the Olympia. I thought
it was great, especially if you could get a couple of cans of lager.
Once the alcohol kicked in the music sounded amazing, on giant
speakers with a bass like you've never heard before, and I would
dance, probably with my fingers in my belt hooks. We never did

it in unison or anything like that – it was an independent thing, more interpretative . . .

Jim

I didn't go to the Olympia because I was younger and a bit of a Nobby No-Mates, then by the time I was old enough punk was happening and things like that became really uncool. But William was more outgoing than me at that time and he went through periods where he had a few mates – I wouldn't quite say a gang, but they all got up to mischief together. There were proper gangs around too, that you had to look out for. One of the Catholic ones was called 'The Shamrock', and 'The Woody' – because they were from Calderwood – were their Protestant counterparts. I don't want to incriminate him too much but I think William was in that organisation for a while.

William

Joining a gang when I was sixteen was the greatest thing I'd done in my life at that time. The crazy young Woody from Calderwood neighbourhood. We weren't all Proddies because the toughest guy in the whole gang – an absolute psycho called 'Messer' – was a Catholic and no one was going to give him any trouble about it. I'll tell you what it was I liked about joining a gang – girls.

I was really shy around girls in my teens. I would go red when a girl spoke to me and super red if I fancied her. It was terrible. Me and my cousin James were both sixteen and you know what that's like when you've got a spotty face and no confidence – we just couldn't get girls to be interested in us. Even though James was a pretty popular character, we could never get to the best parties – we'd only hear about them a couple of days afterwards whereas all the kids that were in gangs got invited to everything and were always getting off with girls. So we joined the gang and that was it, we were in – there was no initiation or anything. James was a bit of a scrapper and had something of a reputation, so maybe that helped get us in under the velvet rope, but the moment we were on the inside our social lives instantly went from zero to hero. Suddenly me and James were going to all these parties where the parents were out and the girls at school thought we were bad boys.

Again, it was probably good preparation for being in a band in terms of the overnight transition to being considered attractive – 'Ye were not attractive last week, but now, I don't know, there's just something about ye . . .' Most of the other guys were just regular dopes like us, as far as I remember. There were only one or two dangerous people. Unfortunately, I crossed the paths of the wrong members of another gang and got quite badly beaten up. Well, they broke my arm and my nose. I wasn't hospitalised at first – I just picked myself up and went away. I didn't even know I had broken my arm till the next morning when I was lying in bed and it was really sore. I'd just left school at sixteen and started work at that point, and when I got there and I couldn't pick things up they sent me to hospital. After that, being in a gang didn't seem like so much fun any more.

Jim

Was East Kilbride a good place to grow up? It certainly could've been worse. If we hadn't bailed from Glasgow at just the right time we'd have ended up in one of those horrible high-rise blocks. As it was there were plenty of amenities and a fair amount of stuff to do. There were several libraries – a couple of which we used to frequent, the main one built into the fabric of the town centre was the only one you could get records from. There was also a big hi-tech swimming pool – one of those ones where when you walked into the reception area and you could see the deep end through the glass – even though legend had it that it was something like two foot short of Olympic size because when they dug out the the hole they didn't take any account of the thickness of the concrete. That seemed very typical of the place and the time that we lived in. We used to piss ourselves laughing at the sign as you came into town that said 'You're entering East Kilbride, the eighth largest town in Scotland'. We'd be thinking 'For fuck's sake! Is that the best you can do for a mark of distinction?' But on reflection, maybe being normal was not so bad – 'You're entering East Kilbride – it's not Shangri-La, but it's not bad at all'.

William

Time gives you a different perspective on the comforting memories of childhood, like the fish and chip vans that came to our street in East Kilbride at the weekends, which were fantastic at the time. It wasn't till I was about forty and watched a documentary which showed the number of people who got badly burnt operating them that I saw the dark side of this great consumer experience. Obviously the oil had to be kept really hot – I think it was 250 degrees – and the van was quite cramped and trying to get to as many stops as possible. So the oil was prone to boiling over anyway, but all that had to happen was for someone to say 'Oh look, there's a squirrel!' The driver would slam on the brakes and the poor guy in the back would have a bucket of boiling oil all over him. It was like medieval torture.

Jim

In *Comfort and Joy*, the film Bill Forsyth made in the eighties that was loosely based around the Glasgow ice cream wars, the story was about a DJ who got caught up in the conflict and brokered some kind of peace. They made it fun and everyone lived happy ever after, but it was only when a TV documentary came out years later that everyone realised how violent it got in real life. People were set upon with machetes and there was a terrible house fire where kids were killed. A lot of Glasgow's enmities made it out to East Kilbride in slightly reduced form, and I do remember rival ice cream van drivers fighting over pitches. Duncan from Duncan's Ices and Davey from Davey's Ices would be knocking seven kinds of shit out of each other in the street and you'd have to wait till the fight was over to see which one of them to go to for your 99 cone and a bottle of Irn-Bru.

Two out-of-shape guys rolling around in the mud trying to throttle each other seemed funny at the time but in retrospect it was quite bleak. There must have been a bit of money in the ice cream business for them to be fighting over it, but it was hard work – as I remember, the guy who came to our road was there three times a day, seven days a week, early afternoon, early evening and later in the evening. Maybe he had the odd day off, but it didn't seem like that. I lived in East Kilbride for eighteen years and he was there that whole time and for years after I left. It was just a part of the culture that people wanted to hold on to. Fair enough in somewhere like Easterhouse where there wasn't much infrastructure, but East Kilbride was pretty well set up for shops – it was only five or ten minutes' walk from our house to any number of pretty decent places, but still everyone waited on Duncan's Ices.

There was another guy called Mr Muir who sold groceries and clothes. My mum would drag me up to his van – it was more of a lorry – and make me try on trousers round the back. There'd be some girl in the neighbourhood you'd been trying to impress for ages and you'd be utterly humiliated as your mum whipped down your trousers so you could try on a pair of Oxford bags. See how I've switched to the second person to try and distance myself from the humiliation, but fucking hell, after six months of trying to impress the girl that lived three doors down in any way possible, this whole painstakingly constructed edifice came crashing down with my trousers . . .

William

Even though she had that lovely apartment, my granny didn't like being left behind in Parkhead when the rest of the family moved out. So eventually she told social services some bullshit about how cruelly her sons and daughters had abandoned her and they responded by taking her out of the high-rise flat and foisting her on her children. Everyone was livid because from that point on she basically went on a tour of the family, staying with each of her children in turn for months on end.

My granny was brilliant and beautiful but she was difficult – she had that type of selective hearing where when you're sitting next to her on the sofa and you say something she can't hear it, but then she can hear the ice cream van from two streets away because she wants an ice cream – 'Go get me one: chocolate.' And don't bother asking how come she can hear the far sound but not the near one, because she'll pretend she can't hear you.

Depending on the time of year, she'd be in the house in East Kilbride for weeks on end. It was horrible in the winter because when it was cold all the windows were shut and if my granny was there that meant it would be my granny, my ma and my da all smoking like chimneys. As a little kid I just thought it was repulsive. I wouldn't let my mother handle my food if she was smoking a cigarette – I'd make her wash her hands 'cos I thought it was disgusting. The closest I got to ever smoking was a friend of mine stole one of their dad's cigars when I was about eight and I might have put that in my mouth, but like Bill Clinton I did not inhale.

I think Jim saw how repulsed I was by their smoking and realised it was a filthy thing we should have nothing to do with, and so did my sister when she was old enough. So we all rebelled by not smoking, which I suppose you could see as evidence of a capacity to go against the grain from quite an early age. Our propaganda worked in the end, because my mother did eventually give up smoking in her fifties, which I respected her for. She gave up drinking as well, which was quite an achievement in our family.

Not smoking was one of the first things Jim and I did that marked us out from the culture of our parents and grandparents. I can't speak for him, but I always felt like I was very different from my ma and da growing up. I argued with their view of the world in so many ways, even though I now hate the thought of having argued with them, because I loved them and it's a long time ago and they're dead now. I can see that my da didn't have a lot of the opportunities to see things in new ways that I had growing up in the late sixties and early seventies, and this was the source of a lot of tension in the household. It was like a culture war before the phrase had even been invented.

The classic example would be the David Bailey documentary about Andy Warhol that was finally broadcast on ITV in 1973 after initially being banned due to a lot of fuss in the media. I really wanted to watch it and I resented the fact that my ma wouldn't let me. I knew it was because she didn't want me to see a man in bed with another man – one of the selling points of the documentary was that it featured David Bailey interviewing Warhol on a bed.

My ma and da weren't bigoted people but they came from a bigoted culture and people were incredibly homophobic in those days, even though I guess life is complicated because More-cambe and Wise could be in bed together on TV in their pyjamas with half the country watching and no one would say a word about it. Over time people's views changed. My ma would have probably had to be considered as quite homophobic in the early seventies, but by the time Boy George was a pop star a decade or so later she wasn't so bothered. Around that time I remem-ber her admitting 'Oh, Bowie's not that bad' – she'd been on a journey!

Jim

One of both my and William's favourite films growing up was Lindsay Anderson's *If.* I was only ten or eleven when I saw that for the first time and it's still one of my favourite movies – I guess that's a clear example of William being older than me and pointing me in a particular direction. You might wonder what a film about a rebellion in an English public school would have to say to a Scottish ten-year-old, but that would be quite a superficial analysis because it's debatable whether those surface details are anything like as significant to the film's meaning as its dreamlike quality, which was mesmerising to me then and still is now.

The first time I saw it I had no idea of what it was about – I guess the school is like a microcosm of the country and the world – but it stuck in my mind. In those days, before video recorders, you could only see a film like that when it came on telly once every four or five years, but when it did come on again, it was an event. Later on I saw the rest of Linsday Anderson's trilogy – *O Lucky Man!* and *Britannia Hospital* (which is not quite as amazing, and very hard to see now because it's not on any streaming sites that I'm aware of) – and got a better idea of how the whole thing fitted together.

If was like a gateway for me into a world of culture that my parents didn't understand.

Not saying anything against them, as I loved them very much, but my parents were terrible philistines . . .

William

Here's a weird thing – me and Jim used to judge things by how much our ma and da hated them. I'm not even joking. If we were out on a Sunday night when a film was on BBC2, and when we came back they said 'Oh it was terrible, we couldnae make head nor tail of it', we would think 'Fuck, we've missed something good.' They were very reliable critics. I remember the night we missed Jack Nicholson in Antonioni's *The Passenger* – 'Oh it was in the desert, there was a lot of sex and we didnae understand the dialogue.' Fuck, that sounds brilliant.

I realise now, although I wouldn't have used that name for it then, that our instinct was always to be drawn towards the counterculture. It's almost like a magnet attracting you to things – you hear about this weird guy called Franz Kafka who wrote this weird book about how he turned into a bug . . . In a working-class environment where the education system gives you no encouragement and your parents are very much in the mainstream, culturally, it's purely a matter of luck, the people you come across who give you tip-offs.

I remember there was a guy at my school called Robert McArthur, although everyone knew him as Gif. I don't want this description to seem unkind, but it's necessary to set the scene in terms of what his standing was in the school. This guy was thought of as being the uncoolest guy – he had greasy hair and a huge nose and he was bullied at a level that was beyond belief. Everyone used to laugh at him and people convinced themselves he had lice. They would go up to him and say 'I nose you, but I don't lice you.' And in the midst of all this cruelty – maybe partly even as a reaction to it, I don't know – this guy was a musical prophet.

At the end-of-year art class where we were allowed to bring in records, he would turn up with things no one had seen before. He had the Velvet Underground banana record, and the first time I ever saw the cover of *The Stooges* was through him. We'd be asking 'What's this?' And he'd be saying 'This is Andy Warhol's *The Velvet Underground*,' or 'This is Iggy and The Stooges.' We didn't know what he was talking about, and the teacher wouldn't let him play them – it's almost like he knew what they might do to our minds. But then five or ten years later I was dancing round my bedroom to these records. I often thought about that, wondering how I would've responded if I'd heard them at that point, instead of later. Would I have been ready for them? Either way, I'd love it if Gif could come to a show in Glasgow one day, and I could tell him 'Hey Gif, you were the coolest guy and nobody fucking knew it.' He was listening to our future – the custodian of the Mary Chain spirit, before the Mary Chain even existed.

Schools can be very small-minded places. There was a girl who was always being teased about her long legs. I saw her again a few years after she'd left and she looked like a supermodel.

Jim

I was one of those kids who spend the summer holidays just lying on the couch watching telly all day every day – enjoying the respite from school. My mum and dad would tell me to 'Go out and do something – join a club', and I'd be shouting back 'Hold on, *The Lone Ranger*'s on in a minute.' Eventually their desire to get me out from under their feet overcame my inertia and they finally succeeded in getting me to join something. It was the karate club and

I went for about six months. My dad paid for me but I still hated karate – absolutely couldn't get into it – because I instinctively knew it was utterly useless to me in terms of defending myself.

Even if I was a black belt and some big tough kid came up to me, he would still just jump on my head and I wasn't going to be able to stop that from happening. The reason I couldn't imagine a way it could ever be a useful tool was that you're either the type of person who can smash your fist into someone's face or you're not. If you're already that type of person you don't need karate anyway, and the reason I knew I wasn't is that there'd been a couple of times at school when I was about thirteen or fourteen where I got into fights and both times I got beaten up – not savagely, but the other guy got the better of me on both occasions. I could've beaten him both times if I really wanted to. I remember thinking 'This is the moment to punch him in the face' but I could not bring myself to do it, so eventually he would do it to me. I knew this was just what I was like and no amount of karate was going to persuade me otherwise. Once you're in that situation and you realise that you'd rather be beaten up yourself than beat someone else up, then the die is kind of cast.

Even though I quit karate after about six months, I carried on going for two years without actually going to the classes – I'd tell my dad 'Yeah, I'm off to karate now', when where I'd actually be was up in the café that overlooked the sports centre where the class was happening. I could buy a bag of crisps and a Coke with the money I was supposed to have spent on my subs and enjoy the social scene. The kids downstairs could do the sweaty bit, it was much more fun hanging around together upstairs.

There was a kid called Ivor who I got on really well with 'cos he liked weird music. You kind of zero in on those people when you're looking for clues about the other more interesting world which you know is out there. In East Kilbride everyone walked and talked and looked the same way, so if you found someone who went against the grain a bit and was into the weird shit that you were starting to be into then you tended to very much gravitate towards them. There's an immediate bond, and Ivor knew this other kid called Douglas, who really was a kid – he looked about eight – but he had the same kind of instincts to be looking for something different, and it was with those two that I had my first thoughts of starting a band.

ii. During Punk

Jim

The education that William and I received didn't send us out into adulthood thinking 'I can take this on – I can conquer the world!' It seemed to encourage feelings of inferiority rather than superiority, and that was not an accident – it was the way it was designed. If we wanted to get better information to prepare us for a fuller kind of life than the one that was earmarked for us, we were going to have to find it for ourselves.

William

When you're sixteen or eighteen you start to realise there's another culture of all these cool people out there in the world, and it was hard to have contact with that in East Kilbride because the only film on at the cinema was *Star Wars*. But I didn't want to see *Star Wars*, I wanted to see this film by this French guy I'd heard of whose name I couldn't pronounce or even quite remember. That's what it's like at that age – you want to explore the options, and East Kilbride was not a great place for doing that. Maybe it's better now, I don't know, but in the seventies it was a cultural graveyard.

Although let me put an asterisk next to that. We used to have a library in the town centre that was run by some pretty cool people. I doubt it exists any more, but libraries in the seventies had a records section, so if there was something me or Jim weren't sure enough about to buy but had a feeling we might like, we would order it from there. That's how we found out about Can, because Can were in the library, and so was Salvador

Dalí's shit book. Have you heard about that one? Salvador Dalí did a load of shits and took photographs of them and somehow they turned up in East Kilbride library to be a part of Jim's and my education. I think that book was worth a fortune and it probably got chucked in a skip when the library was 'modernised'. Hopefully someone who worked there got first dibs on it.

With their encouragement we would go on these literary and musical adventures that were the exact opposite of the frustrating experiences we'd had at school. Like with Albert Goldman. Well, I loved his Lenny Bruce book at first, because Goldman's a great writer, and he goes deep into the speech patterns of people – hipsters from the early sixties, late fifties – and that made reading him very entertaining. But I got sick of Goldman later on, because I realised that every subject he took on, he was determined to destroy them . . .

One of the reasons I mentioned Lenny Bruce at this point is that even though he obviously wasn't a musician, he was still kind of rock 'n' roll. Just like Marlon Brando and James Dean and Andy Warhol and William Burroughs were. I don't know about you, but I include them all in the rock 'n' roll family.

One day you've never heard of William Burroughs and then you hear about him and you go to the library and you read his book and it's like 'OK, there was brilliance in Burroughs for sure'. He was a millionaire's son – the typewriter mogul's kid – and he could've led a life of luxury living in big houses and travelling by air, which in those days was not common, but he chose to be what he was. Once you were done with Burroughs you could move on to Brion Gysin. I still don't know how you pronounce his name because I don't ever remember hearing anyone say it – I've only seen it written down.

Anyway, you pick up these things and then you get interested in these people and you peruse their work and you come away with something. To me, I don't think Gysin himself was a brilliant artist, but if it was him who first came up with the idea of cutting up text and reassembling it then that undoubtedly was brilliant.

I wouldn't claim to be a huge fan of Allen Ginsberg either, but he was one of these people who jolted you. You read his poetry or heard the spoken word albums and you had to think about it twice, and his work led you on to other people's. I'm not saying all this to paint Jim and myself as huge fans of the beat generation. What inspired us the most I think was the examples of people who'd made a life out of art – so you don't have to work in a factory or an office, you can actually survive a whole life doing something creative, whether it's writing or painting or music. You don't have to die in a pit of despair, which at that point looked to be our only option. And of course the thing that blew the whole of life wide open for Jim and I was punk rock. Instead of it just being the next thing, it fucking went to our core.

I only started listening to John Peel when rumours about punk began to circle in 1976. I'd heard him before, but I was never attracted to the music he played – there was a lot of long proggy stuff, and I couldn't really get into his voice, so I never stuck with it for longer than five minutes. Then suddenly you'd be reading the music papers and they'd be talking about this band from New York or this band called the Sex Pistols – of course, if you were in that situation now it'd literally be seconds between hearing about them and knowing what they sounded like. But then, waiting to hear them on John Peel was the only way. He'd play about twenty records that you'd never want to hear again, and then suddenly one that would completely hook you.

Each time something happened, we paid attention. Jim liked this, I liked that. The Sex Pistols, The Clash – that's brilliant, that's amazing. Eventually punk bands started to appear on *Top of the Pops* and the two of us would be sitting there watching them together, knowing even as these moments unfolded how much they meant to us. We experienced that in each other's company and we would talk about it endlessly afterwards, often in strangely formal terms, as if we were in a biopic. Like after watching the video for 'Pretty Vacant' on *Top of the Pops* . . . 'Did you see that? This has just changed my life! I can't believe it – I don't know what to do!' 'Same with me, Jim, same with me!'

Our parents thought we were weirdos. After all those years of studied indifference – when Jim was just my wee brother and we were basically quite nice to each other but we weren't buddies – we suddenly became allies, and the currency of our new-found friendship was punk rock.

Jim

The Sex Pistols were extremely important to me and William, and still are. One of the things they did really well in the TV series *Pistol* was show the positive impact their example had on people. Johnny's become a bit of a dick in real life, to be honest. He's no longer the guy that we thought he was back in the day – smart, articulate, saying everything we wanted to say about how much we despised the life that had been earmarked for us. Now he's become more of a caricature of himself, like Morrissey – he seems to say utterly hateful things just to amuse himself – but then he was everything we wanted to be.

Up until punk, rock music was made by exotic creatures from places like London and New York, and the idea that little shits like me and William in East Kilbride might be able to form a band hadn't even entered our heads. Even when punk hit it still felt like we were a million miles away from where it was all happening, but reading interviews with people like Johnny Rotten or listening to the Ramones it felt like this was suddenly something a bit more achievable. We were no longer just these kids living in this backwater where we might as well have been living on the fucking moon. What punk did – not just through the music but the whole culture around it – was it brought a lot of people together and made you feel like you were less remote and could maybe even participate, without needing Whispering Bob Harris to tell you it was OK.

There was no way I was going to get to see any of those first punk shows. I was only fifteen in 1977, but it wasn't just about my age. We were pretty poor, so the idea of getting the money to go to a gig in Glasgow was out of the question. That's why I was so disappointed when The Clash – who I absolutely loved – said they would never do *Top of the Pops*. We're your fans and we want to see you on it, so why the fuck not?

I understood that when punk came along everybody was loading up the bullets and looking for someone to shoot, but I couldn't see the logic in signing to CBS and then refusing to do *Top of the Pops*. They'd probably all been glued to Slade, Bolan and Bowie when they were growing up the same way that we were, so why would they take that experience away from us? There may have been institutions that needed to be brought down, but I didn't – and still don't – think *Top of the Pops* was one of them.

It was different for William because he was three years older than me – which is such a lot at that age – and had more money at the time, as by then he'd left school and got a job. So he had much more freedom of action.

William

There was a guy called Jim Sinclair who worked in my job at James Lumsden and Company, which made sheet metalwork for air conditioning. He had a ticket for the Clash gig in Glasgow on the White Riot tour, but he couldn't go. He sold me his ticket – I paid him for it – but on the night of the show I'm ashamed to say I just sat there and never left the house. I was scared because I didn't know anybody else who was going, so I missed a legendary gig that ended up being in the Clash movie. I tried to learn a lesson from missing out like that, and my determination not to let life pass me by would lead me to a decision which would shock my ma and da more than anything the Sex Pistols said on Bill Grundy.

Never Understood

Once or twice when I was at school, a cow or a bull escaped the abattoir next door and ran terrified through the school grounds. We worked in an abattoir for a week upgrading the ventilation system and what I saw and heard there left no doubt as to the logic of that terror. I've never forgotten the smell of that place and the sight of the cows hung upside down with the bolts slashing at their throats. It's just brutal, and I don't eat red meat to this day. It did take me ten years after this experience to give it up – you'd have died of malnutrition pretty swiftly if you'd tried to be a vegetarian in East Kilbride in the late seventies – but I couldn't face the gammon rolls my ma had given me for my lunch. The guy I was working with didn't give a fuck, though – he was tearing into them. My mate Gordon Smith who worked at the abattoir by the school in the summer was even worse – he would prank you by putting an eyeball in your coat-pocket.

I don't think I need to make the analogy between myself and the fugitive farm animals too explicit, but I knew I didn't want to be stuck at James Lumsden's for the rest of my life. My job was an apprenticeship learning to making the ducts for ventilation systems. I was an awful sheet metal worker because I was always scared of getting some horrendous industrial injury. It was a dangerous job and I remember thinking 'If I lose the tips of my fingers, I'll never be able to learn to play the guitar.' I know it worked out OK for Tony Iommi of Black Sabbath but that was not light engineering, it was heavy metal.

There were all these old men working there who had half a pinkie or a toe missing and would laugh about it. It was funny to them – or at least that was the way they dealt with mutilation in the line of duty – where I was thinking 'Fucking hell, you're not paying me enough money to lose parts of my body. Offer me ten grand a week and I'll think about it.' I couldn't see me hanging around there for forty years, I just went along with what I thought would please my ma and da. It wasn't that they were trying to limit my horizons – their attitude was 'You get a trade and you can go anywhere', whereas if I left, how was I going to survive? I'd become a part of the 'demi-monde' which my da would call the layabouts of the world.

It was really difficult giving up that apprenticeship. I didn't just throw it away on a whim, because I knew what it meant to other people, most of all to my da. My defence of my position – 'I don't want to work at a job that will destroy my soul!' – seemed ridiculous to him, especially as I was trying to talk to him about punk rock and how it had it changed my views.

That probably just made it sound trivial to his ears, but it wasn't trivial to mine, and it wasn't for thousands of other kids in 1976–77. Maybe music doesn't do that nowadays, but when I was young it had a power that could change your life's direction. It did that for me and for Jim and for a lot of other people I know. But it's hard to tell your working-class ma and da about those things when they just think you're throwing everything away.

Jim

William explaining his decision to give up his job with reference to things Johnny Rotten had said would've been exactly the wrong thing to do. To my mum and dad, we both had our heads in the clouds and absolutely no sense of what the real world was like, so to say 'This man in the bondage trousers has shown me the way' was just pouring petrol on the flames.

William

My ma and da asked me how I was going to make a living if I walked away from the job, and I remember blurting out something like 'I don't know. I don't wanna work in a factory or an office – I wanna try to be a musician.' I was always on the verge of being in a band. Even though I couldn't technically play a musical instrument, it was always something that was being talked about. I bought a bass from my friend Duncan Cameron. It wasn't full-sized, it was a small practice one, but it got me started. In the long run I didn't want to play the bass, I wanted to play the guitar, but the bass was cheap and it was a beginning. I never really had an amp, though, so the whole thing was kind of silly. Gordon Smith, who liked The Stranglers, was pretty much the only other person I knew in East Kilbride apart from Jim who was into punk in 1977, so me and him were going to have a band, but we never really did anything other than talk about how great it would be to go on tour.

There was a certain amount of dreaming going on at that stage. Like when me and my cousin James were really drunk on the Friday night before the England–Scotland game in 1977 and decided to hitch down to Wembley the next day. We had no money or anything but we knew that a car travels at 70mph, so calculated that 'if we get a ride every half an hour we can make it the morra'. Unfortunately the first guy who picked us up seemed to be some kind of serial killer. We didn't realise that at first – when we got in the car and he said 'Yeah, I'll take you to Hamilton', we thought Wembley Way was calling. Then he started driving the car at 100mph and doing this crazy laugh – like a movie villain – and we were absolutely shitting ourselves.

Have you ever been driven by a maniac? It's a horrible experience. Luckily he decided to drop us off in Hamilton rather than driving the car into a wall or burying our bodies in the woods, and so we started to walk towards England, one step at the time. I don't think we'd even reached Motherwell before the sun was up. By then we were starving in the way that does tend to happen when drunk guys sober up, so we raided the milk and the bread rolls the milkman had left out at the back of a café. It was about that time we realised we were not going to make it. I don't even remember how we got home – probably caught the bus.

Either way, we made it back in time to see the pitch invasion when they broke the crossbar and a net got torn after Scotland won 2–1, and the BBC commentators were insulting the whole of Scotland, calling the crowd thugs and hooligans.

The next time I set off for the big city, I was a lot better organised.

Jim

So William's bass guitar sat in the corner of the room gathering cobwebs for two years until the moment was right for him to write another song . . .

William

When I was young and adventurous and wanting to be Jack Kerouac, I thought the biggest adventure available was London, and to be honest London never disappointed me. There's often anti-London feelings in bands who come from outside the capital, but I'm anti anti-London bands. If you're sixteen and you want to see Fellini movies it won't happen in Glasgow – well it might, but it will probably only be for one night and it might be a Tuesday night and you've got school tomorrow . . . when me and Jim started to have our little adventures down to London it was like 'Oh my God – every band or exhibition or film you can think of comes to London!'

As the older brother I was the first to go and I surpassed myself by actually getting a job for a while – in housekeeping at the London School of Economics, the place Mick Jagger went to fifteen years before . . . I had a kick-ass little flat – which came with the job – right under the Post Office Tower. I would go to sleep looking up at that famous London landmark and even though I still had no money, I used to think I was the luckiest person in the world. What a little tube I was. I used to remember all the films set around there that I'd grown up watching in the sixties and seventies and feel like I'd cracked it. OK, the job only paid 99 pence an hour, but it was definitely a good move to be there from East Kilbride. Jim came down for a holiday for a couple of weeks and he loved it down there as well.

Jim

I left school in December of '77. I went to some little building course near Glasgow. There were no jobs to be had in general, but out of the class I was the only one who got a fucking job – what kind of fucking luck is that? No part of me was pleased.

I just thought 'I've got to do this course because they won't give me any dole money if I don't.' So I did it and it turned out I was quite good at it. The guy who was my teacher there said something about me being 'born to be a joiner' which just chilled me to the bone. I was in a zombiefied state for two or three days after that, thinking 'No, no' but still he seemed to go out of his way to get me this job – as an apprentice joiner at the Rolls-Royce factory in East Kilbride.

I started there in March 1978. I wasn't on the production line, it was more like maintenance, so if a forklift truck smashed into a door, we'd make a new door. It was a huge factory with five thousand people working in it, some of whom were old and had spent their whole working lives there. They'd point out 'Wee Willie' – some knackered-looking old fossil who'd been there since before the war. He'd give me a toothless grin and I'd experience an involuntary shudder at the thought that Wee Willie's destiny might also be mine. I spent much of the two years I was there trying to figure a way to get out of this situation – 'No I cannot be doing this, this is not what it's supposed to be.' I wasn't entirely sure how my life was going to pan out, but I knew what I didn't want to do, which was spend the next fifty years in that factory.

The one upside was that for the first time in my life, I actually had some money, so now I could afford to go to gigs. I think the first may have actually been The Jam at Glasgow Apollo, on Bonfire Night, 1978. The band that were playing before them, The Dickies, were the loudest band I've ever seen before or since. They more or less destroyed my eardrums with their version of Simon & Garfunkel's 'The Sound of Silence'. That was pretty much all I could hear by the time they were done, which didn't matter too much because I wasn't the biggest Jam fan. I'm still not, to be honest. The first album had a couple of good punk songs on it, but they used to go on about being a mod band, and I used to think 'But mod bands were in the sixties and they sound fuck all like you.' I appreciated the punky side of it but I was more there for the outing: 'I've started this job so I've got a bit of cash in my pocket for the first time in my life – I'll go to see a band. Who's playing this week? Oh, it's The Jam, I'll go and see them.' A few weeks after that it was The Rezillos, again at the Apollo. That was a much better night out. It was their farewell gig (or at least so we – and they – thought at the time: their 2023 tour schedule was in fact quite extensive) and it really hit the spot. It was actually released as a live album, and it deserved to be. It didn't make any difference to me that The Rezillos were Scottish, they were just really, really good. And getting Fay Fife to make a guest appearance on our 2024 album *Glasgow Eyes* would bring this story full circle forty-five years later.

William

I had this Bert Weedon book with all these pictures of open chords, which I had painstakingly learnt to the point where I could just about stumble through 'She'll Be Coming Round The Mountain'. Then I would listen to punk records and think 'How the fuck do they do that?' I'd be looking at pictures of their hands on the guitars in the music papers and thinking 'What was that chord?' Then I finally worked out what a barre chord was, and once you can play one of those, you've got the key to the door. Bert Weedon goes out the window at that point and you start to realise how all the songs you're listening to on John Peel or Annie Nightingale have been constructed. Once you've grasped the nature of the bricks in the building, you can see how the whole thing has been put together. You learn one song and then another, and next thing you know, you are busking on the London Underground.

I think Jim might have actually done it first, and he did quite well the first time because he still looked quite fresh-faced and people felt sorry for him. But by the time he tried again three years later he looked more like a heroin addict and people were literally walking by on the other side of the tunnel. Me and my friend Davy Campbell had a go one of the times down in London when things were starting to go to shit. He'd got kicked out of his flat, and we'd gone back on the dole and ended up in this place in Earls Court with five smelly blokes in one room. We busked for two days down at Marble Arch and it was pretty awful. We got 65p the first day and 45p the next with me singing punk songs on an acoustic guitar and Davy playing brushes on a snare. We were desperate and it probably showed in our performance. It was mainly Buzzcocks songs from the 'Spiral Scratch' EP and if I'd seen us I would've felt sorry for us. But I did notice a couple of famous people walk past and neither of them gave us a penny.

First there was a guy called Gerald Harper who played Adam Adamant on TV – a sophisticated English gentleman type, a bit like Nigel Havers. He wasn't putting his hand in his pocket for my approximation of Pete Shelley's nasal whine. Then the woman who was in *Abigail's Party* but wasn't Alison Steadman came by – later on she'd be in the Victor Meldrew programme. I loved *Abigail's Party* so I was so impressed to see her coming towards me, but I don't think she appreciated my shout of 'orgasm addict', as she just walked straight past. In hindsight I can see that a mental Scotsman screaming 'You're an orgasm addict' might not have been the experience that she was looking for, but at the time I was pretty annoyed that she wouldn't give me 50p.

Jim

I got myself a crappy Les Paul copy in about 1979. The way I learnt the rudiments of picking out a song on the guitar was by throwing an overnighter similar to the one Steve Jones did in *Pistol* except it looked much sexier on TV. I certainly didn't have an idealised version of Chrissie Hynde coming round to give me the encouragement any man would crave – that would've been nice. I remember sitting up in my room in East Kilbride thinking 'I'm gonna learn "Judy Is A Punk" tonight.' I didn't know how I was gonna do it but I had a chord book and the shape of a barre chord and I just sat there playing for hours and hours.

It must've been when William was in London, because he wasn't there to tell me to knock it off as it sounded awful, but the next day when I went to pick up the guitar I put my hand in the shape and it was much easier. Once you can do a barre chord you can play a punk version of pretty much any song, and I wouldn't say that I ever really got any better as a guitar player from that point on. Nobody would have me in their band as a guitarist, that's for sure, but I was always worried that if I learnt the names of the actual chords it might all get a bit Head, Hands & Feet.

I was still hanging around with the karate crowd at the time and me and Ivor were always trying to get a band together. Different guys would drift in and out but there were was never a real band and there were never any real gigs. We did once play what we called a gig in Ivor's living room with four girls we fancied as our audience. They kept repeating the words 'This isn't music' and throwing the couch cushions at us. 'You've rumbled us, but can we get a snog anyway?' 'No chance.' I can't remember who sang – it's possible we were all too bashful – and I'm not sure which instrument I'd decided to demonstrate my lack of competence by playing on that occasion. It could've been guitar or bass, I was equally bad at both.

William

The closest I got to being in a band before the Mary Chain started to happen was 1979, when me and my friends Davy Campbell – who was the drummer I'd busked with – and Bobby Hamilton, who played the bass, had a go at rehearsing and playing through a little PA. We actually wrote a few songs together and got as far as going to a studio to record three or four of them, but they sounded terrible and I just felt like we'd wasted our money. The idea of recording seemed very difficult – it felt like you only had one shot at it. Luckily that did not turn out to be the case. I found these recordings about ten years ago and thought maybe they weren't that bad, but when I listened to them they were even worse than I'd thought.

Jim

As early as the end of 1977, I remember a feeling that punk had run its course and was going to have to morph into something else. Otherwise it was gonna become as stale as fuck. There was a time where things sort of seemed to stop happening. One of the bands that most hit home with us was Subway Sect – those early records 'Ambition', 'Nobody's Scared', 'Don't Split It' are brilliant. There was such a buzz about them for a while – everybody thought they were going to be the next big thing – well, maybe not everybody but certainly we did. They used to rehearse at The Clash's studio and I remember seeing a video clip of them doing. . . I can't even remember what song it was but it was the perfect punk music to me. Then they just seem to go away. I was waiting on this album that never seemed to happen and when it finally did, it wasn't the album I was waiting on. I still really like *What's the Matter Boy?* But it took too long for them to get it together – I think they lost band members and maybe some of the masters, so by the time it finally came out, music had moved on.

Bands just doing the same old same old wasn't good enough. Punk had to be about ripping it up and starting again, to borrow Orange Juice's phrase for a time before they had even used it. There were a few notable exceptions coming through in 1978 – bands who seemed like they were doing something new and hinting at the direction punk could move into. The Banshees were one of them – their first album was one of my favourites – and PiL, and Joy Division, who were very much a punk band in my book. They were the ones who continued to reinvent what punk had been; it wasn't called punk any more but it made all the guys with the spiked haircuts and the thrashy guitars seem irrelevant.

One of the best gigs I ever went to was Buzzcocks at the Glasgow Apollo with Joy Division opening up for them in the autumn of 1979. When Joy Division came out there was such electricity in the air. I was thinking 'My God, it's like we're watching The Doors or something! I'm going to be telling people for the rest of my life that I saw the Joy Division gig at the Apollo in 1979.' And that premonition was accurate, because that's exactly what I have done . . .

There was a feeling that this was an important musical moment – people were just going fucking crazy. Obviously Joy Division are not the sort of band you jump up and down and rip up seats to – people just stood there open-mouthed. It was kind of sad for the Buzzcocks because they had to come on after and you couldn't possibly follow that. They did their best and they were all right and everyone was into them, but they were already on the way down and being on a bill that was so unbalanced in favour of the support act can't have helped. It was fucking amazing seeing Joy Division, but just a few months later, Ian Curtis was dead.

William

I wasn't as big a fan as Jim of live music. I'm still not, really – I prefer listening to studio recordings. Even though I didn't go and see many live bands because there didn't seem to be much point in it, Joy Division with the Buzzcocks in 1979 was pretty fucking stunning. I think we'd seen them on some teenage TV show before – maybe *Something Else* – doing 'Transmission' and 'She's Lost Control', so we kind of knew what was coming, but a gig like that knocks your world off its axis. I think one of the reasons Joy Division made such a big impression on both of us was because at the time – forty-five-odd years ago – neither of us were exactly virtuosi, and Joy Division were just so fucking uncomplicated and yet the whole thing was incredibly powerful.

The guitar playing of Bernard Sumner, or Barney Albrecht or whatever he was calling himself, was just revolutionary in my mind. He was only playing two or three notes but it wasn't like anything was missing. Him and Peter Hook were just banging out these repetitive but incredibly catchy riffs, and then there was the drumming! In those days your world could get rearranged by some band, and I felt the same way about Public Image Limited. They had the same basic structure – a great drum sound and incredibly simple bass and guitar sounds which just made up this huge complex *thing*. Jah Wobble and Keith Levene were only in the band because they were Rotten's mates, but they just happened to be these amazing fucking musicians. What were the chances? How many more people could there be out there like them, talented to the level of genius, who just never got discovered?

Jim

I only went to see Public Image a bit later, so by the time I got to them John Lydon had already picked up his cabaret band . . . I also went to see The Slits who I loved then and I love now. They were just so fucking uncompromising. I think Ari Up did a piss on the stage and as an eighteen-year-old kid living in East Kilbride that was quite something – 'Oh I say!' They were great sonically, too, but just to do something like that was extraordinary. It made me think 'Oh my God – you can do what you fucking like and nobody cares!' For about three seconds I thought 'Yes, I'm going to be like that' and then I remembered that I was the most timid person on earth and no one was going to want to watch me take a piss onstage anyway.

I saw Altered Images and the Banshees around that time as well. I also went to see The Cure but I have to admit I fell asleep at that gig. Not because they were bad or boring or anything like that, but we were sitting in a box – a lot of the main Glasgow venues were seated – and I was working in that fucking factory and I was shattered. I used to get up at the crack of dawn and be on my feet all day lifting big bits of wood. Once I got to that gig I just couldn't keep my eyes open, so I put my head down on the seat and fell asleep.

When William had gave up his apprenticeship as a sheet metal worker, it caused an almighty hoo-ha in the house, but basically everyone got through it. So two or three years later, when I was thinking about making the same move, I was thinking 'What's the worst that could happen? OK, my dad's going to be pissed off with me for the rest of my life, but I'll cross that bridge when I come to it, just like William did.'

I hadn't reckoned with the fact that it being the second time around would make it worse when I did it. My dad was thinking 'Oh fuck, not this again', so he took a more hard-line approach and basically said 'If you pack that job in, you're going to have to leave this house.' That was a shock – 'Hang on a minute, what about William? He got to stay . . .' But my dad had raised the stakes, so that was it. I understood that he wanted the best for me and he was only trying to stop me giving up what he thought of as a great job, but that didn't make it seem any fairer at the time. And when I left Rolls-Royce after serving just two years of my four-year sentence – in the spring of 1980 – it was next stop London.

William

My da was not a control freak or a bully, he was just a working-class guy who'd been brought up to believe that having a trade is fine and good and honest and skilful. Which of course it is for lots of people, but not for me, and not for Jim either. Or at least, it was another trade we had in mind, we'd just not learnt it yet . . .

Jim

As far as London was concerned, it was all over by Christmas. I must confess to an element of calculation in the timing of my return. I gambled that my mum and dad's hearts wouldn't be cold enough to turn me out on the street if I came home at that magical time of year, and it turned out I was right. There *was* room at the inn. Shortly after I'd got my feet back under the table in East Kilbride in December 1980, a rugged-looking man with razor-sharp cheekbones came to the door.

I asked 'Who the fuck are you?' And he said 'It's me, Douglas.' 'You fucking monster. Who are you and what have you done with little Douglas?' When we first knew him, Douglas looked so young that William used to call him 'The Toddler' – and to this day we still call him Todd . . . He insisted it was really him and so it was. In the six months I'd been away Douglas had gone from being a little twelve-year-old kid who'd ask 'Is Jim in?' in a voice high-pitched enough to make my dad worried I was a paedophile – 'Jim, there's a weird wee boy at the door for ye' – to a full-grown man with stubble.

William

We always thought something might happen if you were in London, but it never did, at least not until we came to London as a band with a bunch of real ideas and a few decent songs. Before that, why would anyone want to pick me and Jim out and give us a record contract and access to the world? The returns from our London trips before the band happened diminished starkly, from the heady excitement of our first visits in the punk era to a couple of pretty fucking grim abortive attempts in the very early eighties.

I tried to go down again in 1981 and I got off the bus to find that the friend I was going to stay with had been kicked out of his flat and we had to sleep in an underground garage for the night. I knew about a secret laundry room that was meant to be open from my time working at the LSE – how far I'd fallen from those happy days contemplating the wonder of the Post Office Tower – but when we got there it was locked and we had no option but to sleep in the concrete car park. There was no romance to it, it was awful.

Jim

I gave London one more go in the middle of what turned out to be my five-year dole period. I just got fed up with everything and me and Davy Campbell said 'Fuck it, let's go to London and see what we can get up to.' I should've realised by then that the solution to that conundrum was 'not a lot', especially when you're stuck in the same set-up of signing on and living in a shit-hole. We only lasted about six weeks, which left time for one more busking episode but by that time our youthful charms had faded. I didn't look like Oliver any more, I looked like the Artful Dodger's dodgy older brother and our takings plummeted accordingly.

We were staying in some shitty place in Earl's Court and when they found out we were signing on we got chucked out and ended up sleeping rough, which even though it was summer was not a good experience. Davy knew a few guys in squats so we lasted a couple more nights there, but by that time I'd got a terrible cold and I felt like I was going to die, so I staggered down to King's Cross and got the bus home. Normally I could never sleep on those bus rides but on that one I kind of keeled over and the next thing I knew I was back in Scotland. There'd been someone next to me when I fell asleep but they were gone by the time I woke up. I wouldn't have wanted to sit next to me either. On top of the cold I hadn't had a bath for a couple of weeks and I probably looked like I'd shot up before I got on the bus. I realise this is not quite Iggy Pop's autobiography, but it still felt like several levels of degradation below anything I was comfortable with.

William

The first time I heard The Velvet Underground was on the Annie Nightingale show – she played 'I'm Waiting For The Man' and it was just incredible. Annie Nightingale didn't get as much credit as John Peel, but I think she introduced a lot of people to a lot of things. Another song she played which I couldn't quite wrap my head around was 'Seven And Seven Is' by Love – it was so fucking punky and yet it came out in the first Summer of

Love, but there I was, just discovering it more than ten years later.

Jim

Everybody was always name-checking The Velvet Underground in the punk era, but it took us ages to get to hear them. William had *Transformer* left over from his glam days but by that time all the Velvet Underground back catalogue had been deleted and the closest we could get to them at the library was a Lou Reed compilation with a couple of Velvets songs on. I remember us going into Glasgow and trying to buy the first Velvets album at the end of the seventies but I think the only one that was actually in print at that time was *Squeeze* which didn't have Lou Reed or any of the original band members on. It was maybe a year later that the original albums were released and the banana album was blinding revelation number four. First we'd had The Beatles, then glam, then punk rock and now the Velvets. I remember bringing that record home and thinking 'This is everything we could ever possibly want to get to. It's the best record I've ever heard in my life and nothing else matters.'

I know there's nothing that is 100 per cent original or new, but there are a few bands that it's hard to figure out exactly where their music had its roots and The Velvet Underground were a good example of that. Obviously it didn't come from nowhere – Lou Reed was clearly very into Bob Dylan and also very into a lot of early soul music, so the way I hear the Velvets is as Bob Dylan singing with a Motown band who are all on fucking speed and their equipment doesn't quite work.

This stuff wasn't coming to us in chronological order. When *Raw Power* was reissued in 1977 – and it was cheap, like £1.99 or something – the cover sold it to me from the off. I remember looking at the picture of Iggy on the front and thinking 'If David Bowie fucked Johnny Rotten, this would be their child.' Lots of albums you had to get up and lift that needle to the next track every once in a while, but with *Raw Power* you only had to shift your lazy arse once every twenty minutes because it was all just fucking great. It was like one single after another – my God, the quality of that record.

The Stooges were another great example of an unsuccessful copy band. They wanted to be The Doors so badly but in a wonderfully incompetent way – because they weren't so accomplished as musicians, they were more primal and had to use their imaginations and came up with something brand new which ended up being just as good. If they had been better at being The Doors, they'd have been worse at being The Stooges. When their first album was reissued I remember seeing it in a Glasgow shop with a little sticker in the corner that had the word 'Punk' written on it, just to let the young punks know that regardless of them appearing to be long-haired dudes from a bygone era, it was OK for their record to be in the punk section. And this was true, because it was actually a lot more punk than a lot of the punk music that was coming out.

It was actually William who bought a lot of those records, because he was working at that time, so he could afford to. But we shared the collection – and did so remarkably harmoniously, given how much we used to bicker about everything when we were younger – so what was his was mine. Then when he left his job and I started at Rolls-Royce, it was me doing the bulk of the buying, so what was mine was his too. We had very understanding neighbours – at least, they never complained – but we'd be up in the bedroom listening with my dad shouting up the stairs 'Turn that fucking racket down.'

You went to London with stuff you could chuck in your bag. You didn't take records, just a few cassette compilations and maybe a small tape recorder. Then when we returned, the record collection would be there waiting for us with maybe a couple of new additions.

William

It wasn't just liking the same music – specifically punk – that brought me and Jim together, it was talking about it . . . for hours. One of the bands we bonded over most was Suicide. Neither of us could understand why Clash fans had booed them when they toured together – to the point where Joe Strummer had to come out and defend them – when it was obvious they were as punk as the Ramones, they just used synthesisers instead of guitars. I loved their stripped-back iconography, which seemed to boil down to a guy called Johnny in an old film who wore a leather jacket, and the tunes, which were incredibly repetitive but in a very hypnotic way.

Jim

Suicide's first album to me is one of the best records ever made, but it's very, very hard to get the reference points. How did they come up with that? I do have an idea actually, in that I think it came out of desperation. I think those guys just wanted to be in a band but didn't know how to do it, so they found these elements they could work with and created something that was utterly unique. To me that's essentially what rock 'n' roll is – people finding bits and pieces and reassembling them into something else that makes sense for the time they're living in. That's what pretty much every band that I admire did, and that's what William and I would eventually try to do, too.

When you're fifteen and your older brother's eighteen, that's such a big gap, but once you're eighteen and he's twenty-one and you've both been away from home for a while and come back, that's somehow not such a great divide. Where once we couldn't agree on anything, we suddenly started to get along much better. After spending our childhoods more or less steering clear of each other, we began to realise how much we had in common – specifically, being outsiders. We had these little golden nuggets that we shared in music and art – just things that made sense to us. We were misfits clinging together. It was us against the world, and it felt like we'd be that way for life.

iii. After Punk

Jim

Not smoking, giving up my apprenticeship, going to London, coming back – these were all choices I made for myself which aligned with decisions William had made before me, but there was one area where I trod entirely my own path, and that was alcohol. All of the men in my family were what at the time would've been called 'drinkers' – a propensity that was deeply embedded in Scottish ideas of masculinity, and which entailed a level of alcohol consumption which would now probably be deemed consistent with addiction. The culture back then was that men drank whisky and that was how they dealt with their problems, and I kicked against that a bit as a teenager.

It was my own slight rebellion and while it might not seem like a big thing, I know it hurt my dad's feelings. He would've liked his sons to go to the pub with him so he could've said 'Oh, that's my boys', just like all his mates did. But I just couldn't do that at the time – I hated the whole idea of being drunk in the corner with no purpose in life other than to be drinking. My subsequent experiences with alcoholism would show me just how right I'd been to be wary of it, but for the moment I stuck to my guns. Much as I liked my uncles, I didn't want to be like them, singing songs at family parties. I'd seen what people were like when they were drunk, and I didn't want that to be me. And that's why I decided to take drugs before I drank. Fuck the hors d'oeuvres, let's go straight to the main course.

William

Jim did miss that whole thing of being sixteen and getting steaming at the weekend and vomiting Pernod and black. He's a cool guy, so he had the strength of character to resist that conditioning. I, on the other hand, was more of a traditionalist. The thing that made alcohol unfortunately irresistible to me was that it gave me confidence with girls. The very first time I got a bottle of Olde English cider and drank it all and was drunk, I walked a girl home and gave her a kiss at her door. I'd been chatting her up and it had miraculously worked. I thought 'That's it – I've found the secret.' Usually I struggled to talk to girls – I just had no conversation with them – but all I had to do was drink this magic liquid and not only could I talk to them, but they actually seemed to like me. What a terrible lesson I learnt . . .

Jim

I knew why people drank. People drank because they hated their shitty, everyday humdrum existence, and I got that, because that was exactly how I felt – first at school and then at work. But I didn't want to just numb that pain, I wanted to get away from it, escape that reality and replace it with something else. So I got into speed and I got into mushrooms and I got into acid, whenever I could afford them, which as I was now unemployed wasn't very often. The logic of this move is pretty hard to refute even now – given that all the music and the books and the art and the films that we were into at the time seemed to be made by people who took drugs, why wouldn't we want to find out what that felt like?

I'd read a lot of interviews with punk bands and everybody seemed to be speeding, so I thought 'Well, if it's good enough for Johnny Rotten and Joe Strummer, it's good enough for Jim Reid.'

Left to my own devices I wouldn't have had the first idea of how to get it, but luckily one of my cousins hung around with a biker crowd for a while so I could go to her and ask her to get me a gram of speed and that would be it. It was pretty straightforward, and compared to other drugs relatively cheap.

It would've been great if I could've just taken a little snort every now and again, but looking back I can see this as the first manifestation of my inability to do anything in moderation. I tend to do too much of anything I like and with speed I was a bit full on from the word go – I would do my gram in an hour, get really twitchy and then feel horrible afterwards.

Although William and I had grown much closer by this time as music had begun to bring us together, we still had separate little hang-out groups. I would be off with Douglas experimenting with speed and mushrooms and then acid, while William and his friends used to sit around in smoking jackets and discuss Oscar Wilde together. 'I wonder what my little brother's up to? Holy fuck, he's just flown in through the window!' It was only once the band started that who was friends with who became irrelevant and our social circles became as interchangeable as our record collection.

For the moment, it was me and Douglas who were off on our little psychedelic odyssey. Magic mushrooms were everywhere in East Kilbride and I hope for the sake of the younger generations coming through that they still are. Our little council house had a tiny bit of lawn wrapped around it and when the mushrooms were in season there was a carpet of them. We bought a couple of pamphlets from a bookshop in Glasgow that helped us identify which were the right ones to pick and we were delighted to find such a plentiful supply so close to home. First we tried making them into tea but I wouldn't recommend that, as you had to use loads to get your trip, whereas if you dried them out in the oven it would only take a handful to get you high.

In those pre-internet times reliable sources of information on such important topics were hard to come by. I remember *Alternative*

London being a very useful handbook one of either me or William had brought back from a trip to the capital. We'd also read in there about these morning glory seeds that you could get high on if you just crushed them and ate them. We were so desperate to get out of it that we tracked some down in the gardening section of the big Boots in East Kilbride town centre that also sold records and cameras. *Alternative London* had warned us of the downside, which was that before they got you high they made you feel sick. Me and Douglas were sitting there thinking 'Oh fuck, we've poisoned ourselves', and then suddenly the nausea subsided and I said 'Wow, Douglas, you're glowing.'

We were in Douglas's house and his mother came home to find us sat there with big grins on our faces. Everything she said just cracked us up. She must've been thinking 'Oh God, I'm on a roll today – these guys are mesmerised by my wit.' She only had to ask 'Do you want a wee sandwich, doll?', and we'd be rolling on the floor laughing. It was good. Was it worth the nausea? Probably not, because we only did it that one time. There was none of your glue sniffing with us, although my dad did think that was what we were doing, because being a bit of a late developer I had bad acne at the time – around the ages of eighteen to twenty – and thanks to Scottish public information campaigns, every parent knew that one of the side-effects of glue sniffing was terrible spots around your face. My dad would say 'What have you been up to? You're sniffing that glue . . .' To be honest, knowing that my skin problems were bad enough already probably helped keep me off it.

Solvents were more of a thing in Glasgow. In East Kilbride we had bounty the earth was giving us. It was organic, it was back to nature. We'd been walking over those little mushrooms our whole lives without knowing what they were – most people still didn't, but now we did. It was like we'd tapped into a new landscape of forbidden pleasure. We'd found the magic wardrobe that could take us to a psychedelic Narnia and the fact that it was packets of seeds you could buy at Boots and mushrooms you could pick on the way back from the dole office just enhanced the sense of being in on some secret knowledge. You've got this stuff you know about that no one else does, and that is half the fun. It seemed strange that these things weren't more widely understood, but we weren't complaining. Being stuck at home on the dole was a bad situation, but we were making the fucking best of it.

There were people in East Kilbride who sold acid. It was easier to find than some other drugs and it was also relatively cheap – about two quid a trip back then – which made it quite accessible for an experience which should probably not be undertaken lightly. I remember reading the relevant section of *Alternative London* before I took acid for the first time and it said words along the lines of 'be careful because you might not like what you find'. The idea of this being not so much a visual experience as an internal journey alarmed and intrigued me at the same time, and when I did it I saw exactly what they meant. When you see people tripping in the movies it's a purely visual thing, but the experience is actually nothing like that. It's more that it takes you out of the physical realm and makes you look inside yourself in a way that can be quite terrifying.

I'm not sure if it was the first time but it was certainly quite early on in our tripping history that there was a rather comical episode where me and Douglas had the bright idea of getting on a train and going to the seaside when we were under the influence. The non dumb-assed way of doing that would have been to get to the seaside first and then drop the acid, but we dropped the acid first. We had literally a few yards more to walk to get to East Kilbride station when we started to come up. We just looked at each other and thought 'Oh fuck, we can't do this.'

There was a little bare patch of grass next to the station and we lay down on this forlorn dog shit-bedecked postage stamp for about the next five hours listening to music on the little slab of a tape machine which I used to carry with me everywhere. It wasn't a boom box, it was one of those flat rectangular ones with big buttons. We always listened to the same stuff – compilations we'd made of The Velvet Underground, Syd Barrett, a smattering of punk rock. I would say music that made sense when we were tripping, but any music makes sense when you're tripping, because it just weaves itself into the trip. The more intense the trip, the better the music sounds. We could've been listening to The Brotherhood of Man or a guy digging a hole in the road with a pneumatic drill and it would've seemed profound to us.

It was a scorching hot summer's day – I know people might be thinking, 'But it's Scotland, what are you talking about?' But we did get them every now and then. So we dropped down on this scrubby little piece of grass and disappeared inside ourselves for about five hours. It was kind of amazing but the stupid thing was we got sunburnt to hell. Worse than that was that being cool dudes and potential rock stars in our own minds, we were wearing sunglasses. So when we took these cool shades off, our fucking faces were bright red but the skin around our eyes was peely-wally white. We looked like drugged-up pandas. I took my sunglasses off and Douglas looked at me and started pissing himself. He kept saying 'Your eyes, man' and then when he took his off I thought 'Oh, right.'

We were still off our tits and hyper-sensitive to everything but had realised by now that the beach was out of the question, so we just started walking around the town. It felt like everybody was staring at us, which no doubt they were because of our bright-red sunburn, but we were getting really paranoid, thinking 'Fuck, these people can all see what's happening to us – we've got to get off the streets.' So we went back to my house and William, who wasn't quite down with the programme yet as far as psychedelic exploration was concerned, opened the door and said 'Ye fucking idiot – look at your bloody face.' I was utterly fragile and looking for someone to hug me and all I got was this fraternal animosity . . . Acid would have the last laugh as far as William was concerned, but we'll get to that later.

Douglas and I sometimes used to trip while walking round the town late at night. It was just more pleasant because you saw less people and East Kilbride felt like a different place in the early hours. I used to take a plastic bag with me, full of little things that it would amuse me to look at once I was off my face. One night it was pishing with rain and we took shelter under the canopy of a garage forecourt. It was probably three in the morning so obviously they weren't open – good luck finding an all-night garage in East Kilbride in 1982. We were standing there seeing all sorts – I remember the sky seemed to be flicking from day to night time like a broken strip light – when a police car pulled into the garage and one of the policemen got out and slowly walked over to us.

Douglas was just muttering 'Oh fuck! Oh fuck!' I told him to shut up, because for some reason on this occasion I was confident I could keep it together. The policeman asked 'So whose is the car?' And we both answered 'What car?' Then he pointed literally five yards to one side of us where there was a car some joyriders had abandoned with all its doors open and its lights flashing. Maybe that had been the source of the sky switching on and off. Either way, we were tripping to the extent that it had eluded our notice.

At this point, just as I was trying very hard not to say anything too idiotic, the policeman asked what was in my bag. 'Just a few things,' I answered mysteriously. When he insisted I show him, there was a light-up yo-yo and a Sindy doll and a series of other equally random objects.

He asked what we were doing there and we told him we were on the dole and a bit depressed and had nothing better to do than walk around town late at night. I guess it was the element of truth in that which saved us, as I don't understand why else a policeman would let two weirdos with pupils the size of saucers walk away from an obviously stolen car at three in the morning. Unless he'd just had a message from the station saying 'The buttered scones have just been toasted and you'd better get back quick or Fat Bob's gonna scoff the lot . . .'

William

I don't see the sunrise. Ever since I was eighteen I've gone to sleep at two or three or four in the morning and I haven't deviated from that. At first my ma used to tell me it was a phase, and I would say 'Why is it a phase, ma?' After midnight there was a weird atmosphere and everything was different, which was what I like. I used to take our dog Patch out for walks late at night and they were some of the most incredible experiences of my life. I loved that dog so much and she was such a big part of our lives growing up that even now I cry when I think about her not being here any more.

Patch was just a member of the family who'd been there since I was twelve, but then after she died and Jim and I were away, my ma and da got another dog and called it Candy. I never got on with that dog, because they treated it completely differently. Patch had never been allowed to go on the couch – my da was a wee bit lenient but my ma would go nuts if Patch even tried to get up there. To my ma, a dog was just a dog, until that fucking idiot Candy came along. She wasn't just allowed on the couch, she slept with them in the bed!

My ma would go, 'That's my baby, that's my baby', and it wasn't hard to understand why, because by that time we'd all left – not just me and Jim, but Linda as well – and my ma was a very motherly woman. Jim and one of our cousins were born at around the same time, and because my aunt was plagued with illness and couldn't breast-feed, my ma breast-fed the both of them.

Jim

Patch was a little mutt who looked like a border collie. We used to pound the pavements of East Kilbride endlessly with her. That was the excuse to get out of the house – 'Let's take the dog for a walk' – and we'd be back five hours later.

We weren't pasty-faced wastrels who never left the sofa. I probably had quite a healthy lifestyle back then – lots of exercise because I was always walking, didn't drink, not enough money to buy as many drugs as I would've liked . . . And we never reached that level of being on the dole where you lose the will to live. I would've probably got there eventually had I not found my way out of East Kilbride, but at that stage of your life, there's still hope. We always felt there was something just around the corner – I guess if you turned enough of those corners and there was nothing there, you'd eventually get that sense of hopelessness, but thankfully we got lucky before it got that bad.

William

Around the time Channel 4 first came on – in 1982 – we got a video recorder which changed our whole lives. My ma and da were beautiful people but they were very middle-of-the-road. They liked Dick Emery, for fuck's sake. Some kids with hippy parents might've been finding dog-eared volumes of Allen Ginsberg's poetry lying around the house to enlighten them, but that was never going to happen to us (although some of my ma's Arthur Hailey books were quite shocking, not to say educational). When you're coming from a very mainstream household like we grew up in you have to find out for yourself about this other world of books and plays and music and drugs and sex – stuff that's always been there but you never saw much of except when you went to the library. You realise there's this secret society of coolness where there's a guy called William Burroughs who's a morphine addict and he writes these weird junkie books and he killed his wife when he was shooting the apple and you think 'Yeah, these are my people!'

It's a lineage that's goes back through Orson Welles and Oscar Wilde all the way to Roman times. Is it cool? Is it clever? Whatever you want to call it, it's the difference between The Rolling Stones and Freddie and the Dreamers. You feel like everyone else is into Freddie and the Dreamers. As you're growing up you're trying to tell your ma and da about this alternative dimension, this magical other world of cool things, but they're not really listening. For me and Jim, BBC2, Channel 4 and the video recorder were portals to that dimension.

Did you ever watch that Channel 4 comedy show *Frasier*? My ma used to say that Frasier and Niles were me and Jim, and my da was the old guy with the Jack Russell. I think maybe he wanted us to be all rough and tough and football players or else guys who lifted things, but it turned out we were aesthetes who wrote beautiful little indie songs and that wasn't what he was expecting.

Jim

There were a few honourable exceptions – *Gregory's Girl* would be one, Alex Harvey, Billy Connolly and Ivor Cutler would be others – but when I was in my teens and early twenties I always cringed whenever Scotland was represented anywhere. At the point where anyone made a big deal about being Scottish, it always seemed really twee – it was all tartan and shortbread and the charming old guy with the whiskers who likes a wee dram. The great thing about people like Orange Juice – who I didn't see live in their Postcard era, but I did go to a show in Glasgow in 1981 and very good it was too – and Josef K (and Simple Minds for that matter, who I really liked, and not just in their early days) was that they could've been from anywhere, they weren't making a big deal out of being Scottish.

William

Both Jim and I really liked Orange Juice, but we liked them because they made amazing music, not because they grew up in Glasgow. The Fire Engines came from Edinburgh, but they still made a couple of my favourite records. If I went on *Desert Island Discs* I would definitely have to pick 'Candyskin'. The first time I heard it I thought it was a newly discovered Velvet Underground song, and when John Peel said they came from Edinburgh I thought 'What the fuck?! *Edinburgh*!? Why are you doing this to me?'

I always feel a wee bit guilty because I don't really like Josef K. People from all over the world have said 'Here's a Josef K cassette for you, William', and I've said 'No, I don't want it.' Then they get all freaked out – 'Why not? Why not, man?' 'I don't know, I'm just not into 'em.'

Jim

We absolutely did share our record collection and there wasn't a record – with the possible exception of Josef K – that we didn't consider that we jointly owned. I wasn't saying 'Ah, The Smiths, I don't like them as much as William does, so that belongs to him.' Suddenly we understood each other in ways we never had before. I knew what he liked and he knew what I liked and I knew what he thought before he said anything, and likewise. It was almost as if it wasn't just a record collection we shared. It reached a point where it might have appeared to some people as if we shared one personality – right down to the single snorkel anorak we used to take turns wearing when we took the dog for a walk.

William

That parka was one of the dark-blue ones you could find in every home-shopping catalogue. What was funny about it was that when we put the hood up, the neighbours couldn't tell which one of us was wearing it – which we loved. We'd pass them in the street and they'd say 'Which fucking one of them was that?' Because we looked the same without a face. We were Kenny before *South Park*. . . I guess the odd *Beavis and Butthead* element might've crept in as well.

Jim

When video cameras suddenly came on the market you could rent them from the Granada shop on the high street, and because me and William had always been interested in film we pooled our dole money to hire one and went around just shooting loads of experimental stuff, like some revolutionary footage of our granny on the toilet, which she wasn't too bothered by. It was one of those cameras where you had to carry the video recorder with you on a strap, so it was like walking round town with five phone books strapped together . . .

We also went through a short-lived Cabaret Voltaire phase when William got hold of a reel-to-reel tape recorder that you could do reverb and echo on and then overdub separately, and I ordered a Stockhausen album from the library. That was fun but it wasn't really us.

There was still no idea of us being in a band together at that point – we thought we would bicker too much (later developments would prove this assessment was totally on the money) and it wasn't until we started trying to write songs for the two separate bands that we were trying to get together that actual songs came about.

William

At first, the songs I was writing were just bad versions of songs that existed already. They sounded just like whatever I was listening to at the time and everything was too noticeably some-one else's style. When I'd had a few goes at moving away from home – in the late seventies, and again in 1981 – I'd always had vague hopes of starting a band or doing something interesting, but it was only once I was kind of stuck in East Kilbride that I started to make progress with songwriting. It wasn't such a bad place to be. I knew I had a little bit of talent and if I just stuck at it and carried on writing songs, maybe the bad ones would get better.

By the time the eighties were properly underway, the inspir-ational components I was missing when I was younger had started to come into play. As well as the Pistols, The Clash and Subway Sect, there were The Velvet Underground, The Thirteenth Floor Elevators, Love and The Seeds. The bulk of the pre-punk stuff actually came to my attention after punk was done, but that glitch in chronology kept things fresh. Obviously this hasn't been true of all songwriters through the ages, but it turned out I needed all this stuff in my creative system before I could do anything good myself.

I was getting better on the guitar – you learn one song and then another, and then eventually you can pick it up and vaguely pick something out. You're making an effort but you're also learning naturally because you've just heard Can and last week when you were writing songs there wasn't Can in your head but now there is. 'Mushroom' is part of your artis-tic artillery. So you're sitting down and you still don't really like what you're doing but you can feel it moving towards something.

I never found it easy to write lyrics. To this day, that's the hardest bit – lyrics are fucking bastards. But having written hundreds of terrible songs, the first good one popped out in 1983. It was a song called 'Sowing Seeds' that a couple of years later ended up on *Psychocandy* – that was the first time I started to think I might be getting somewhere . . .

I was pretty good at playing football, informally, as a kid. I'm not saying I was a great footballer – I couldn't have made a living at it – but I was a little bit talented and half decent with my pals. So I thought I'd go for the school team, but when I tried to up my game I was just fucking awful. It was embarrassing, like I'd never seen a football before. It was just one of those humiliations where you thought you were good at something but then you discover you're not.

With music, it was the other way round. I don't know if Jim's the same, but in my life in general I never felt that strong. I'm neurotic as fuck and I'm quite a small guy – five foot seven and three quarters, and only small people need to mention the three quarters. Music's the only place where I've felt like a giant – 'I know this shit, I'm not scared of anything here' – and outside that realm I'm not quite so confident.

Jim

We'd had an old acoustic guitar for a while that we used to just make bits of songs up on.

William

It takes a lot to get a song to the point where you're willing to let someone else hear it, and as dismissive as he had been about 'My Name Is Jonathan', Jim was always the first person I'd play something new to.

Jim

Although we used to complain about East Kilbride at the time, in a way the fact that we were separate and cut off from everything else was ultimately what made our band what it was. You're in this little place that is nowhere near the centre of things and that not only makes you try a bit harder, it also gives you room to develop what you're doing on your own terms and not as part of a scene.

If there was a film playing at the East Kilbride cinema in the 1980s it was going to be *Rambo*, and it felt like everyone else liked it except us – we were the neighbourhood weirdos, the guys that looked a bit odd and didn't fit in with mass tastes or the pattern of expected behaviour. Especially as far as our parents were concerned.

Our parents were straight-down-the-middle kind of people and we were a bit bizarre to them – we were kind of unusual in the neighbourhood full stop. For a long time my mum and dad used to wonder 'Where did you two come from?' It started off as a joke. My mum would ask herself 'How the fuck did I end up with a pair of queeries like you?' At first those things were said in a tongue-in-cheek way, but after a few years of us being cooped up in the house together, wry amusement had turned to bitter sarcasm, and William and I cultivating an outer shell of arrogance to cover up our many insecurities probably didn't help.

The fact that we'd both given up what our parents considered to be very good apprenticeships had caused a certain amount of friction in the house even before my dad got made redundant. But then the shit really hit the fan. Factories were closing down everywhere in the Thatcher era, and in 1983 the Caterpillar plant in Uddingston in Glasgow where my dad had been a machine operator since I was a small boy was next on the casualty list. My dad was only in his forties at the time – still quite young – and he expected it would be easy for him to get another job, as it had been when he'd changed jobs a few times in the sixties, but it wasn't and he never worked again after that.

For him this was a massive blow, and even though it was never officially acknowledged within the family, I think what he went through in the years after that was something akin to a breakdown. For all those years he'd been 'Jimmy from the Caterpillar' and now he had to reinvent himself, but it was hard for him – as it was for a lot of men of that generation. The education system had taught them to think work was what gave a man value, but now as hard as he tried to get a job, there just weren't any.

In that context a couple of layabout sons quoting Baudelaire and Arthur Lee at him while they hoarded every penny of their dole money to buy musical accessories for an as-yet grounded mission to stardom must have been the very last thing he needed. The only jobs I remember my mum having in East Kilbride were in a wallpaper shop in the sixties and then from the seventies onwards she worked in the Manhattan chip shop for about twenty-five years. When I look back I can totally see this whole situation from my parents' point of view – 'What's your plan?' 'Oh, we're gonna be rock stars' 'Yeah, right.' It must have sounded insane, because it actually was insane. The fact that it did ultimately happen didn't make it any less improbable.

You can picture the early-eighties scene – a big chunky telly in the corner with a video recorder underneath it, mum and dad's nicotine-stained wallpaper all around us. Everyone else would go to bed, and me and William would sit there till the early hours listening to records, making plans and drinking cups of tea because that was all that was on offer. It had to be done quietly because everyone else was trying to sleep and it was a small house. There was no doubt about who was in charge. We knew we were a couple of wasters who were signing on and our mum and dad were quite capable of throwing us out at any moment – because in my case they'd done that already – so there was no playing records loud at two in the morning.

We'd start talking about films – 'Why don't people make films like this?' And pretty much plan a movie overnight. It was the same thing with books and most of all with bands. The make-up of the perfect band was discussed many times and ultimately that perfect band went on to be us. I understand that everyone's perfect band would be different, but ours turned out to be The Jesus and Mary Chain, and those late-night discussions where we'd be putting the world – or our world, anyway – to rights at three in the morning, they were the crucible in which the band was forged.

The actual sound of the band was something me and William didn't even need to talk about very much. We were both very much into sixties garage rock but also sixties pop, and we wondered why no one had ever previously tried to put the most offensive, loud, screeching guitars over the top of the bittersweet melodies of The Shangri-Las. We couldn't understand why no one had done that before, but it gave us our opportunity – the thought was there between us that this was a gap in the market, but we'd need the right technology to deliver on our vision.

William

My da gave his all for that factory but Caterpillar didn't give a fuck. They used a loophole to pay him about a tenth of the redundancy he was meant to get – not just him, it was all his mates as well. This made what he did next even more generous. He gave me and Jim three hundred quid each of his redundancy money. He thought we were gonna pool our money to buy a motor or maybe get driving lessons so we could pass our tests and have licences, all of which was a normal aspiration and in his and my ma's assessment would've expanded our range of employment opportunities. But motors and driving lessons were the last thing on our minds. We bought a Portastudio – which did ultimately prove to be a very wise investment, although my da at that point could be forgiven for thinking otherwise.

In fact there was total disbelief in his voice as he tried to process what we'd done. 'You've bought a tape recorder?!' We were like 'No, it's not just a tape recorder, da, it records on four tracks and you can overdub so you can have eight tracks or twelve or sixteen!' He was horrified and just kept repeating – 'You bought a tape recorder?!' He couldn't believe we'd bought one for three hundred quid when you could get one for fifteen.

'It's not a tape recorder – well, it is, but it's a special kind of tape recorder with magical powers . . .' He thought we'd wasted his money, and we actually did come perilously close to doing that, because it was a terrible wee Portastudio – one of the very early Tascam ones from a high-end place called Victor Morris in Glasgow. It was a little miracle when it worked, but it used to break down all the time so we had to keep taking it back and paying for repairs because the warranty ran out really quickly – Victor Morris, you're a bastard.

I found out later when I got to know other people who'd used them that there was a design fault on the early models – if it had been the internet age people would've been going online and sharing their pain that their Portastudio kept breaking down every two or three months, but as it was, ours was the only one in East Kilbride – at least as far as we knew – and we just thought it was cursed. It was also the thing that made our band possible, and a lifeline we were able to let other bands use. That Tascam was the greatest gift that our da could've given us and it was ironic that his misfortune was our opportunity.

Jim

Once we got the Portastudio we both started making four-track demos – William would go into the bedroom saying 'I'm going to make a demo', then I would do it the next night. And those were the songs that would end up being on *Psychocandy*. We never wrote songs together at that stage. Meanwhile, Davy Campbell's dad had an old-fashioned looking Gretsch Tennessean guitar which Davy sold to William for twenty quid behind his dad's back. This was not a bad price at all, as even then it was probably worth at least two hundred, so Davy's dad was kicking him up and down the street when he found out . . .

William

Not long after I got the guitar, I heard that this kid Queenie was selling a Shin-ei fuzz pedal for a tenner. That was actually quite a lot of money at the time – it should've been a fiver because it was nineteen eighty fucking three. His full name was McQueen but we called him Queenie, and God save McQueen, because he gave us a loan of this pedal, I plugged it into a horrible little Marshall transistor amp and it sounded fucking amazing right from the off. It's hard to describe even now but there was an almost orchestral sound coming through my newly acquired Gretsch.

I gave him a tenner straight away before he changed his mind, and word came back not long after that he called me a sucker 'cos he'd sold me a broke pedal. Of course it wasn't broke – he just didn't know how to use it, because he didn't appreciate its insanity. He thought it was useless because the frequencies were jumping everywhere, but I thought it was beautiful and so did Jim. At certain settings it definitely sounded out of control but that was what made it so exciting. I don't think we even properly had a band at the time, so it was almost more like the pedal recruited us to do its work.

Jim

I'll tell you one thing – we made those fuzz pedals famous. Those wonderful fizzing, exploding sounds don't come cheap any more. If you try and find a Shin-ei fuzz wah pedal on eBay now you'll pay hundreds for one, but what with the pedal and William's guitar, we'd essentially bought our career for thirty quid. We may not have had two shirt buttons to rub together, but the one and a half we had, we'd put to good use. The Gretsch Tennessean, the Shin-ei pedal and the Portastudio from my dad's redundancy payment, that was our roadmap out of hell.

William

We'd watch *Lou Grant* till about half one and then put the telly off and get down to our scheming. It was funny because it was so stupid – we'd talk about 'My group's gonna be like this' and 'My group's gonna be like that', and it was basically the same fucking group. But we didn't realise for a long time that we were talking about the same thing. So we'd be telling people we knew, 'I need a drummer', or 'I need a bass player', and they'd just be looking at us, thinking 'Why are you trying to do two bands, you fucking idiots?'

It took me a long time to see it. My motivation at that point was quite clear in my mind – I wanted to a) make brilliant records and get them out there so people could hear them, b) get a wee bit of money, and c) get a bunch of girls . . . and c) was the reason I didn't want my brother there while I was doing it.

You know that special face you pull when you're young and you're trying to get off with a girl? Maybe Jim was completely himself in an amorous setting, but I wasn't, so I'd be chatting someone up and then Jim would walk past and I would just turn back into myself – I could not sustain the illusion. I didn't want that to keep happening throughout a major pop career . . .

Jim

The idea of us not being able to be in a band together because we would've cramped each other's style around girls is completely ridiculous and I am surprised William would say that.

The reason The Jesus and Mary Chain ultimately came into being was as much about what we hated as what we loved. There was a real mood of disenchantment in 1982–83. It seemed like there was a thread that ran through great popular music, from the blues to Elvis Presley to Dylan to The Beatles and the Stones to Bowie and glam up to punk and post-punk, and it seemed that somehow this thread had broken. We detested what was going on in the charts and on *Top of the Pops* at that point, and our mission in so far as we had one was to try to restore music to what it once had been. I remember one thing that really kicked us up the arse was Kid Creole and The Coconuts being on the cover of the *NME* – we thought 'Fuck this! We are not going to have this, we are going to have to start a band to get rid of this kind of shite!'

William

It wasn't like it was Jim's dream to be the singer either – we basically had a big fight about who was gonna sing and he lost.

Jim

We actually tossed a coin for it, but the outcome was the same: William won. I was the singer.

I was and still am one of the shyest human beings in the world, so the idea of stepping out on a stage in any capacity was terrifying enough. The idea of going up to the middle of the stage and singing was something that I could not get my fucking head around, but someone was going to have to do it.

After Ivor dropped out of the picture for reasons I can't really remember, that left me, William and Douglas. We just needed a drummer, which was quite difficult, but eventually we found Murray Dalglish through the friend of a friend. He was a bit younger than us and there was some overlap in terms of musical taste, but not that much. He was more into goth music but he could play the drums and he wanted to be in the band, so from that point we were able to rehearse.

We hated rehearsing but we knew that it was necessary. Everyone thinks that being in a band is all just the good stuff, and there is good stuff but in order to get access to that you have to put a bit of work in. If you want to play in front of a crowd you can't just show up and start playing, you have to know what you're doing and that takes gruelling preparation. We would practise wherever we could find little community centres in East Kilbride that would give us a room for an afternoon for nothing. It was a pain in the arse to get the gear there – obviously we had no transport, so we would have to take our guitars and amps on those little trolleys that pensioners carry their shopping in. So there'd be the four of us lifting this gear half a mile down the road to the community centre where we could just let it rip and play as loud as we liked to try to get the songs into a kind of playable shape.

I remember at first it was a bit disappointing, because you've got your wee demos that you've lived with for a while and you think they're quite good and you've got it in your head how this is all gonna sound. But then you plug in and you try and play those songs and they don't come out how you thought. There's no mixing desk and there's no PA and it's all spilling out of the amps in different parts of the room, so you sound like a total rabble. But then you start to learn a few things, like how to stack the gear up and where to point it and how badly you need a separate amp for the vocal, and it doesn't take long to get from 'Oh fuck, we're never gonna be able to do this' to a point where it's coming together enough for you to think 'This is OK – it's a version of something which we could play to an audience, if we ever get one.'

I suppose just because it had always seemed like a dream or at best an idea, once it started to become something that could actually happen – we're in a band, we've got a drummer and a bass player and a bunch of songs and it actually sounds pretty good – we had a very clear sense that this was our chance. Now we'd finally got the ball rolling, we seemed to instinctively know what the next move was, but there were still some pretty big obstacles to overcome, like the fact that there was a scene in Glasgow at the time that was essentially the opposite of us.

William

That mini wave of shit Glasgow pop-soul was just breaking – Hipsway, Love and Money, Hue and Cry, all those type of people playing the guitar in what Douglas called 'the wank rhythm'. Because that clique of bands had the live circuit virtually sewn up, it was almost impossible for us to get a gig.

Jim

We knew the demo was good, and looking back now the lineage of us being the next thing after Orange Juice and Josef K and the Fire Engines kind of makes sense, but people at the time didn't see it that way. The Glasgow scene – in its own mind at least – had moved on. The problem was the direction that it had moved in. The great thing about Orange Juice's Al Green cover was that it actually had soul, whereas all those Hipsway and Hue and Cry type of bands were making the most soulless music you could think of. They probably thought they were putting a new twist on soul, but they were wrong. Nonetheless, they saw it as progress, and I think – although it was never said like this at the time – people considered what we were trying to do to be a backward step. Either way, no one in the long list of every mover and shaker in Glasgow that we sent our demo to would even reply to us.

The guy from the Candy Club was a typical example – he just wasn't interested. But luckily he was a friend of Bobby Gillespie's, who we didn't know yet, but whose own band Primal Scream were – we would later discover – at the same stage as us of banging their heads against the wall of a Glasgow scene which hated everything we (and they) were about. Seeing that we'd recorded our demo on the other side of a Syd Barrett tape, the Candy Club guy said 'Here, Bobby, you like Syd Barrett don't you, you can have this . . .'

William

I can't remember which two early songs of ours were on that demo, but I know it was *The Madcap Laughs* on the other side. And because Bobby did indeed like Syd Barrett, his curiosity was aroused. He played our side and thought it was interesting, so he phoned up Douglas – whose mum's phone number was on the tape – and he and Douglas chatted for ages. Then Douglas called us and said 'Some guy in Glasgow has heard our tape and thinks it's pretty good and he's into a lot of really good music . . .' It wasn't just about him liking our songs. We hardly knew anybody who was into all the stuff that we liked, so it felt as if we'd found a kindred spirit.

Jim

Bobby ringing to tell us he liked our demo was the first bit of encouragement we'd ever had. And in the same breath he started telling us about this mate of his in London called Alan McGee who had a club and a label and he was sure would put us on down there if we'd only send him the tape. We followed his instructions and even though as it turned out Alan wasn't instantly won over, he still said he'd put us on as a favour to Bobby.

Bobby Gillespie's autobiography claims that East Kilbride at that time was full of guys with air rifles, and it's true there was a phase in the early eighties where that kind of low-impact weaponry seemed to be ubiquitous, especially in the ned community. You'd be walking down the road and you'd hear a report and a milk bottle would explode. You'd know it was those fucking neds with their air rifle so you'd have to jump over a wall and take cover for a while – 'Is it OK to go out yet?' I have to say that I don't remember anyone ever suffering a serious injury . . .

There was a country park near us called Calder Glen which was a beautiful place in every respect except it was also the place all the hoodlums went for their target practice so you'd have to be careful. That was where Douglas and I would go down to the place we called The Acid Factory. It was an old abandoned paint factory that was about forty minutes' walk away from our house.

It was a huge place which must've had a couple of thousand people working there when it was open, but now it was derelict we had it all to ourselves. It was the opposite of all the love and peace stuff which people generally associate with acid, because we used to get wrecked and trash the place. It was like something out of *Apocalypse Now* – we'd be going mental, off our heads, smashing metal poles into walls with no one to stop us and no reason not to carry on, because the factory was going to get levelled and it eventually did. We were just the first phase of the demolition. We got the job started and a few years later they came in with the wrecking balls.

The musical landscape was quite bleak for a while at that time but one new band that really made an impression on us was Einstürzende Neubauten. We didn't get to see them till a couple of years later, after we'd moved down to London, but I saw an early interview with Blixa Bargeld on *The Whistle Test* (I think it'd lost the 'Old Grey' by then, but they weren't fooling anyone – I hated the show by that time) where he said 'You don't need musical instruments to make music.' I remember thinking 'Of course, you don't. What is a musical instrument other than just an object that makes noise? So is a fucking road drill, so is an angle-grinder, so is a hammer bashing off a washing machine – yeah, this is great.' It was almost like the ultimate form of punk rock – just noise with a voice on top – and there were lots of lesser bands proclaiming different versions of that gospel around that time.

Helping that old building collapse while tripping was a way of tapping into that powerful destructive energy. It was very liberating to be left to your own devices in that state and just get into what was happening in that exact moment. There was something very primal about it – you could lose yourself, and the time we took William down there to take acid with Primal Scream, he had some difficulty finding himself again.

William

Jim and Douglas had already done loads of mushrooms and LSD, and they'd also met Primal Scream a couple of times and got on great with them, but the old paint factory was my first time on both counts and I must say that it was a terrible experience. It was pretty embarrassing for me when the acid we'd scored in Glasgow took hold. I'd only just met Bobby Gillespie and twenty minutes later I was jumping around hitting one arm with the other trying to dislodge imaginary insects. And then it got worse. I think Jim felt a bit of guilt about it afterwards because he just assumed I'd be OK, as he'd done it before so what could possibly go wrong?

Jim

When William asked me 'How much should I take?', I said 'Oh, just take a whole one.' I did feel a little responsible afterwards that I just dropped him into a full trip thinking 'Oh, he'll be all right', where we probably should have built him up to it gradually by taking a half a tab a few times to see how it went, which was what me and Douglas had done. As it was, he had a bad trip and kind of freaked out and I had to take him away from everyone to talk him down.

There was a Cramps song playing on the cassette player – 'Beautiful Gardens' – that has a lyric about 'spiders in my eyelids', and because obviously the thing about acid is you're very suggestible, William was shouting 'That is happening! That is happening!' And I'd have to say 'No, that is not real'. There were loads of things like that. There was one point where he was looking at a tree and he became convinced there was someone inside it, pushing, trying to get out – I remember looking at the tree, thinking 'Fuck, don't let me see it too.'

William

Everybody was saying this was the strongest acid they'd ever had and as a first-timer the intensity of the hallucinations was overwhelming.

It was a very hot day for Scotland and I remember thinking that somehow I'd gone back to the sixties and I was in Vietnam. My freckles became like horrible little insects crawling all over my arms and nobody wants that. I got all the clichéd things like looking up into the sky and all these birds turning into bats. One that was quite special was doing a pee and it lasting what seemed like twenty minutes. 'When is it going to end? This can't be pee, this must be like my . . . *life juice*! Everything's pouring out of me!' I remember thinking that the tree I was peeing against was going to come to life (in a way beyond the life it already had as a tree) . . .

When it wasn't terrifying, some of it was incredible. Jim took me away from everyone to sit in a park so he could calm me down and on the way there I swear to this day we were talking without talking – telepathically, without using words. Jim said the same thing when we came back to earth. It was actually an important bonding experience for us. As we were walking back to our house and the drug was starting to wear off so we were seeing normal things again, about twenty kids with Down's syndrome came past us on an outing and I was watching these kids walking by, not knowing if I was hallucinating – it sent me back over the line.

I had another strange flashback experience about a year or so later. In the summer of 1985, I was walking with my girlfriend down by Putney Bridge in London where there are benches alongside the river when we saw a businessman get up on the bridge. He stood up, put his briefcase down and jumped off the bridge into the Thames. I thought it was a hallucination but my girlfriend said 'No, he really did fall', and at that point I went into this kind of free-form hallucination as if I was on acid again. It was insane – the birds started turning into bats again and it all started with this man jumping off the fucking bridge. We never knew what happened – we went home and looked on the local news and there was nothing. I said 'This is London – people do make films here. Is there any chance this was a film?', but my girlfriend said no, it had definitely happened.

This did send me a little crazy for half an hour and I was pretty traumatised after the original Acid Factory incident too. I didn't like looking at birds in the sky for weeks – in fact the sky in general I had a problem with, to the point where I resolved that I was never going to take a hallucinogenic drug again (although as it turned out, I would have some very positive experiences with mushrooms and then one with acid in the nineties).

Jim

The reason I didn't do acid too many more times was that I found the process of self-examination it would open up inside my head to be a little too harsh for something I was theoretically doing for entertainment. 'Wait a minute, aren't we supposed to be having fun here? And yet suddenly I'm questioning the fundamentals of my existence and I'm not liking the answers I'm getting . . .'

Music was a problem too, after a while . . . because acid makes whatever you are listening to sound amazing and profound, you might as well just switch off the tape machine and listen to the birdsong. In a way that's much more entertaining, because when you're on acid the birds will be talking to you – you can hear what they're saying, you really can, you just don't remember it when the drug wears off.

That was the other thing that started to frustrate me about tripping. It felt like the secrets of the universe were laid bare to you – you could see them and you could understand them – but only at that moment, in that frame of mind. When the drug wore off, you remembered that you had had a profound experience, you just couldn't remember what it was. So you've got the keys to the kingdom, but you had to hand them back when you left the hotel, and I found that very frustrating. There were words I could hear in my head when I was tripping that I couldn't say out loud. I'd sit there for hours, thinking 'Why can't I fucking say this?' I could hear it in my head, but when I would try to say it, it didn't mean anything and it wasn't even a word. That started to happen every time I was tripping – it was the same fucking word every time, or at least it was the same shadow where a word ought to be – but I couldn't say it, never mind write it down. It started to really freak me out.

In the end I just thought 'Fuck it, maybe I'll try some other drugs that give me confidence and make it easier to talk to girls.' Unfortunately, alcohol and cocaine were lying in wait for me . . . and being in the band would be the key that opened the door for them.

The early versions of us making music were just fumbling around in the dark, really. It only came into focus – the light was turned on, you could say – when there was a band called The Jesus and Mary Chain. There was definitely a sense that we were running out of time to finalise it in time for our first show down in London. The tracks Bobby got hold of and talked to McGee about were probably sent out as The Poppy Seeds. We knew that wasn't the name but if you're sending demos out you have to put something.

The name didn't come to us in a blinding flash of light, but it wasn't far off that. It was William's idea. The two of us were throwing possibilities about and he suddenly said 'Oh, what about The Jesus and Mary Chain?' I started off a sentence where I was going to say 'What the fuck are you on about?', but then changed my mind before the end of it to 'That's fucking brilliant.' It doesn't sound like a band name, that's what I was going to say to him, but then I realised that was what was great about it: it was actually original. Once we had the band's name, the whole identity we'd been looking for all those years was ready to go – we were already rehearsing, we had demos, we had gigs lined up – the name just lit the blue touch paper.

To get around the fact that no one in Glasgow would give us a gig, we'd already shot some fake 'live photos' that were actually done in our bedroom. We were very into photography at that time – we'd bought a Pentax SLR camera that we paid a pound a week on for about a year and a half. Then we saw an advert in the local paper saying that some old geezer was selling an enlarger. So we went round to his flat and he was so pleased that his equipment was going to young people who were keen that he let us have it for about £2 and gave us loads of the printing paper as a bonus. We got books from the library and worked out that developing black and white negatives and printing them is just about doable, and it turned out to be relatively easy. I would love to have done colour as well, but the temperatures have to be much more precise in the processing so we never went down that road.

We had a blackout sheet to put over the window so we could use the bedroom as a darkroom, and this doubled as a backdrop to simulate being onstage. Obviously there were no pictures of us 'performing' together because one of us had to be taking the photo. I'd be standing on one of our beds with William holding the micstand up from underneath (because the stand wouldn't fit on the bed), and we used the light from the enlarger to create the illusion of a spotlight.

We fully realised at the time how ludicrous this was – it's one step away from singing into your hairbrush in front of the mirror – but the irony was we were only doing it because we wanted to be taken seriously. If someone had given us a gig earlier, we wouldn't have had to do it, but since we'd still never played one at this point we had to make it look like this was a real band. Sometimes you've got to dream it to be it. And as ridiculous as playing imaginary gigs and taking photos of them might sound, it actually worked. Because when we got a friend who worked in a print shop to do us a few thousand of those posters and we stuck them up all around Glasgow, they created quite a buzz: 'Oh my God, these Jesus and Mary Chain guys look great and they've played shows – I wish I'd have been there!'

We actually did two of those poster runs with the same image, which was a collage of those photos of us supposedly playing live. The first lot – which actually got the biggest reaction – just had the name The Jesus and Mary Chain at the bottom, the second batch had the date of our first gig in Glasgow, at some club in Argyll Street, which we had finally managed to line up, but which wasn't going to happen till after we'd gone down to London to do our debut show for McGee.

It was ridiculous that we had to go to London to get our first fucking gig but it also helped to define us as outsiders from the very beginning. That was something which would continue throughout our whole career. We always struggled to find a place where we could fit comfortably, and as the years went on we would learn to take a strange kind of comfort from that and even to enjoy it. Fuck you, here we are, we're The Jesus and Mary Chain.

Part 3
Creation (1984)

Jim

It was a scorching hot summer day in June 1984 when we went to London for that first meeting with McGee. We'd got the overnight bus down from Glasgow and turned up early at the gig at his club the Living Room, which was a little shit-hole of a room upstairs at The Roebuck Arms near Tottenham Court Road. We set up our gear and waited for McGee to show up before attempting our first formal soundcheck. Because we didn't even know what Alan looked like at that point, we were hanging out of the first-floor window assessing all these interesting characters walking up the street towards the pub and thinking 'Is that him there?' 'Oh yeah, that guy who looks like Jim Morrison. I bet that's him . . .' It wasn't, though.

This went on for quite a while until finally this frizzy red-headed lunatic character was heading in our direction. Nobody pegged him as McGee until he came up the stairs saying 'Hi, I'm Alan, how you doing?' The 'For fuck's sakes' were barely out of our mouths before his enthusiasm began to grow on us.

We made the introductions and started playing our soundcheck. We'd got through about half a not very musical song when William and I had a big blazing row over something that was nothing – which was something we used to do a lot. This screaming match almost came to blows before we started playing the song again, and by that time even the vaguest contact with the intended rhythm and chord structure had probably been lost.

McGee was watching sort of spellbound – I think he just thought we were nuts, but he was going crazy for it. He'd been quite luke-warm when we sent him the demos and he'd only put the gig on as a favour to Bobby, but as soon as he saw us doing that soundcheck, everything changed for the better. Because he used to salivate a lot when he got excited, he was literally frothing at the mouth.

We couldn't believe it, as we thought we'd ruined our chance – we were standing there ready to headbutt each other, thinking 'That's that opportunity lost – they probably won't even let us play this gig tonight.' Alan had walked in to find these two guys with big floppy fringes swinging at each other and we couldn't have blamed him if he'd just walked straight out again. Instead he was rushing over saying 'Fuck yeah. Let's make albums!' Talk about validating destructive behaviour patterns!

It was the first time apart from our initial contact with Bobby Gillespie that anyone had said anything positive about anything we'd done, and here was this guy calling us 'genius'. Of course it wasn't long before we realised that everything was 'genius' to McGee – he overused the word to an extent that made it utterly meaningless – but his intentions were good, and at that point any positivity was welcome.

It wasn't that we needed other people's approval, because we were very sure of ourselves in terms of what we were doing. There's a ridiculous implication in some accounts of this first gig that our sound was some kind of happy accident arising out of our not knowing how to work the equipment, where in fact it was more like the opposite of that – a carefully planned operation that left space inside itself for the chaos to be real. There were a lot of accidental occurrences that led to the sound of the Mary Chain – things like chancing on that fuzz pedal and the noise it made when we plugged it in. That was an accident that was given to us, but we still had to work with it.

It was a mark of our confidence that after arriving in London early in the morning, we'd gone down to the *NME* offices in Holborn to hassle them into coming to the gig. This was our first ever live show, remember. McGee laughed at us and said that would never work, but when the guy we spoke to – who turned out to be the music journalist David Quantick – asked why he should come along, we said: 'Because if you don't, you'll be pretending you were there in five years time.' Those words obviously struck a chord with him, because he did actually turn up to review the gig. We weren't just a couple of wide-eyed country bumpkins that got lucky. Well, we did get lucky – the dice really landed in the right place for us – but for that to happen we had to have them in our hands to throw. It helped that we really knew our music, and also that we'd already spent a certain amount of time in London – we'd been there when we had a bit of money and when we had absolutely fuck all, so we weren't going to be overwhelmed by it. It was a place that we understood and kind of knew our way around.

It would be strange to say that being Scottish made us exotic, but it was certainly a point of difference that we could play upon as we started to establish ourselves, and being from out of town and not like everyone else, but also not being tourists, did actually give us a bit of an advantage. David Quantick admitted later that one reason he came along to our show was because he hadn't been able to understand more than the odd word we were saying, and he wanted to make sure he hadn't missed anything.

William

I always feel weird talking about myself in a historical context, especially when you're talking about something you've done forty years ago: your whole skin and your body have changed since then. I don't like discussing the minutiae of what happened in 1984. Because my recollections feel like conjecture instead of fact, all you're hearing is feelings – how I felt it was.

Quite a lot of it, I'll be honest, I forgot – wine is beautiful but I don't think it's good for the memory. I do have some slight remembrance, tiny stems of whatever happened, but the point where looking back at all this stuff really began to depress me was when people started to write books about it. If you ask people what happened on a night when you did something together forty years ago, one of them will say 'We went and got a Burger King', but another will counter 'Oh no, we just went home – we never ate.' And once those different perspectives start to appear on the page between hard covers, they start to acquire an authority they shouldn't really have.

Where this realisation really hit home was when David Cavanagh's Creation book, *My Magpie Eyes Are Hungry for the Prize* came out. Until that book was written – I know Dave was a good writer and a lot of people really like that book, but bear with me – I used to love music biographies. I would devour them – three or four a year easily – until I became the subject of one. I was racing through the bits about us, thinking 'No way, you're painting this as black and white, but there were so many nuances to this situation!' It spoilt me, or rather it spoilt them, because after that I just couldn't read music biographies any more.

You know if somebody punched somebody in the face and five people saw it? Their account will depend not only on their relationship with the puncher or the punchee, but also something as basic as where they were standing. Everyone will have their own different viewpoint, but let's say two of the five people agree, and they're the only ones whose version gets quoted, then it will very quickly become the definitive account. And if you're one of the three people who haven't been asked, then being faced with the official version given by the other two people can be a very painful experience.

And that's why I'll be leaving most of the nuts and bolts of what happened in this first public phase of the band to Jim. Our interests were so closely aligned in the common cause of The Jesus and Mary Chain at that time that – even though we'd still sometimes get on each other's nerves to the point of physical conflict, like we did at that first soundcheck – you couldn't really get a piece of tissue paper between our opinions on anything to do with the band.

Jim

So when we plugged our guitars in to play the actual gig, it was just screeching feedback that filled the room. Beneath the cacophony it was a massive relief to finally get that creative outlet for all our frustration after all that time of nobody being interested or wanting to give us a gig in Glasgow. Somewhere inside that noise were the skeletons of songs that ended up on *Psychocandy* – 'Never Understand', 'Inside Me' and 'The Living End' – but if you hadn't heard the demos, they'd probably just sound like people punching the shit out of their guitars while an actual nutter screamed into a mic.

There were a few covers in there as well – just songs we liked and thought we could play, like Subway Sect's 'Ambition', 'Love Battery' by Buzzcocks and Syd Barrett's 'Vegetable Man'. A bit of Jefferson Airplane's 'Somebody To Love' probably crept in, too, but for people hearing us for the first time that night the covers probably weren't much more recognisable than the original material. There certainly wasn't anything particularly musical about what we were doing. David Quantick's review said we sounded like a bee in a lift shaft, which probably wasn't a bad shout.

As far as going onstage was concerned, we'd rehearsed many times and we knew what we were fucking doing. The element of chaos – the drinking, arguing and falling over – was something we knew we had to leave space for. By definition we couldn't control how that chaos was going to turn out, and our failure to control it was part of the excitement. So it was kind of orchestrated, but if it was too orchestrated it wouldn't be chaos. And the fact that we sort of knew what we were doing, and sort of didn't, gave us the perfectly unsure foundation on which to construct our rickety edifice.

William

One reason we only played short gigs in the beginning was because we only had about five songs of our own. The other was that we felt it should be like an explosion, and explosions can't last too long . . .

Jim

How did two total introverts staging fake live photos of imaginary gigs in their bedroom get up the courage to actually face the London gig-going public (or at least the tiny proportion of it that was in The Roebuck that night)? The mystery ingredient, in my case at least, was alcohol.

The first time I got drunk, it was like somebody had flicked a switch in my soul. Do you know that film *Whisky Galore* where Gordon Jackson's overbearing mother won't let him do anything, but then one day he has a couple of whiskies and goes and tells her a thing or two and the other guys are saying 'Some fellows are just born two or three drinks below par' and that explains everything? Well, that's me, I was born two or three drinks below par . . . In fact, I think I'm going to have that on my fucking headstone: 'Jim Reid – he was born two or three drinks below par . . .'

I'm not saying I'd never drunk a beer before the band, but the process of me taking to drinking like a duck to water, the feeling of 'Oh my God, where have you been all my life? Now I know why people do this – why did I resist it for so long?' That was totally bound up with our first live shows and the fact that alcohol was the only thing that gave me the confidence to get up and do them. I realised right from the start that this wasn't something I was going to be able to do sober – the only way I could manage it was to get wasted, hopefully not so drunk that I'd be falling over and unable to remember the words, but drunk enough to overcome my high level of natural resistance to doing anything in public, never mind singing on a stage.

Even the most experienced drinker will tell you that this dividing line can be a difficult one to get right, and I was not an experienced drinker. I told you before I was a late developer, and those embarrassing memories of the first flush of alcohol consumption that most people tend to gather in their mid to late teens still lay ahead of me in my early twenties. The fact that I would accumulate them as the lead singer of what was about to become the most notorious rock band in Britain was just the icing on the booze-laced cake.

From that first show at The Roebuck to the night The Jesus and Mary Chain imploded onstage in LA fourteen years later, I was off my tits every gig we played. Or if not fully off my tits, certainly very much under the influence of something – whether that something be drink, or drugs, or most usually a combination of the two. Booze and drugs – I couldn't have done any of it without them. Left to my own devices, I struggled with going outside my own house and walking down the road, but with the help of booze and drugs, all things were possible.

Virtually overnight, with alcohol's assistance, I'd gone from being the kid who spent his entire adolescence trying not to stand out from the crowd in any way, to the (on the surface at least) reckless and provocative frontman who could be pulled off the stage by the bouncers in the middle of his second-ever gig, then kicked down the stairs, then thrown out of the venue, and somehow not turn a hair. That last scenario is not a theoretical one, it's exactly what happened when we played at Night Moves in Glasgow, a few days after our London debut. Not everyone hated us that night – Bobby Gillespie, who was there to see us for the first time, thought it was the best thing he'd seen since punk rock. So with him and Alan McGee on board, it felt like we had a gang now.

After that gig we went home and wrote a load of letters to Billy Sloan, a DJ who had a show on Radio Clyde. He was like a 'Glasgow's John Peel' type of character who played the indie music of the time at midnight on a Thursday. Basically these letters divided down the middle – half of them said 'I've just been to Night Moves and seen the best band you could ever imagine,' and the other half said 'I've just been to Night Moves and seen the vilest creatures that have ever picked up a guitar and called themselves a band. I've never been so offended in my life.' He read a bunch of these letters out, not realising that we had written them. Years later I was interviewed by Billy and he said 'I knew you guys were gonna be big, because our mailbag was always empty until you came along and then it was full.' I didn't have the heart to tell him we'd written all those letters, but I think Douglas did a few years later.

William

You couldn't just write gushing letters in that situation – it was important to have a range of views. Not just to cover your tracks, but also because you want to divide opinion when you're starting out. I guess we were Marmite in the beginning, because when we got reviews of the same gig in *Sounds* and *NME*, they were at 180 degrees to each other – *NME* said we were the new Sex Pistols or some bullshit, and *Sounds* said we were just the worst thing ever. That couldn't have gone any better.

Jim

It felt like nobody was taking any chances any more. William and I watched a Doors documentary around that time, where they were playing the Hollywood Bowl – it was after 'Light My Fire' was a massive hit, but Jim Morrison just turned up really late and did a forty-minute version of 'When The Music's Over' and then left the stage. I remember us thinking 'My God – why don't people do things like that now?' It shouldn't just be about pandering to your audience's demands. If we felt like doing a song called 'Jesus Fuck' for half an hour, we thought that should be up to us: 'You've come to see us and this is what we want to do, we won't do it like this every night, but tonight we are, so just sit back and enjoy the ride because this is what you're getting.'

It never seemed to go smoothly, not least because we were absolutely fucking rat-arsed onstage and we'd not been playing together long enough to have any certainty about what was going to happen from one minute to the next anyway. It was always chaotic and there was an incident of some kind at pretty much every show, whether that meant me getting punched in the face by a bouncer or us getting threatened by someone in the crowd. People didn't sit there and politely clap their hands afterwards, some of them would really want to beat the shit out of us for what we were doing – that was the norm back then – and with the help of my new best friend, alcohol, I wasn't seeing that as a problem. This devil-may-care spirit wasn't everything the band was about – we knew we had the actual songs to back up the attitude – but it was an element we really loved. The idea that we could do that and get away with it was really important to us.

Half the people in the room wanted to kill me, but the other half thought it was really cool, and I couldn't let that go. After a couple of months, when I started to attract an increasing amount of female attention, William was saying 'I want to be the singer', but no deal – we'd tossed that coin, I'm afraid.

William

I was fine with being in the shadows. I did sing once at an early gig in London – when Jim had lost his voice – and I really enjoyed it, but being the frontman wasn't for me. Jim was born for that role, even though he would never admit it.

Jim

Everything we were doing just seemed to make more sense in London. People in Glasgow weren't really entertaining the kind of music that we wanted to make, but as soon as we got out of there, things began to click very quickly. It was almost overnight, or at least within a couple of weeks of us playing down in London – there was a buzz about the band in a way we would never have dreamt of back home. And yet as soon as we started to make it a bit, Glasgow was trying to claim us – 'Local boys The Jesus and Mary Chain have made good'. We used to think: 'No fucking thanks to you. When we needed a break, Glasgow wasn't giving us one.' We resented that bitterly for years afterwards. Were we going to start flying the St Andrew's cross? No fucking way.

It wasn't just Glasgow we were angry with. Sonically, the early to mid 1980s was about the worst period for music that I can think of. We listened to what was coming out of the radio and thought 'Fuck, the radio's broke'. Then, when we realised the radio wasn't broke – it was music that was broke. That was when we decided to fix things.

The fundamental problem was what me and William called 'the standard non-guitar rock sound' of the eighties. We used to watch *Top of the Pops* and there'd be bands going mental – jumping up and down and thrashing their guitars – and you'd think 'Hold on a minute, I don't think there's a guitar on that song . . .'

Van Halen's 'Jump' would be a good example – I quite like that song, but is there a guitar on it? If there is, I can't hear it. Remember this is Eddie Van Halen we're talking about – one of the most famous guitarists in the world. He's practically doing the Pete Townshend windmills in the video, but if you listen to the record, it's a synthesiser playing the actual riff.

'Born In The USA' is another one. Now I quite like Bruce Springsteen for my sins and I think 'Born In The USA' is a great fucking song, but it's got the soulless 'p'chow-p'chow' drum beat and a load of synthesiser and OK, maybe a tiny smattering of guitar. But that was one of those records where you'd think 'Christ, if this had been recorded in 1975, it would've been one of the greats.' I know a lot of people think it is anyway, but I don't. It's a great song, it's just not a great record.

That chronic mid-eighties guitar deficit was what The Jesus and Mary Chain were born to make good. Whatever else you might think about our first single, 'Upside Down', no one can deny there's a guitar on it.

The vocal as it turned out would be more of a stretch. I already had a throat infection before we got on the overnight Scottish Express bus down to London. That was a hellish ride through the night at the best of times – get on at midnight and arrive at seven in the morning – but you could still smoke on buses back then, and I was sitting next to this fat fucker who chain-smoked all the way down. I begged someone to swap seats with me – 'I've got to fucking sing tomorrow' – but the rest of the band just said 'No deal', as he carried on lighting cigarette after cigarette. By the time I got to London my throat was totally fucked – 'Oh God, somebody kill me.'

I just about managed the vocal on the single, but McGee had set us up two or three shows on the same trip, so one of those ended up being the gig where William had to step in as reluctant lead vocalist. I still think I would've been happier as a musician rather than a singer, but much as even now I still don't like everyone looking at me, it was clear from my brother's one-off showing as a stand-in frontman that he was even more uncomfortable with it than I was.

Our first experience in a proper studio was a much more positive learning curve. Because it was the first time we had ever made a record, Murray's drums didn't sound very good at first, so we got the guy whose studio it was – Pat Collier – to twiddle a few knobs and put loads of effects on to make it sound weird and a bit interesting. I'm not snobbish about anything when it comes to music – there's a pair of speakers and if what I'm hearing coming out of them sounds good, then that's it, it's job done as far as I'm concerned.

I don't care what piece of equipment anyone was using or who pressed what button to make it sound that way. Joe Foster was in the studio when we made 'Upside Down', but he was there on the invitation of Alan McGee, not The Jesus and Mary Chain, because for some reason McGee had this idea that Joe was going to be Creation's 'in-house producer' – like it was Motown or Blue Note or something, even though that concept didn't really sit easily with the kind of music we were making. It wasn't just us who had a problem with McGee's determination to foreground Joe's contribution. The Pastels had the same sort of situation where McGee had insisted he produce their single but they felt he did fuck all. So when they did the artwork for it – I think it was 'A Million Tears' – they didn't give him a credit.

Now that I think of it, that trip down to London to record 'Upside Down' was actually the very one where The Pastels met us at Glasgow bus station to hand over this lovely professionally produced artwork before we got on the nicotine express down to London, so we could give it to McGee. When Alan saw it he got a pencil out and scribbled 'produced by Joe Foster' all over it. We asked him 'Should you really be doing that?' And he said 'Oh for fuck's sake, those Pastels are a pain in the arse.' We should have known from that point how things were going to go, because The Pastels were (and are) not a pain in the arse, they're a fucking great band. But for some reason – and I have no idea why – McGee would have pet people, and Joe was one of his longest living pets.

We did make one classic beginners' mistake the first time we went in the studio, which is to listen back to what you've done on the giant speakers inside the studio and think it's really powerful, then get it home and realise your mistake. What we'd done sounded immense on the giant motherfucking tannoys in Pat Collier's control room. Then when we played the tape back on a normal cassette recorder, it sounded like Dire Straits. We knew we had to remix it, so William put loads of extra layers of feedback on and it sounded much better.

We were determined to be the antidote to the mid eighties, not just in terms of how we sounded, but also in terms of how we looked. It wasn't like we sat down and thought about it – nobody discussed what was going to be worn onstage – but we were very interested in the look, and it was a look that we already had. We'd read something in *NME* about The Beatles in Hamburg at some point – when Stuart Sutcliffe was still in the band. They all wore leather and they just looked so fucking cool in the pictures – I wished they'd never worn suits – and there was a definite crossover from there to those photographs of The Velvet Underground in the John Cale period. The 1966 look that launched a million indie bands. Then when punk came in you had the Ramones in their leather jackets and Billy Idol in his leather trousers in Generation X, and Johnny Rotten wearing those pointy brothel creepers, and all of that kind of came together as our look, with a bit of Echo and the Bunnymen long mac fashion in there too.

The missing ingredient – visually and sonically – was Bobby Gillespie. We did already have a drummer, and Murray Dalglish was – and is – a good guy who I still see from time to time, but he wasn't really a kindred spirit. He was a younger goth kid who was happy to be in a band but would've been even happier if we could've done a Bauhaus cover every now and then. We couldn't have got started without him, but it was obvious he didn't really fit in, and I think he realised we were probably going to get rid of him, so he did all the early shows – and the recording of 'Upside Down' – and then jumped before he was pushed. He just told us he didn't want to do it any more and we agreed quite readily.

I don't even remember seeing Bobby play drums before we asked him to take Murray's place. I think we probably asked him if he could do it and when he answered in the affirmative, that was good enough for us. There was a Creation tour of Europe looming – just a bunch of Creation bands including us playing these little dives all across the continent for a couple of weeks – and when we asked Bobby if he fancied doing it with us, he said yes straight away. I don't remember any rehearsals, never mind an audition. There was a gig at the Three Johns pub in Islington just before we left for the tour. That was Bobby's chance to show us he had the chops, and he passed the test with flying colours. It could've and perhaps should've been a disaster, but it just felt like the final piece of the puzzle.

I don't think Bobby could've played a full kit, but we didn't need him to. Stand-up drums felt natural and that was the way things were with us at the time – if it felt right, we did it. If Bobby hadn't agreed to help us out we would probably have ended up using a drum machine, because we had no problems with the idea of that and we wanted quite a mechanical sound. Bobby was so fucking tight on those drums that he might as well have been a drum machine, and the minimal element of it was very important to us on our 'antidote to the mid eighties' crusade.

You'd go to see most bands at that time and the stage was basically like a musical instrument shop – there's guitars on one side, a whole fucking gigantic drum kit filling the stage and blah blah blah. When you went to see the Mary Chain, William had one guitar, that was it. He didn't change it. He still doesn't, which is why I have to stand there like a fucking idiot telling jokes while he tunes up. But anyway, it was William with his one guitar, Douglas with his two-string bass, and Bobby standing just behind us with two drums, not on a riser or anything. Stripped down to the bone, it looked great and it sounded great. Simple, powerful, (ahem) primal. There was almost a bit of a Suicide vibe to it, which we were happy with – no fat on it, just the bare essentials, but then also sometimes a vocal that was a kind of panic attack over the top, like in 'Frankie Teardrop'.

The Three Johns gig was packed because 'Upside Down' had just come out and there was a buzz about us, so the music papers were there to review it. The reviews – one great, one terrible, as William mentioned – would be waiting for us when we got off the train back from the European tour at Victoria. Bobby picking up *NME* and *Sounds* and saying 'Oh, there's reviews in here' – very matter-of-factly like it happened every day – was a big moment in the history of the band, and we pissed ourselves laughing at the conjunction of the terrible review and the great review, because after all those long nights of hatching plans together, we couldn't have designed it any better. Basically, we were the new Sex Pistols. However ludicrous that felt to us – and in fact was – for the time being it was a done deal.

That was when the men in Armani suits came looking for us. It turned out those two weeks in Europe had been the beginning and the end of our rock 'n' roll dues-paying experience. Other bands have to slog around doing that for ages, but we only roughed it for a fortnight. After all those years of not much going on, everything suddenly seemed to be happening at the double for the Mary Chain.

We figured that all this was as new to Bobby as it was to us. He'd vaguely mentioned something about the Factory band he'd been in called The Wake, but he didn't go on about it much. It was only when we read his book years later that we found out that compared to us he had actually already been around the block a few times in terms of live music. But he was so wide eyed and fresh faced about it all on that first European tour that it seemed like it must be his first time driving hundreds of miles in a draughty old Transit to play a gig with only eight people watching, too.

William

The thing with Bobby was that at heart he's not a drummer, he's a singer, and we always knew Primal Scream were going to be his priority in the long run. But somehow knowing that he was going to have to go back – feeling like we were borrowing him – made the whole thing brilliant. The ad hoc feel of it totally fitted with the way we wanted things to be, so it was almost like a dream.

Me and Bobby had a pretty intense relationship onstage. I think you'd have to be a musician to know what I was talking about but it's a thing called being 'simpatico'. We would just look at each other while we were playing and burst out laughing. He was the same with Jim as well. People thought of the Mary Chain as a bunch of miserable bastards, but there was a lot of joy in what we were doing – there were so many moments when I'd be playing, out of my mind with the intensity of it, then I'd see Bobby hammering away at his two drums and it was just an incredible amount of fun.

Jim

Bobby was like the engine in the back. I'm not talking about his drumming because I honestly think anyone could have done that, but it was his energy and the way he looked the part. We'd be doing some gig in the wilds of Germany where no one had ever heard of us and there'd be a bunch of lukewarm people dressed in black giving out that 'Come on, show us what you've got, impress us', vibe. I'd be feeling momentarily crushed until I turned around and saw Bobby with that manic mental smile on his face, then I'd just think 'Fuck it, here goes.' And the gig would kick off from there. He was kind of our onstage barometer of 'How's this going?' Sometimes in the more free-form improv sections he'd just flick his hair across his face and go 'whew' and then you'd know it was going well – the electricity of the show seemed to course through him, and I could always turn to Bobby if I needed a pick-me-up. Then I'd look at William with his head stuck in the speaker and his arse up in in the air like a monkey as he bent down to get the feedback out of the amp and that would give me the energy to do what I needed. Well, that and the alcohol and the drugs – I would just start rolling around on the floor screaming blue bloody murder and that would be it.

I was basically drunk for the entire two weeks of that European tour so my memories of it are a little foggy, but there were were definitely a bunch of us – Biff Bang Pow, The Jasmine Minks and the Mary Chain – crammed together in two small vans. It wasn't like we enjoyed experiencing the local culture, it was egg and chips and lager all the way as we breezed across Europe in our little British bubble. The broadening of our horizons would come later but it didn't happen on that tour. We had more of a *Pulp Fiction* vibe going on – fucking hell, the Europeans are putting mayo on chips! Our minds were blown.

I guess these were the kinds of experiences that middle-class kids would've had on French exchanges, but even though William and I had both gone abroad on school trips as kids, I'd not been drinking for very long. Mind you, I took to it like a duck to water. In retrospect, that tour was probably the beginning of my wrestling with alcohol for the next forty fucking years, but it was also very enjoyable. Not glamorous, but exciting – disorganised, utterly chaotic and strangely fun.

One of the reasons the drinking had to be so relentless was because of the kind of places McGee made us stay in. He'd give the big build-up to the hotel we were heading for in Düsseldorf, then when you'd get there the place would literally be a doss house. 'McGee, this isn't a hotel – there's an old man over there in a bunk bed drinking methylated spirits, for fuck's sake.' The next night we'd be staying with someone McGee had met five years before who had misguidedly said 'If you're ever near Frankfurt, drop in', only for Alan to call by with twenty people in tow. It was like the Monty Python sketch – 'You said drop in any time and here we are . . . now you've got three bands sleeping on your floor.'

Some bands would start off on that circuit and stay there for forty years, but even my very brief experience of that lifestyle cured me of any inclination to romanticise it. I have to admit to quite enjoying the fact that we progressed to a more comfortable touring set-up almost straight away. And if you are sensing the beginnings of a divide between the Mary Chain and the ideological construct that no one really ever calls 'indie orthodoxy' – even though they probably could if they wanted – then you are right on the money.

Creation at the point where we came into contact with it was more of a hobby than a proper record label. Alan McGee still worked for British Rail and the records were stacked up in the spare room of his flat in Tottenham. It was one of those two-bedroom conversions on the ground floor of a house that's been divided into two so someone else can live above. We stayed over there sometimes, like when we played two nights at Alan's club, The Living Room, but his wife at the time was (understandably) not all that keen on having weird guys in bands cluttering up her spare room and eating her out of house and home, so we weren't always that welcome. Primal Scream had an unflattering nickname for her, but I could see her point and the constant requirement to play host to hard-living rock 'n' rollers like us might've been one reason that marriage didn't last.

Either way, it wasn't that luxurious from our point of view, and Alan's Creation right-hand man Dick Green lived just round the corner on Seven Sisters Road, so we would usually angle to relocate in his direction, as that was a slightly more relaxed environment. In terms of the records Alan and Dick had released before we came along, you'd have to say the talent pool wasn't that deep. No one they'd worked with was ever going to be on *Top of the Pops*, especially not The Legend! A fanzine writer and indie scenester who was in the process of becoming a music journalist, The Legend! (his exclamation mark) was also the man responsible for the first single ever released on Creation – a record so bad it can only be safely transported in a lead-lined casket. He really liked The Jesus and Mary Chain initially but then turned very much against us for reasons I never quite understood – possibly connected to us buying a pair of leather trousers.

This was one of the earliest examples of a response which would affect us throughout our career – where dyed-in-the-wool indie guys (and it is always guys) thought we'd sold out because we had a bit of get up and go about us. The irony of it was that it was our first single which turned Creation from a cottage industry into something almost like a record company. 'Upside Down' came out just before we went off to Europe and by the time we came back it was selling in quantities Alan and Dick hadn't had to deal with before. That's how we found ourselves in McGee's flat, folding up the paper sleeves with the Jackson Pollock paint spatters that would make such a big impression on The Stone Roses and putting them in the seven-inch plastic bags. Me, William, Douglas, Bobby and McGee as well were sat in that back room of his flat doing that for hours. When we got bored we started writing abusive messages on them for fun so if you've got one of those arcane scribblings you know you've got a reasonably early pressing.

William

By the time we were making our first record, there was this ethos among the kind of indie bands the *NME* liked of failure being a badge of honour – when people made a record they were proud if it sold 200 copies while anything that looked like success would be considered an embarrassing lapse in taste. Whereas how we were thinking was 'If we make a record it's going to be fucking great and why the fuck can't we be on *Top of the Pops* like the bands we loved when we were growing up?' We still considered what we were doing to be pop music, even if our version of that was laced with poisonous feedback. It had strychnine in it as well as a cocktail umbrella, it was a nun in a mini-skirt – that's why it affronted the hierarchy.

Jim

We were very anti-indie at the time, because the indie crowd seemed to be underachievers who aimed low. It's hard to say this without sounding Thatcherite, but the problem with indie music in 1984 was it had no ambition. As this musical realm was experienced at McGee's Living Room and many other similar clubs around the country, what it meant was a bunch of people in Oxfam clothes playing to eighteen of their friends in a room above a pub and thinking that was good enough. I love lo-fi music but I don't like music that doesn't seem to have any self-belief, and a lot of that eighties indie stuff that was getting played on John Peel at the time seemed to be almost an exercise in futility – it didn't seem to have any end destination.

Me and William knew what a pop star looked like and it wasn't some indie kid in Oxfam clothes – any more than it was Simon Le Bon or one of the clowns out of Spandau Ballet like everyone else in the mid-eighties seemed to have decided. We wanted to bring cool-looking people and aggressive-sounding music back to the forefront, because the whole scene seemed to have been hijacked by all these fucking twats in two thousand pound suits, and that wasn't what we'd signed up for when we'd watched

Marc Bolan or Generation X on *Top of the Pops*.

There was a strand of indie thinking which almost didn't want success because somehow that was considered too ostentatious or embarrassing. I think that was a very middle-class attitude perpetrated by kids who thought it was cool to wear charity shop clothes with holes in them when in fact they could have afforded brand-new Benetton. I realise this is probably sounding like a rant now but I actually think it's quite a fundamental divide.

Musicians from working-class backgrounds who knew what it was to have nothing – like me and William and Douglas and Bobby – weren't signing up for any of that nonsense. We wanted to be big stars and we didn't care who knew it, and the hostility this brought down on our heads was very real. You can see this enduring even now in some of the treatment Bobby gets.

I understand there was an ideological undercurrent to it in the eighties. Because of the state of Western politics in the era of Thatcher and Reagan, where everything seemed to be about greed and pushing people out of the way to succeed, there was value in showing things didn't have to be that way. But that didn't mean anyone with an ounce of drive or ambition should be lumped in with Gordon Gekko from *Wall Street*. 'Greed is good' certainly wasn't what The Jesus and Mary Chain were about. Collective self-improvement was our watchword, and it was following that particular yellow brick road which led us to make the biggest fuck-up of our career.

The first time Rough Trade boss Geoff Travis came to see us was a gig at the squatted ambulance station on Old Kent Road. It was quite an edgy night – the element of aggression in audience responses to what we were doing was starting to come to the fore by then – but Geoff didn't seem to mind.

We were totally aware of all the things he had done at Rough Trade – he was kind of the king of post-punk, in so far as the patriarchal concept of kingship could be incorporated into Rough Trade's Notting Hill brown-rice feminist world view – and I liked him as a person, but he was always kind of aloof. You were never going to be mates with Geoff. There was no nattering away telling each other your backstory while you went for a pint the way we did with McGee, it was always going to be business. And we were fine with that, because contrary to what you might have read in Alan McGee's autobiography, William and I were (and are) actually very business-like people.

Yes, we were very, very shy back then, yet there was one thing that was guaranteed to bring us out of our shells (apart from drugs and drink, but I'm talking about when we were sober) and that was discussing our band and its future. The Jesus and Mary Chain was a matter of life and death to us. Without making us sound too desperate, 'If this doesn't work we'll just have to kill ourselves' was a thought process to which we were not strangers, so we certainly weren't going to be letting anybody else make key career decisions for us.

On the fateful day when Geoff was flown up to McGee's mum's house in Glasgow to offer us whatever he was going to offer us – Alan's mum may well have made us a cream tea – William and I did not just sit there in silence, looking down at her carpet like a couple of sulky teenagers while the adults took care of business. There's been some bullshit to this effect from McGee but there usually is – bullshit is his currency, for Christ's sake. (For the sake of full disclosure, I've never read Alan's book or seen the film of it, but this is one of several warped notions that have drifted through to me at second hand that I'd really like to set straight.)

That meeting at Alan's mum's house was me, William and Geoff Travis, with McGee sat in the corner while the three of us had a discussion about what we wanted for the Mary Chain. We told Geoff that we wanted to be rock stars and as far as we were concerned that meant having a major label and a bankroll behind us. He kept telling us 'You can do that on Rough Trade', but we weren't really believing him, and there was a tempting option B, because Geoff was pitching us two alternative deals. Rough Trade, which was the one he was heavily leaning towards, or a bigger money situation with Blanco y Negro, a new faux-indie subsidiary of the international corporate conglomerate Warner/Reprise, which Geoff had helped set up.

This would give us all the clout of a major label deal, but with Geoff – a guy we had quickly come to feel that we knew and trusted – as the translator and middleman. It seemed like a no-brainer, and we duly left that room with a deal for a one-off second single on Warners (via Blanco y Negro) – basically a 'Dip your toe in the water to see how this is going to go down' major label situation – for which The Jesus and Mary Chain would be paid a thousand pounds each. The big time was calling and it was very exciting.

It was also a colossal mistake. Elektra was part of Warner Brothers, and The Doors and Love were on Elektra, so we thought that was the kind of label we needed to be on, but of course the major record labels of the mid eighties were very different places to the ones that had signed the bands we loved twenty years before. The world had changed and now (with the power of some exceptionally painful hindsight) I can see that this should have been obvious to us, but at that time, because we were naive idealists with no experience of the music industry, it wasn't.

Much as I'd like to be able to blame Alan McGee for this defining wrong turn in the life of the band, unfortunately it was all our own doing. Events would ultimately prove that Geoff Travis had been right all along – Rough Trade would've been a much better home than Warners for The Jesus and Mary Chain in the Eighties, just as it was for The Smiths, but there's no going back, so fuck it.

Part 4
Warners

i. Psychocandy

Jim

Because we still had that punk rock mindset, we felt that it was our duty to shake things up a bit as we stepped out of our bedroom and into the limelight. So the first time we went to the Warners offices – we'd flown down from Glasgow and it was also the first time we'd ever been on a plane – we couldn't just go in there and shake those guys' hands. We were quite drunk and there was a little bit of vandalism. A moustache was drawn on a picture of Rod Stewart and a few gold discs were knocked off the walls, not intentionally, just by Douglas stumbling against them on the stairs.

As we were escorted from the building, the security guard, who was a Scottish guy, was telling us we were a bunch of stupid little arses – 'If you're going to make it in this business, you can't carry on like that . . .' We were thinking 'Fuck it, we didn't mean any harm', but he was OK about it and we got on all right with him.

On subsequent visits to the building we would come to realise that we had a lot more in common with him than we did with any of the jackals in Armani suits who worked upstairs. It was obvious from the start that they were businessmen and music was a product – it might as well have been fish fingers – you couldn't have a conversation with them about your favourite bands, because no one was interested. All they cared about was where their next Rolex was coming from.

William

This guy at a marketing meeting at Warners early on made a joke that wasn't a joke – you know the way someone says something with a smile, but really it's exactly what they're thinking? He said 'If there wasn't feedback, these would be really commercial songs.' There was that sense right from the beginning of 'Why do they have to do this? Why can't they just make records like other people?' Our response to that was 'Well, you knew who we were when you signed us.'

Because we had no experience of the whole cynical world of the music business, we thought everyone was cool and on the level, and that when people told you they liked you, they actually liked you, and when they told you they were gonna do something, that meant they were gonna do it. We certainly had a lot to learn!

Jim

It was Alan McGee's first sniff of the big time as well as ours, and he was even more wildly overexcited than we were. On paper at least, our signing to Warners was going to allow us all to live out our fantasies. We wanted to be rock 'n' roll stars like Marc Bolan and make the best music anyone had ever heard, whereas Alan wanted to be Malcolm McLaren Mk 2.

At first, the yawning gap between these two ambitions didn't seem to be a problem. We weren't averse to a bit of media manipulation either, as we'd shown by sending all those fake letters to Radio Clyde, so when Alan started planting made-up stories about us in the music press and the tabloids – for example, exaggerating the extent of the damage we'd caused on that first drunken visit to the record company to the point of falsely claiming that we'd stolen Warners boss Rob Dickins's wallet – it just seemed like a bit of a laugh.

The first time we'd met McGee we joked around that we were younger than we were. I was a late developer who still couldn't go anywhere without ID – and would occasionally get thrown out of pubs on principle even when I did have it on me – so it wasn't stretching credulity too far for me to claim that I was only eighteen years old. Unfortunately Alan picked up the baton of my invention and ran so far so fast with it – 'Fuck, that's mental, man!' – that it was hard for me to get it back. We hadn't thought he would take us seriously but the more he told us how amazing it was that we were 'so fucking young', the more it started to feel like it was a key element in our appeal, and the harder it got to tell him the slightly less interesting truth.

His disappointment when all was finally revealed – I think it happened when we had to get passports for that first Creation European tour – had been embarrassing on all sides. 'But you said you were eighteen – you're *ancient!*' 'I'm not ancient, I'm twenty-two.'

There probably was a lesson here about the potentially awkward consequences of playful myth-making, but we weren't quite ready to learn it yet. So as Alan's Malcolm McLaren fixation spiralled out of control, it just seemed like another source of amusement rather than anything to be concerned about. We'd often catch him repeating lines of dialogue from *The Great Rock 'n' Roll Swindle,* as if these piercing insights had only just come to him – he turned round to me one day and actually said 'Jim, we're not going to play any of these rock 'n' roll houses.' 'For fuck's sake, McGee – that's like lesson number seven in the *Rock 'n' Roll Swindle!*'

Of course, Alan wasn't the only one making a bit of a twat of himself. When I look back on that period, I often wish I could go back in time and give myself a good slap. To suddenly be getting so much attention after a lifetime of being basically ignored was a bit of a shock to the system, and although we felt very confident about our music in the early days of the Mary Chain, when it came to how to present ourselves we weren't so sure, so we tended to overcompensate by making grandiose statements: 'Yeah, we're fantastic and everybody knows it – all the other bands aren't fit to wipe our boots.' Or words to that effect – those early interviews I did make me cringe so much that I can't bear to read them.

When I wasn't bigging us up to a ludicrous extent or spraying unearned vitriol on our contemporaries, I sometimes used to get drunk and say outrageous things just to get a reaction. There are hundreds of statements I made in interviews which I came to regret – one of the worst, which William constantly reminds me of to this day, was when I said 'Mark Chapman shot the wrong Beatle.' I fucking adore The Beatles – all of them – so why would I ever have said something like that? I guess in my mind I was trying to cause a stir, and there was also an element of the naughty schoolboy going 'Tee hee hee, did you hear what I said?' But it was dumb and it was pathetic and I wish I could take those things back.

The one card we did play very close to our chest was how much fun we were having. The first year of the band was probably the best time to be in The Jesus and Mary Chain, because we existed in a state of utter freedom – we didn't owe anyone anything, so we just did whatever we wanted and didn't care who we pissed off. But you wouldn't have guessed how carefree we were to look at us, because we didn't think it was the done thing for a band to look like they were enjoying themselves. I remembered reading that Ian Curtis had a great sense of humour and used to act like a total arse, but surely Joy Division sat around all day reading Gogol? We had an idea of what the Mary Chain should be about that went along similar lines, so although there was a lot of humour in what we were doing, we didn't ever really put that across.

You create an image of how you want people to see you, and on top of that none of us was particularly outgoing by nature anyway. So we'd be having a laugh in the dressing room, then someone would come in with a camera and we'd all suck our cheeks in and start looking miserable. If it was a formal photo or video shoot situation, we'd be even more intimidated. As shy as we were of the stills camera – and we were all too aware that a photograph was forever – video cameras were even worse. So

Butter wouldn't melt . . . at Hunter Primary School,
East Kilbride, 1966 or 67.

Graffiti on the wall outside our parents' bedroom window in East Kilbride.

Learning the guitar in William's Post Office Tower flat, August 1979.
William *above*, Jim *below*.

Sightseeing in London when Jim went to visit William, August 1979.

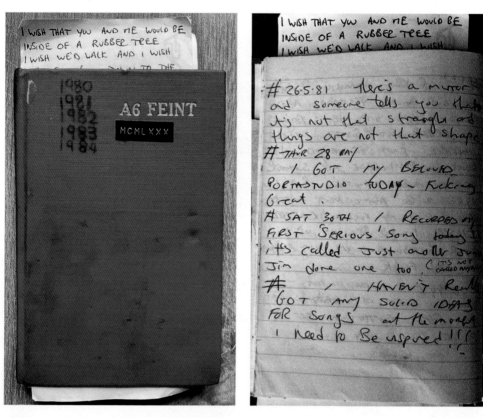

William's diary entry on the Portastudio purchase, 28 May 1981.

William studying his Beatles songbook, 24 August 1982.

William with Patch, and Jim at home in East Kilbride – we shared that jumper – March 1982.

Above William out walking Patch, 28 March 1983.

Left William sitting on his Marshall amp, 10 August 1983.

Jim on the train to George Square, looking like the anti-hero of an East European art film, 26 May 1983.

Fake live poster templates.

The PO proof of posting receipt for the demo sent
to Alan McGee – the rest was history!

Above and left Auditioning Murray, Scout Hall, East Mains, 13 May 1984. He's the one on the drums. And check out Douglas's biker boots as he marvels at William's instrumental prowess.

Above Another rehearsal a few weeks later.

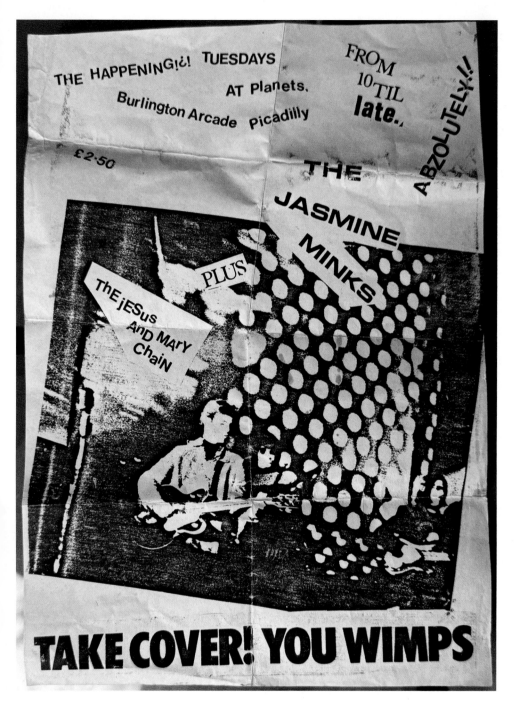

We played two gigs on 12 June 1984 – one in Camden, then this one – before going home to East Kilbride the next day (see diary entry overleaf). We'd been in London for five days, since our live debut at The Roebuck.

I WISH THAT YOU AND ME WOULD BE
INSIDE OF A RUBBER TREE
I WISH WE'D WALK AND I WISH

= USUAL
WED 13TH SLEEP IN GET UP RUSH
FOR BUS HOME ~~JUST~~ MAKE IT IN
TIME ARRIVE HOME IN A
STRANGE MOOD. 14TH PLAY NIGHT
MOVES
MON 9TH JULY 1984
ON SATERDAY ME + JIM AND
DOUGLAS ~~GOT~~ TOOK A TAB OF
L.S.D. WITH BOBBY GILLESPIE
AND HIS PRIMAL SCREAM MATES. I
HAD A TERRIBLE TRIP FOR MOST
OF THE, IMAGINING I WAS IN
A TROPICAL JUNGLE BEING
ATTACKED BY INSECTS ETC. THE
GOOD BITS WERE FANTASTIC AND
~~THE~~ BAD BITS WERE TERRIFYING.
KISSING THE TOILET SEAT

~~Friday~~. SUNDAY

FEBRUARY 3

19 RECORDED A JOHN Peel
SESSION TODAY AT MAIDA VALE
STUDIOS NO 5. WE DONE
19 THE LIVING END, INSIDE ME
JUST LIKE HONEY. APART FROM
JUST LIKE HONEY WE DIDN'T
LIKE THE SESSION AT ALL. KAREN
19 SANG BACKING VOCALS ON
JUST LIKE HONEY.

19

19

Above William's diary entry from the second Peel session, 3 February 1985.

Opposite William's diary entries after returning home from our London gigs.
13 June, noted our first Scottish gig at Night Moves in Glasgow. Four weeks
later, on 9 July, the LSD took hold . . .

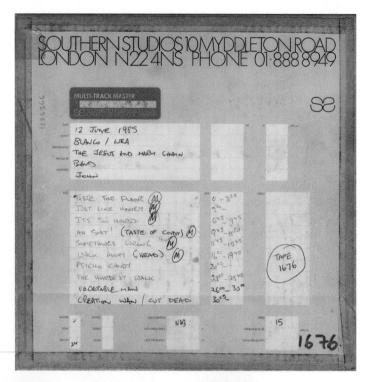

Above
Psychocandy recording label.

Left The first pressing of 'Upside Down' was the black paint-spattered one and the colours followed later. The SUCK sign is from the video for 'Just Like Honey'.

Bobby in LA (*above*), and Jim living his best life buying records in the sunshine (*below*). US tour, December 1985.

Above and left In the studio with Alan Moulder (middle) and Flood (right), recording 'Some Candy Talking', 14 April 1986.

Right William's 'Some Candy Talking' lyrics.

Above Jim on the 'April Skies' video shoot in Hastings, 3 April 1987.

Left William songwriting at breakfast while on tour in America (probably in Philadelphia), later in 1987.

Memorial to Patch on the run-out groove of
'Happy When It Rains' – it's only on the 7 inch, not the 12.

once we started making videos my discomfort could be captured for all eternity. You can actually see me wrestling with my own uncertainty on the screen – 'Fuck, I don't know what to do. You're expecting me to move my lips in time to a record?' The whole thing just seemed ridiculous.

William

I don't think we were meant for actual fame, I think we were meant for some weird outlier version of celebrity where we were too shy for people to actually look at us.

Jim

A lot of the stuff we did at that time was idiotic schoolboy prankishness, but at many other times all we had to do to cause problems was just show up. It was a reflection of how sanitised everything was becoming in the mid eighties that a bunch of little scruff-bags like us could actually be perceived as a threat.

The Sex Pistols actually did shake things up – they were a genuine threat to the Establishment, to the point where John Lydon could get banned from the BBC for daring to speak out against the Establishment's favourite paedophile, Jimmy Savile – but the fact that it now took so little to wind people up was a reflection on how successfully ranks had been closed. A certain kind of person seemed to think 'Thank goodness we got rid of all that nastiness and everything's gone back to the way it should be. We've got nice chaps like Spandau Ballet now – look at the way they dress, they're so well turned out.' And in that atmosphere even our vague, drunken sense of a need to disrupt the placid surface of Thatcher's decade became a self-fulfilling prophecy – we could get on people's nerves without even doing anything.

Even our very hazy and unfocused notion of wanting to shake things up was enough to make some people think 'They're the bastard sons of the Sex Pistols, kill, kill, destroy!' It was almost like a muscle memory. The first time we definitely felt that was when we went in to do our debut Peel session. We weren't fussed about the bad reception we got at Maida Vale at the time – it just seemed like a weird blip that BBC technicians were so totally out of touch with the world around them that they greeted us like lepers at the barbecue. But that not especially happy occasion actually set the tone for the bulk of our future dealings with TV and radio. The second Peel session – where we had the temerity to want to record the sound of actual breaking glass rather than using a sound effect – was even worse.

William

Then there was the time we got banned from Capital Radio because they said we smashed the glass table in reception, when what actually happened was Geoff fucking Travis sat on this table and it collapsed. Warners were livid, but we were innocent bystanders and it was the wild man Geoff Travis who wrecked the joint . . .

Jim

Much as we resented being blamed for things we hadn't actually done, it was rather exciting being the scourge of respectable society. Meanwhile, a lot of good stuff was happening to us – once the ball started rolling, it rolled bloody quickly. Take 29 December 1984, for example. It was my twenty-third birthday and I bought two guitars with the first instalment of the Warners money – a little Kay one from the Record and Tape Exchange, which I've still got to this day, and a Vox Phantom off McGee that I loved but which got nicked in America years later when our tour van had a break-in. In the evening we headlined the ICA Rock Week to a triumphantly mixed response and I met Laurence Verfaillie for the first time, who would become the girlfriend who helped me make the transition from scruffy herbert to international gallery-going sophisticate.

In the new year, Douglas, William and I moved down to London. The fact that Bobby Gillespie stayed in Glasgow with Primal Scream was a straw in the wind in terms of where things were ultimately going, and we kind of knew that at the time. Obviously this big move down south meant breaking up mine and William's shared record collection, and we did have the odd tussle about it – 'I bought that one.' 'No you didn't, it was me – I bought *Mix Up* by Cabaret Voltaire.' – but the cash from Warners meant we at least both had the resources to fill any gaping holes left in our side of the record collection.

There was no competitive atmosphere between William and I in those days – we were totally on the same page, excepting the odd momentary flare-up – to the extent that people who came across us for the first time at that point seemed to have seen us as being like those weird twins who finish each other's sentences. By that stage I no longer thought of William as my elder brother – we were equals and friends.

William

I always thought of Jim as my younger brother – you would if you were older, wouldn't you?

Jim

It was actually Douglas I ended up living with when we moved to London in January of 1985, because the flat he got was damp and horrible so he shared a bedsit with me until he could find somewhere else (William's place, which was just around the corner, had mushrooms growing up the walls too, but it didn't seem to bother him). We'd spent most of our first week in the capital queuing up in Fulham Broadway dole office to get the kind of accommodation that supplementary benefit would pay your rent for. I realise this will sound like an impossible dream to young people hoping to move to London four decades later, but at the time we didn't realise how lucky we were.

It was a pretty basic situation, with a communal toilet on the landing to stop us losing touch with our Glasgow tenement roots, but I loved being in Fulham. Douglas and I would be sitting up in the double bed in our pyjamas like Morecambe and Wise listening to all the madness unfolding around us. It was mental in that house – like *The Young Ones* without the living room.

On the first floor there was a psychotic drug dealer who everyone was terrified of. Across the corridor from me was a very disturbed woman. I don't know exactly what her deal was but I think she was schizophrenic because you would hear her having screaming arguments with herself – shouting 'Cunt!', and then 'I didn't say that.' Between me and her – and a buffer wasn't a bad idea – was a very middle-class guy called Adrian who used to bring his friends over for a cheese and wine party and a game of charades on a Friday night. I know Fulham has quite a swanky reputation but our particular bit was the old working-class Irish area and far from the kind of environment in which you'd expect that sort of soirée to be taking place, especially with the nutty lady screaming obscenities at herself and the east European handyman who the landlord generously allowed to sleep in the cupboard under the stairs in return for doing the occasional ham-fisted bit of maintenance – Alexei Sayle would've had to play that guy.

Superficially it was quite grim but it was also a completely different vibe to mine and William's earlier failed attempts to move to London. Before, we were where we wanted to be but with no prospects, no money and no hope, and now we not only had better things on the horizon, they were happening on a daily basis as we headed out into the big city to do gigs and record singles. Obviously this was what we'd been aiming for all along, but just because you plan something is no indicator that it's actually going to happen, so there was a constant sense of being pleasantly surprised – which was not something our previous years of earthly existence had necessarily prepared us for.

The next step, which was recording our second single 'Never Understand', took a little while to get right. Stephen Street, the producer Warners initially tried to foist on us, was a big name at the time on account of his big commercial breakthrough with The Smiths. He was also everything we were trying to avoid. It was like he was on Warner Brothers' payroll (which was obviously true in a literal sense, but I'm talking about the spirit of the law as well as the letter).

We turned up at the studio with a crate of beer, saying 'Let's make a good record', and he looked at us like we'd stepped in something. It was one of those situations where you'd get the music sounding pretty much like you wanted then pop off to the toilet and by the time you came back all the guitars had been turned down. 'Oh, weren't the guitars a bit louder a few minutes ago?' You bet they fucking were!

We ended up going to Geoff Travis and telling him Stephen Street was not a road we wanted to be going down – 'This guy is trying to turn us into a fucking pub rock band.' At this tense mo-ment Geoff had one of his occasional brainwaves and came up with the idea of John Loder at Southern Studios. That was it – a meeting of kindred spirits, and *Psychocandy* was born from that suggestion.

William

The reason John Loder was the perfect fit for us was that the record company would be telling us we needed a producer and John would say just say 'I'm the producer.'

Jim

John Loder's studio was a very basic converted garage in the back of a house in Wood Green, for fuck's sake. John was very connected in the anarcho-punk world, so he'd have Crass doing all the DIY and cleaning the kitchen. They were all right, although they did get really pissed off with us frying bacon for bacon butties. We couldn't be sure if it was their vegan convictions or the deliciousness of the smell that was driving them crazy.

John was pretty much the opposite of every other studio technician that we'd come across at that point. Once we'd made the long trek across town from Fulham (in a cab of course – we were living so large we were buying our lunchtime sandwiches from Marks & Spencer) he'd set up all the equipment, then tell us 'Right, I'm going up to my office – if you've got any problems give me a buzz.' We'd tell him 'But we don't know how to work any of this stuff', and he'd say 'You'll figure it out.'

We thought 'Fuck, this is perfect.' John let us loose on his equipment and every now and again he'd come down and show us which button did what – he was brilliant. We'd give him a buzz every couple of days to say 'All the needles are going into the red and this little machine is making a whistling sound', and he'd ask 'Does it sound good what you're doing?' We'd tell him 'Yeah' and he'd say 'Well, fuck it.' 'Cheers John, just checking.'

William

John was a bit of a hippy but his connection to all those direct-action people was real. One time we were having a meal with him in Pizza Express in Islington and there was some music playing that was offensive to his ears. It wasn't Kylie, because this was just before Kylie, but it was something in that area he didn't like, and rather than just grit his teeth and get through it like you would, there was a lead hanging clumsily down from a really big speaker above us that he started trying to pull down so he could tear the speaker off the wall. Me and Jim were thinking 'That's a fucking big speaker, if it comes down on our heads we won't be too happy.' Luckily we managed to persuade him to knock it off or we'd have been blamed for the Pizza Express riot as well.

Jim

Although we were very happy with our second single 'Never Understand' – the first fruits of our collaboration with John – not everyone felt the same way. It was the first chance the Warners guys had had to tell us what they really thought of the music we had made, and what they mainly thought was 'We're going to get Don Was to do a remix'. We said 'Uh, I don't think so' and they said 'But he's a world-class producer!' 'We don't give a fuck. The record's made, now put the thing out and shut the fuck up'.

That was our attitude and that was their attitude and it basically stayed that way for the next twelve years we were at Warners. Luckily the idea of doing something that wasn't accepted had been hard-wired into our DNA in The Jesus and Mary Chain's pre-success epoch, so the 'us against them' mood came naturally to us. But after all the enthusiasm we'd so appreciated from McGee (say what you like about Alan, he was totally into what we were doing) and Bobby and – in a more restrained, middle-class kind of way – Geoff Travis, it was a bit of a sickener to find out that was not how things were going to be for the foreseeable future. It almost felt like we'd walked into a trap.

As it turned out, the real problem with 'Never Understand' was not with the A-side, it was with the B-side. We'd decided the time was right to give our free-form live staple 'Jesus Fuck' an outing on record. It wasn't about shock value – otherwise we'd have put it on the A-side. Putting those two words together was a comment on the absurdity of blasphemy.

This was the sort of thing I used to enjoy discussing with the priest when I occasionally went to my Catholic friend Stuart's church with him back in East Kilbride as a teenager. St Bride's was one of those imposing brutalist churches that look like they ought to be prisons, and I used to enjoy testing the theological parole conditions by getting into debates with the man in the dog collar. To be fair, he was quite receptive to what I had to say, and at least the Catholics actually believed in something, not like the godless Protestant realm we came from, where people could barely be arsed to drag themselves to church unless it was a wedding or a funeral. And now we had the chance to take that kind of intellectual discussion to a broader platform, it wasn't an opportunity I planned to miss. Neither William nor I are religious people, but we both hated the way a residue of what I can only think of as superstition still impacted on our lives.

William

If I went to Marks & Spencer for sandwiches and the bill came to £6.66 – and this is not a hypothetical, it did actually happen – it would send me into a tailspin for weeks, because that was the number of the devil and somewhere inside of me I was still afraid of it. Also, and I still don't know why this was, I couldn't countenance sexual activity on a Sunday till I was about thirty years old. Of course I'm talking mainly about masturbation here, but it was still very limiting.

Jim

Unfortunately our bold plan to widen the parameters of inter-faith discussion came to nothing. The people who worked at the pressing plant refused to manufacture copies of 'Never Understand' if 'Jesus Fuck' was on the B-side, so we had to substitute it for the less controversial 'Suck'. In retrospect those philistines probably did us a favour, because the recorded version we came up with wasn't a patch on the live experience anyway. I think that song possibly required the presence of a confused and angry crowd to really operate at full strength.

The live shows we played around the release of 'Never Understand' in the winter of 1985 were the point at which audience's responses to us started to get violent enough to be a problem. In Brighton we walked out into a hail of missiles and Bobby's girlfriend Karen caught a bottle full in the face. She was OK but it could've been nasty, and that was a warning we should've paid heed to, instead of doing what we actually did, which was play a very angry twenty-minute show culminating in me getting McGee to give me the money we'd been paid so I could wave it at the angry crowd.

'If we're shite, what does that make you? We're getting pretty well paid for this and this is your money, you gave it to us!' I think this was just before Harry Enfield's 'Loadsamoney' so I was ahead of the curve, culturally. Looking back on incidents like this obviously involves a measure of embarrassment, but there were also some very funny moments which were like being in one of those old Frankenstein movies where the rabble are coming for you holding flaming torches, and if you're tanked up enough there is a temptation to just scream 'Fuck you!' at everyone and then go down in a blaze of glory.

I was certainly tanked up enough that night. When I rewind the booze-degraded film stock of my memories of that day in Brighton I can see myself going down to the sea before the gig and being so drunk I actually fall in the water – with my leather trousers on and all – then when I came back into the venue like the Creature from the Black Lagoon I couldn't find the stage door so I had to climb up the front of the stage dripping with water and go back to the dressing room to dry out. Obviously this took a while, to the point where we hadn't really noticed – or didn't really care – that we'd been supposed to be onstage an hour ago. I remember a nervous promoter kept putting his head round the door and saying, 'Things are getting ugly – you guys really ought to get out there'. 'Yeah, five more minutes . . .' By the time we did finally stumble out onto the stage, the crowd just went berserk.

Because none of us except Bobby had been in a band before, we didn't really know what the rules were. Obviously we were aware to a certain extent of the fact that we were going on late and it was going to piss people off, but we naively thought that because we were the band, we could do what the fuck we wanted. Ours was a volatile combination of bravado, booze and nerves – I really did have to be pretty out of it before I could consider offering the world the approximation of being a frontman that I had put together from close study of Iggy Pop and Jim Morrison – and it wasn't long before that Molotov cocktail would go off in our faces.

There was a gig at Liverpool Poly where we'd got so drunk we had to take a load of speed to sober up, but the industrial quantity probably wasn't our smartest move so we went onstage totally off our tits and played 'Jesus Fuck' for about half an hour. It wasn't music in any recognisable sense, just pure aggression, but we were pretty happy with the way it turned out. In fact we felt so good about it that we went out to mingle with the crowd afterwards to feel the love, but instead were faced with people going 'Before we kick the shit out of you, what makes you think that you can get away with this?' 'But what on earth could you mean by that? You have witnessed something special tonight . . .'

Our appearance on the *Old Grey Whistle Test* – on 12 March 1985 – was a textbook example of The Jesus and Mary Chain's tendency to fall foul of the rock 'n' roll gatekeepers, the guys in cowboy boots who knew the way things should be done. So alert were the Whispering Bob posse to the danger of us turning up at their studio in a state of inebriation that they insisted on us arriving at a ridiculously early hour of the morning, but this ruse backfired because it just meant we didn't go to bed the night before and the party was still very much ongoing at the time we staggered into the BBC.

We'd figured it would be one of those situations where they'd just be looking for a reason to get upset, and so it proved. As part of their unsuccessful attempt to stop the show looking like it was a fossil from the seventies, they had a little mannequin wearing a pair of sunglasses on the set at that time. Me borrowing those sunglasses to use as part of my stage-wear while we played 'In A Hole' was about as outrageous as we got, but they were on the brink of throwing us off the show for that, and there was an unfortunate accident afterwards – and I swear it was an accident – when one of the arms of the glasses got broken as I was putting it back on the dummy. This was hardly the Sex Pistols on Bill Grundy, but nonetheless elicited an outburst from the *OGWT* top brass along the lines of 'For fuck's sake – do you call yourselves professional?' It had never occurred to me to do that before, but I guess we were getting there.

Three days later, the 'Jesus and Mary Chain riot' (as the *NME* called it with their customary knack for hyperbole) at North London Poly on Holloway Road would put our band on the map in a way it would take us years to live down. This was the one where our preference for staying that little bit too long in the dressing room before a show – getting ourselves in the mood with a few beers and listening to compilation tapes of whatever music we were into at the time on the ghetto blaster – really bit us in the arse. The venue was massively oversold – say what you like about the Mary Chain at that time, but we could really pack out a big room – a situation not eased when someone, possibly Douglas, opened a fire door to let in a load of people who were queuing up outside without tickets.

The first sign that people were getting pissed off with us not being onstage was the ominous stamping of boots – it sounded like a marching army. That fearsome sound, combined with the increasingly desperate entreaties of the promoter, left us with only one option – having another drink and listening to a few more tunes. It does seem fucking stupid thinking back on it, but that was the high-wire act we were walking at the time and this was the night we fell off.

When we finally walked out onstage, it didn't take long for the penny to drop – 'Oh fuck, this is not good, I thought they were fans but they look like they want to kill us.' At that point, rather than doing anything to try and calm the situation we obviously kicked into 'fuck you' mode. That whipped the crowd into even more of a frenzy, to the point where when we left the stage people really did want to kill us, and because they couldn't get to us to kill us (and there were people trying to smash down the barricaded door of the dressing room with fire extinguishers, so this wasn't for want of trying), they decided to tear the venue apart instead.

Both Alan and Joe Foster have testified to their own heroics in jumping into the fray but the one whose fearlessness really impressed me, even though nothing has ever been said about it in public as far as I know, was Geoff Travis. You (or at least I) wouldn't really think of him as a physical guy, but he was right out there in the thick of it, identifying the ringleaders who were trying to destroy our PA, and doing everything he could to stop them. It wasn't a full-on riot, but it was certainly an out-of-control situation where people could easily have been badly hurt, and the sensationalist way the incident was reported in the music press did nothing to dampen the enthusiasm of people who liked a bit of a ruck for the opportunities future Jesus and Mary Chain live shows might offer them. Alan gave a quote describing the situation as 'art as terrorism' which didn't do anything to help defuse things either.

By this time, some of the archaic local licensing rules which had been used to stop the Sex Pistols playing were being invoked against us, to the extent of gigs being cancelled. Obviously this only poured paraffin on the fire of McGee's McLaren fixation. We were not in agreement with his view that whether we actually played gigs or not 'didn't matter', because the publicity generated by us being banned was just as good if not better than any response our music could elicit. We wanted people to hear our music – that was the whole point of being in a band after all – but because I was such good friends with Alan, it took me longer than it should've to realise the extent to which his svengali fantasies were actually starting to work against the band's interests.

In the meantime, there were a couple of uncomfortable brushes with the tabloid media where we got slightly suckered into playing Alan's game. I remember particularly not enjoying a conversation I was obliged to have with Garry Bushell after Alan had spun him some yarn about us getting thrown off the plane. I resolved to never speak to *The Sun* again because they'd only make their own stories up anyway, which, it later transpired, was exactly what they did do.

When the going gets tough, the tough fuck off to New York. It'd only been three months since signing off the dole before we were crossing the Atlantic for the first time, in April 1985. It would've been nice to have had a bit of time to take stock of all the things that were happening, but that's not how rock 'n' roll trajectories tend to play out. And for the moment it was pretty much non-stop excitement. Sometimes when we woke up in the morning it was hard to believe what the next day ahead held in store. What was that Lou Reed album, *Growing Up in Public?* That's certainly what we were doing. Although at this point you might look in vain for signs of new-found maturity, there were some hard lessons coming down the track.

We were in New York less than a week that first time, and I can remember everything that happened with almost hallucinatory clarity. Everyone always says 'It's like you've walked onto a movie set', and the reason they always say that is because that is exactly what it feels like. 'Hey, William, we're not in East Kilbride any more.'

William

I don't wanna be a Debbie Downer but I remember coming into New York at night for the first time and thinking 'Is that all there is?' Oh my God, I love and hate that Peggy Lee song at the same time. There would be plenty of later occasions when we'd go to America and I'd be practically fainting about how amazing it was – that's why I ended up living here after all – for example, the time we got the helicopter over the Grand Canyon, that was one of the greatest moments of my life . But that first trip when we came into the city in the darkness I was thinking 'Oh, OK – it's *fine.*'

Jim

The promoter Ruth Polsky had brought us over to play two nights at the Danceteria, the sort of happening downtown location where you'd expect to see Madonna hanging out with the Beastie Boys. The first night we played there it was packed out with indie kids who looked a bit like us and were really into what we were doing. The second night, there were a handful of b-boys trying to breakdance to 'You Trip Me Up'. That pretty much set the tone for our career in America. Excepting a couple of glitches when we would momentarily feel the heat of the spotlight, in general the people that liked us, liked us, and in sufficient numbers to keep us coming back, but the rest of the culture that had been the power source for so many of our inspirations managed to get along just fine without the Mary Chain.

We were OK with that, because we were having a great time. Now that the Warners deal had been extended to include publishing, we had money to buy brothel-creepers and the cool-looking guitars we could previously only salivate over in Glasgow pawn shop windows. I say cool-*looking* 'cos we weren't even that bothered about how they sounded. They went through a fuzz pedal that made everything sound like a fucking aircraft taking off anyway, so all they had to have was visual appeal. There was one in particular which you can see planted in the sand of the Algarve in the video for 'You Trip Me Up' – our *The Monkees* moment – it's got all these big knobs on it that made it looked like part of a tank, or an east European cooker hob from the mid 1950s. I think William ended up giving it away to a fan.

Back at John Loder's studio, we were working full steam ahead on the album. Of course, sometimes the steam was coming out of our ears. We were always screaming at each other, but when me and William argued in the early days of the band it was always about how to make the music better and it usually seemed to be over as soon as it began. What would happen would be that no one would concede that they'd lost the argument – or claim to have won it, that would be a surefire way of starting another one – but each of us would've taken on board what the other one had said, and things would go in the direction of the person who was right. The penny dropped and suddenly everything went back to normal, as if the argument had never happened. No one said sorry but no one bore grudges either. At this point we just got on with stuff – nothing simmered. That part would come later.

William

One time we were throwing each other around, having a bit of a scuffle, and somehow the studio door came off its hinges. I don't know how that happened, because we probably both weighed about nine stone at the time – we certainly weren't working out – and those doors are totally soundproofed so they're really fucking heavy. We weren't trying to hurt each other – it was more like a violent hug – and John Loder was quite anti-corporate so he probably billed Warners for it.

He was a great guy – very caring in some quite strange and unexpected ways. Once, when I told him I had a sore tooth at the back of my mouth, he bundled us both into his car and took us to this dentist who was some kind of rock 'n' roll weirdo. John made us both have detailed examinations even though I was the only one with toothache. The dentist offered us this laughing gas and said 'I can play bass, I can be in the band.' It was quite hard fobbing him off while his hands were in your mouth.

We had some other funny encounters while we were in that studio. Jah Wobble and Keith Levene from PiL dropped by to see us, which was great as I think they are both geniuses. Keith was talking to us in the way people who've been successful for a while often do to people who have just started out – not quite patronising, but like he was explaining the mysteries of the universe. I remember him telling us how Geoff Travis was trying to act like his dad was a coal miner even though in real life he was the ambassador to Washington. There may have been a little bit of exaggeration involved in that statement.

Jim

As well as Crass being vegans – and no one normal knew what vegans were then, we thought it was something to do with the Starship *Enterprise* – the other alternative lifestyle on display at John's studio was that of Chicago industrial pioneers Ministry, who were time-sharing the studio with us. They'd take speed and be up all night recording, then we'd come in all sedate in the morning. Even including those luxurious cabs from Fulham, the total cost for recording the whole of *Psychocandy* and the singles and B-sides that went with it would end up being about seventeen grand. So we'd been wrong about needing a major label's bankroll – at least in recording terms. At the time we were wondering how we could possibly even justify that much expense, until we heard that Lloyd Cole and the Commotions' album had cost a quarter of a million.

William

We developed a different way of working on the B-sides, which I really liked because it was much more collaborative and off the cuff. That was the only time we wrote together rather than as individuals really – when we had to knock something up from scratch, like on 'F. Hole' which came out later on the twelve-inch of 'Happy When It Rains'. It was pishing with rain that day, we'd recorded a little bit of feedback for the end of the EP, and John said 'Why don't we just stick a mic outside, record the rain and stick it over the top?', which we did and it sounded great.

I loved doing that kind of thing and wished we could have done it more. I'll tell you what's happened way too often over the years – and the first time I noticed it happening was in John Loder's studio – is that Jim will be sitting there playing his guitar, then I pick mine up and join in with him and I think it sounds beautiful and amazing but he always gets uncomfortable and just stops. The little thing he was playing that first time at John's was great and the bit I added was nice and really fitted, but then after about eight to ten seconds Jim put his guitar down and walked away. It's always annoyed me when he does that but I guess it comes down to confidence. I've told Jim hundreds of times that he is a pretty good guitar player, and I know it's said half in jest when he says he never wants to go beyond a certain level, but it's only half in jest and I guess I have to respect it, even though it's really annoying – 'This guy doesn't want to jam, even when he's in the middle of a great jam!'

Jim

On the day of Live Aid, in July 1985, I remember going from Fulham pub to Fulham pub, trying to find a place where people weren't watching it on the telly. It was quite claustrophobic because it did feel even while it was happening as if there was a lot of cynicism involved. Was this more about helping people who were starving or reviving bands' careers? It was hard to be sure.

I knew someone who worked at the Virgin Megastore on Oxford Street and he said that the week Queen played Live Aid, their back catalogue started selling four times what it had previously. It seemed like everyone who participated got a massive boost to their careers, especially Bob Geldof who was going nowhere before Live Aid but then suddenly became Sir Bob, this multimillionaire media star.

The phrase 'disaster capitalism' hadn't been coined yet, but I guess Live Aid was the ultimate example of that before the concept even existed. If you look at the imperial phase of the mid- and late-eighties music industry, when the guys in Armani suits were having a fantastic time selling everyone their record collections again on CD, Live Aid was definitely a big part of that. In musical terms,

I wouldn't go as far as the people who say 'Live Aid killed pop music', because I think pop music was already in trouble before Live Aid came along, but it certainly rubber-stamped a drift away from spontaneity and invention and towards a world where everything had to be stadium-sized so it could shift the maximum number of units.

It'd all started with Martin Hannett doing something new. Then people – and I guess the main person would be Steve Lillywhite, but there were others so it wouldn't be fair to blame him entirely – grabbed on to what Hannett did with Joy Division, misunderstood it, and before we knew it, everyone was wearing big coats with shoulder-pads and filming their videos in the open air.

At a time when everybody was doing these generic great big rock productions in the hope of being as big as U2 – and it seemed to be a reflection of the Thatcher/Reagan/Madonna era that people were pursuing success at all costs – we were determined to keep things scaled down and do our own thing, which was to stay as far from that new arena-friendly template of how a rock band was supposed to sound as possible, and make sure there was room for a little bit of spontaneity. That's why we asked Bobby's girlfriend Karen Parker to sing the backing vocals on 'Just Like Honey' (my girlfriend Laurence had a go, too, and got a credit even though her efforts didn't actually make the cut), and at a gig at the Haçienda we got her to play the drums for a whole show on the spur of the moment, even though we had no idea if she could do it. How well that worked out was very exciting, and I still got to turn around and see Bobby's enraptured 'Whew!' face, but this time on the side of the stage instead of behind the drums. It wasn't until years later, when Bobby's book came out, that we found out he was actually quite upset by this.

Bobby and Karen also had walk-on parts in an episode which does the Mary Chain – and specifically me – even less credit. In fact it's so embarrassing I'd rather not mention it at all, but YouTube has ensured it's never gone away, and I guess the only way it makes sense is in the context of our determination to roughen up the surface of the mid-eighties. I fucking hate that clip and if I'd known it was gonna be haunting me for the next forty fucking years I'd have taken a different approach

We were being interviewed on Belgian TV by a guy who we had, for some reason, been warned was an utterly obsessive fan of Joy Division and would not hear a word against them. Contrarian that I was trying to be, I took that as my cue to launch into a savage and entirely unwarranted assault on the reputation of Ian Curtis and co. (a band that of course I loved as much as the presenter did) while (and hard to believe as it is, we had actually planned this) Karen and Bobby made out on the couch next to me. I can laugh about this now, so long as I never have to watch it again.

The interval between North London Poly and our next show in the capital – at the Electric Ballroom in Camden – should have given people time to cool off. Unfortunately it seemed to have had the opposite effect, giving more of the kind of people who like to go around carrying baseball bats the time to hear about riots at Mary Chain shows – 'Ooh, right, riots at Mary Chain shows, I want to be part of this.' How they got those bats past the guys on the door I don't know – presumably they said they were just pleased to see them – but the results (at least after we'd done our customary late-starting, quick-finishing burst of feedback-drenched provocation) were so ugly that the two ex-SAS security guards McGee had hired to protect us handed in their notice on the spot.

The whole situation was started to feel dangerously out of control. I'd already taken a pasting at a Nick Cave gig from some guys who'd been at the earlier 'riot' show (the sad part was, when one of them asked me if I was in the Mary Chain I assumed he was wanting an autograph when what he actually wanted was to punch me in the face), and while you could make a case that our behaviour was courting this kind of response, we didn't want it on our conscience for someone in the audience to get badly hurt – the band would've deserved it, but the audience didn't. At the Electric Ballroom it was Laurence who was lucky to escape serious injury after being hit by a bottle, and this time we, perhaps belatedly, decided that enough was enough and action needed to be taken.

The timing was certainly right, in that whereas a year before we didn't really feel that we owed our audiences anything, now we were on the brink of releasing an album we'd worked really hard to make as good as it could possibly be. In the future we wanted audiences to come and see us because they wanted to hear the songs we were really proud of, not in the vague hope of being part of a violent melee. The strategy we adopted had three different strands to it, which bound together into a guide rope that would eventually pull us into the next phase of the band.

The first was to leave it a few months without playing any gigs in the UK at all, in the hope that the hooligan element which had suddenly attached itself to us would find another focus for its yearning for ultra-violence. The second was to sideline McGee. We'd got totally fed up with him making incendiary statements 'on behalf of' the band in newspaper interviews and we made it clear to him that while we were happy for him to carry on being our manager, we would speak for ourselves from now on and were no longer willing to be portrayed as putty in his McLaren-esque hands. To be fair to Alan, he actually took this demotion pretty well. He'd go on to find plenty of other ways of getting the rock-star levels of attention he'd always craved without having to have actual recourse to musical talent or a charismatic stage presence, and that was fine by us, so long as he wasn't trying to turn our band's name into a byword for civic disorder in the process.

The third element in our self re-invention strategy was to put our faith in Mick Houghton, the old-school press guy who was one of the only people we'd met at Warners who seemed to love and understand music the same way we did. Mick was older than us, and dressed very differently, but within about five minutes of meeting him for the first time we'd been deep in conversation about the various sixties psych bands we all revered. He'd had experience of helping independent-minded bands through the minefield of major-label politics while working with Echo and The Bunnymen, who were one of our favourite bands of the era, and we were confident that with his help we could swap the tabloid profile McGee's fly-by-night manoeuvrings had bought us for something more consistent with the long-term career we were hell-bent on having. People were always asking us the implicitly very insulting question 'What do you think you'll be doing in five years' time?' And we urgently needed them to stop being surprised when we answered 'Making our next album.' We'd also learnt that if you spend your whole time telling people how amazing you are, you're going to end up looking like a fucking idiot, so it's generally best to let the music do the talking.

Although the stigma of being the band who inspired angry mobs to smash up the PA system did take a while to shake off, this three-point plan did ultimately prove to be pretty successful. The next time we played in London, at Hammersmith Palais in the spring of 1986, there were no psychos waving baseball bats waiting for us, just a bunch of Mary Chain fans wearing Mary Chain t-shirts. We went onstage on time and played a full show, and from that point on we took our responsibilities much more seriously as a successful band that people would come to see because they actually liked us. I'd still have to get off my tits before I could go onstage, but I'd make sure that process was completed within the scheduled time frame.

The one major hurdle we had to get over in the intervening months was how to convince Warners to release our album as it was, without fucking it up. We'd been told all sorts of horror stories by other bands on the label about hearing their singles on the radio in totally unrecognisable form because the record company had remixed them without asking. Strawberry Switchblade – a band I'd loved when I saw them supporting Orange Juice at Night Moves years before – were a good example. If you listen to their Peel session they were fantastic, but as soon as Warners got their mitts on them it all went pear-shaped. There were other people whose records had been rejected but they weren't allowed to take them anywhere else, so you'd have these bands that were stuck in some awful limbo like flies in a web. It was horrifying stuff, and having realised fairly early on in our time at Warners that we'd done a deal with the devil, we focused all our energies on protecting our record. It was a high-stakes game, and the guy holding all the cards was Warners boss Rob Dickins, whose status as a true aristocrat of the music industry was underlined by the fact that he was married to one of Pan's People.

William

When we first went into Warners, we'd said to Rob 'You're not going to remix our records are you? You're not going to bring in other musicians to fix them?' At that point me and Jim were like 'Oh fuck, what have we done?' To be fair to him, he did ultimately keep his word, although he did often have very strong – and often unfavourable – opinions about the music we made.

Jim

We actually got on better with Rob than most of the other people at Warners, because at least he would tell us what he thought to our faces. The rest of them had all these different not-so-subtle strategies for letting us know they despised us without actually saying it. Our name was the first thing they wanted to change – 'Just call yourselves The Mary Chain'. 'We are The Mary Chain, but it's short for The Jesus and Mary Chain.'

Radio 1 didn't play our records very much, but the fact that they did every now and then showed that the name wasn't the thing that was holding them back. The reason Radio 1 didn't play our records was because they hated them. The people at Warners felt the same way. You should've seen the looks on their faces when we took *Psychocandy* down to the office to play it to them for the first time. Their bewildered expressions said 'Is this a joke? When are you going to make the real record?'

This was where the real chess game began with Dickins. We knew there was a good chance he was going to pull the plug on the album, because he kept telling us it was a piece of shit, so we had to figure out a way to get him to release it into the world in the form we'd intended. Somehow we managed to convince him that it was the record we needed to make and something we had to get out of our system, and if he could only see his way to not fuck with it, we'd be much more willing to take his thoughts on board in the future. Obviously this was storing up trouble for our next record, but we'd cross that bridge when we came to it, and in some ways I'm as proud of the political campaign we waged to get *Psychocandy* out into the world as I am of the record itself. If somebody had said 'boo' to me on the way home from that meeting I would still have jumped, but somehow we'd gone into a room with Rob and came out with what we wanted.

William

We thought *Psychocandy* was a big success, but Warners didn't agree, 'cos it only sold 100 or 120 thousand in the first couple of months and they want you to do that in the first week.

Jim

A lot of the music we were listening to in 1985 was from ten, twenty, even thirty years before, and we always thought of ourselves as being in it for the long haul in the same way. The idea of *Psychocandy* wasn't just to entertain people in the year it came out. We wanted to be a band that when we weren't around any longer, little misfits in their bedrooms would be finding our records and thinking 'God, that was amazing, we want to do something like that.' We had it in mind that this music would last, and it has done.

What we didn't realise at the time was that *Psychocandy* would be the easiest record we ever made. It turned out exactly the way it needed to, and we'd been making it in our heads for a couple of years before we did it anyway, so the idea of anyone seriously thinking it could be any other way was just ridiculous to us. We knew that whole record inside out – we could actually hear it in our heads – before we'd even started recording it, and the whole process of putting it together was, in a way, almost effortless. The hardest walk lay ahead of us.

ii. The Pino Palladino Years

Jim

The deal with the devil we had been forced to strike to save *Psycho-candy* required much more record company input into the albums that followed. The idea that The Jesus and Mary Chain's music might be improved by a contribution from the session bass player Pino Palladino is a representative sample of the kind of helpful suggestions we would face over the coming years. We never gave in, but it was very draining.

I don't think the music suffered, but we suffered, as after a while the relentless bad vibes with the record company ground us down, and the thought that we wouldn't have received such unsympathetic handling from Rough Trade was one of several reasons to be slightly jealous of The Smiths. Geoff Travis was a great help to us as a point-man with Warners, but his presence in our camp was also a constant reminder of what might've been.

The big leftover from the *Psychocandy* era – 'Some Candy Talking', which had first seen the light of day on the acoustic session we did for John Peel in October of 1985 – would be our biggest hit to date when a rerecorded version came out in the summer of 1986. Although 'Some Candy Talking' itself had a drum machine on it, the rest of the session tracks which we included on the double seven-inch – and the B-sides, which included the track 'Psychocandy' which we had opted not to put on the album – would be our last records with Bobby Gillespie on them. The drums weren't the problem with the new recording, it was the bass.

William

When we did 'Some Candy Talking', for some reason – maybe because we sensed it was going to be a big song for us – me and Jim just got an incredible case of nerves. I wrote the song and yet somehow I couldn't play the bass line. Jim's quite a good bass player – it's actually him on most of the records – but when I said 'For fuck's sake, Jim, you do it', he couldn't manage it either.

It was just one of those weird sorts of anxiety that seemed to affect everyone. I'm not going to go so far as to call it a mass psychosis, but we did ask several of our friends to try it and they all failed as well. We even asked Douglas, who was technically our bass player, but usually more in the live arena than on record. If you listen to the song, it's not like there's anything complicated about the bass line – it's basically just one note – but when we got a top session guy in (not Pino Palladino, maybe that was our mistake), he couldn't do it either. He asked us what we wanted and we said 'Basically "boom, boom boom" then "boom boom boom boom, boom, boom"', and he said 'No problem.' But as it turned out, there was a problem. By the end everyone in the fucking building had had a go – we weren't in John Loder's studio any more, so we couldn't ask one of Ministry or Crass to do it. We did this one with Flood and Alan Moulder at Trident Studios in St Anne's Court in Soho, and we were up to double figures of unsuccessful try-outs before we found the right man for the job. Dick Green from Creation was the one who finally got it right. We certainly weren't going to be asking anyone from Warners.

Around that time we did our last American trip with Bobby, where we played at The Ritz in New York. That was a weird one, because we were the talk of the town and everyone treated us like stars but we had really bad jet lag, so when Andy Warhol invited us over to The Factory, we didn't go.

This is what pussies we were. Not only did Warhol's people send that invite over and we didn't go, but we were so much the hot band of the moment that the pimp in the neighbourhood where we were staying said 'Come down and pick out the girl of your choice.' I had a girlfriend back in London at that point so both offers were rejected – 'Sorry Andy, we're not coming out 'cos we're really tired', and no one had sex with prostitutes in the flat across the street, because we had girlfriends at home and we didn't think they'd be very pleased. It's no wonder we never made it into the Rock and Roll Hall of Fame.

I always knew that Jim was a good-looking guy, and people were attracted to singers. I'm more of a plain man, but I've loved and been loved, which is all you want anyway. Women were definitely a big part of my motivation for being in a band at the start. Obviously my most motivating thing was wanting to write songs and for people to like them, but when you're young you've also got huge reserves of desire and horniness, and it did turn out to be true that being in a band takes you instantly from being a four to a ten.

The first few times it was like 'Here I am, I've come from East Kilbride and I'm not particularly fucking gorgeous. The only thing I've got going for me is that I can write a couple of decent songs . . . Oh, good, you're saying that's enough?' But pretty soon I started to hate it because it's so phoney – when you're in a band you can have sex with hundreds of women if you want to, but you'll end up thinking, 'If I sold tins of beans at the local convenience store, would I really have my cock up your whatever?' So I really distrusted it. I just wanted someone who wanted to be with me – a good girlfriend, which is what I got in Rona McIntosh.

Jim

Because I'd started going out with Laurence Verfaillie and she was – initially at least – still living in Paris, I spent a lot of time in France in the first flush of the band's success. It was amazing to be able to go and spend a month or two there doing all the things I'd always wanted to but hadn't been able to, either because I was stuck in East Kilbride or because I was tied to the band's schedule. Being in Paris on your own is very different to having someone who lives there to take you around – it's like you were locked out before but now someone's given you the keys so you can get in and see everything close-up. As time went on I would treasure those moments being on tour when it was less frantic – being in Milan, looking out of the window at the cathedral and thinking 'Fuck, look where I am!' Or walking around Rome on my day off, being so fucking happy and thinking 'Christ, this is the most beautiful place I've ever seen.' That, to me, was the rock 'n' roll dream. I always knew there was more to life than Butlin's in Ayr, and now here I was.

When we had a day off on tour my favourite thing to do was just get lost in a city I didn't know. Sometimes I really did get lost and would've had to make sure I had the hotel's address in my pocket so I could get a cab back – I almost needed a name tag like Paddington. I don't think people would've guessed that's how we would spend our days off – they'd have imagined us getting in arguments and petulantly slamming doors before ordering unhealthy food from room service. But we all have our simple pleasures that don't need to surface in a song – if The Jesus and Mary Chain had started releasing concept albums called *Before the Dawn, I Saw You in Rio* , we instinctively knew that would've bored the bejesus out of everyone – Duran Duran had kicked that shit out of us.

William

When we'd get back from tour people would ask 'Oh did you see the architecture in Prague? It's wonderful', and I'd be thinking 'But I only saw the Holiday Inn.' Touring for me was more like travelling to watch Rangers when I was a kid – you got there, you saw the game, then you went home.

Jim

After Laurence came to live with me in London, in 1986, we moved out of the Fulham bedsit and into William's old flat in Stoke New-ington, as he and Rona had moved on to Archway by that time. Because I couldn't find anywhere decent, we stayed there about six months before a place in Kentish Town came up where we lived for a few years before we broke up. After living in bedsits for a while a one-bedroom flat in Kentish Town seemed like luxury, because it was luxury. William and I were happy our dues-paying period was brief, and obviously everyone wants the best standard of living they can manage, but we didn't have unreasonable material ex-pectations. We weren't looking for mansions in Buckinghamshire – London was where we wanted to be. And to have mortgages we could afford on decent places of our own where we didn't have to share a bog on the landing was enough – it felt like things were going all right. Obviously William got bored with touring pretty quickly and became quite domesticated. Him and Rona even had two cats called Jim and William . . .

William

They were full brothers – both of them grey tabbies – and they squabbled, but it wasn't vicious. Basically they had fights like Jim and I do where you push each other around, going 'You fucking idiot' 'No, *you* fucking idiot.' William was the Smiths fan with glasses and Jim was the lovable accident-prone little dope who got electrocuted through his whiskers. One night he was standing next to an electrical socket and his whisker got stuck in the plug so he got a massive shock – he did survive but he jumped about twelve feet in the air . . .

Jim

The way John Moore joined the band as drummer in Bobby's place was basically like a stray cat that gets itself adopted. He was a stalker.

William

John just sort of charmed us. I don't think he'd mind me saying – and I love John, so this is nothing against him – that he was kind of ridiculous. He would always act so rock 'n' roll but then his mother would still drive him to the airport and pick him up after touring. One of his most endearing qualities is that he thinks he's a badass but he's not.

Jim

As Primal Scream had started to make records – for Creation, of course – it reached a point with Bobby where it was becoming clear that him being in two bands wasn't going to work. We knew his heart was with his own band but we thought we owed it to him to formally ask him to join The Jesus and Mary Chain (up to that point he'd not wanted to take a cut of our Warners advances, so we were paying him like a session player), even though we were pretty sure he'd turn us down. It would have been great if he'd agreed, but then there wouldn't have been Primal Scream so it wouldn't have been that great. It was a very polite sort of request – 'We'd love you to join the Mary Chain, you're perfectly welcome, but we totally understand if you don't want to' – and the parting of the ways that followed after he gave us the response we expected was consensual and even loving.

Once John Moore had planted himself in our subconscious – turning up at gigs and film screenings we were going to, looking like he was already in the band (*Entertaining Mr Sloane* at the Scala was one of them, and come to think of it his whole pursuit of us is a bit Orton-esque). I don't think we talked to him at that point, just looked at each other awkwardly. Shortly after that he used his family connections in the courier industry to travel to East Kilbride and buy a black shirt from Top Man, just as he had imagined us doing. There's not much you can do in the face of that kind of commitment, is there?

When we eventually asked him to join, the interview went along very similar lines to how Bobby's had gone – 'Hi, can you play the drums?' He wasn't going to say no, was he, even though like Gillespie before him, he wasn't actually a drummer (in John's case the guitar was his main instrument). 'OK, do you want to go on tour in couple of weeks?' 'Sure, yeah.' Bobby came along to John's first gig – at Nottingham Rock City – to give him some hints on how to do it. He did fine, playing a stripped-down stand-up kit, the same way Bobby had, and Bobby left the band after that show. A lot of those little looks and glances and unspoken moments on-stage – that thing which was almost like telepathy – went with him, but we'd always known Bobby being in the band was temporary, and him leaving was something that had to happen so we could become more business-like about what we did.

We knew we had to figure out how to put the show across in a different way, so that being in The Jesus and Mary Chain could become more like a job, which was what we wanted it to be. So we put John Moore in the video for 'Some Candy Talking' – even though it was a drum machine on the record – and the EP went straight into the top 20 and the next week climbed to number 13. And then Radio 1 Breakfast Show DJ Mike Smith got it banned from the BBC for being 'about heroin'.

William

People thought that song was full of heroin references, when in fact it wasn't, but who am I to question Mike Smith's perceptions? The reason I try not to get to get drawn into discussing what songs are 'about' is because a song is not just a set of instructions. Isn't a song something that just vibrates and anyone can look into it and get what energy they want? That's why I don't want to take away someone else's version of a song I've written – even if they are a Radio 1 DJ making a decision which does my band long-term commercial damage – because I hate it when that's been done to me.

I was in a taxi once and Robbie Robertson was on the radio talking about 'Bessie Smith', which is one of my favourite songs from *The Basement Tapes*. Now I don't know what that song's about – well, I have a little idea, but I also like the mystery of it.

But the DJ asked him to explain it and, oh my God, what he said was horrific to me, to the point where I was sitting there almost crying – 'You just ruined it for me and that was my favourite Band song.'

But thank goodness for early onset dementia caused by excessive drinking and dope smoking, because now I've totally forgotten what he said and I love the song just as much as I always did. It took me ages to get back to it, and I know there's a reason I don't feel the same way about it as I used to, but I can't remember what it is, so I can return to the state of innocence in which I didn't even have an opinion and I was just listening to something beautiful.

The hardest thing when you write songs is that people want explanations which are not necessarily in their interests to have. Sometimes the subject of a song is obvious and you'll tell them and sometimes you just don't fucking know – 'I never thought about it, I just did it, then I went on to the next one' – but that's too boring for people. 'Oh, come on, surely it was about your cousin who was a prostitute?' Everyone always wants it to be a big story, but why can't the story just be the song? What I used to say to people – and some people got it and some people didn't – was 'Just pretend I'm dead and then figure it out for yourself.'

Jim

If the 'Some Candy Talking' ban had happened a year earlier, McGee would've been popping up in all our interviews telling everyone it was a McLaren-esque promotional masterstroke. Luckily we had relieved him of that duty, and things had plodded along quite well for a while once it was established that the band spoke for itself and we didn't need our manager to do it for us. But it didn't take long before the dial started to turn the other way, and as Alan started managing other bands and trying to set up his Elevation deal with Warners, we began to feel as it we no longer had his full attention. If I'm honest about the impact this had on us, I'd have to say it made us feel neglected and even a little bit jealous. The time had come for a parting of the ways. William – who had never been as close to Alan as I was – went with me to do the deed in the discreet West End Wendy's burger joint where we used to hold most of our business meetings. It all seemed reasonably functional and amicable at the time, except that Alan – perhaps understandably given how much he'd believed in us when no one else did – didn't take it too well and there were a few years where we didn't really speak.

William

Once we made the break with McGee, that was it in financial terms. There were no legal issues, he never owed us any money and vice versa. But there was one investment I couldn't quite bring myself to write off. Do you remember how Tottenham Court Road in the eighties was all shops that sold technical things like fax machines and video recorders? I'd gone into one of those shops and bought Alan an answering machine to make the Creation office in Clerkenwell a bit more professional when they were first setting it up. It was a pretty good one and cost a bit of money – maybe £170 – and I couldn't stop thinking about it, because the one we had at home at the time was awful and never seemed to pick up any messages – we used to go out to the pub and ring our home number to test it.

One day me and Rona were down near the office and I suddenly thought: 'You know what, we're not with Alan any more, why don't we go and pick up that answering machine so I can stop missing calls?' I should emphasise that this was one of the worst ideas I'd ever had in my life because it just caused so much stress and grief. I went into the office and Alan's wife Yvonne was there as they'd had one of their temporary reconciliations. She tried to stop me when I picked the answering machine up and took it out of the wall – 'What are you doing?' 'It's my answering machine so I'm taking it.' 'No you're not.' 'Yes I am, I bought this answering machine with my own money' etc.

I've heard a version of this story where the answering machine ended up in a bin up the road, but what would have been the point of taking it just to do that? The happy ending was that once Rona and I got it home, it did work much better than the defective one so we were no longer missing messages, but if I had my time over again I think I'd probably just leave it where it was.

Jim

There was an enormous amount of pressure on us after *Psychocandy* which, because we'd got rid of Alan without any kind of successor in place, we ended up having to deal with pretty much on our own. If *Psychocandy* had come out and been just the singles and the B-sides, the *NME* would've said we were a busted flush. But for some reason the extent to which it surpassed expectations – in that pretty much every track on it could've been a single – ended up becoming a problem. There was a period of time where everyone in the music press seemed to be saying 'They should split up now, because they're never gonna be able to top that record.' What the fuck were we supposed to do? All these people seemed to have an idea of what the Mary Chain ought to be, but all we knew was that, much as we loved the Ramones, we didn't want to be like them and make the same record over and over. But before we could reach that point where we could just make the album we needed to make, we had to go through a lot of rigmarole with Warners.

William

We never lost our taste for destruction – we were still going out to Einstürzende Neubauten shows – but we wanted to make a different kind of record second time around. Jim and I were listening to a lot of Van Morrison at the time and even though no one would say *Darklands* ended up sounding like him, we definitely wanted to do something with a certain vibe to it. We'd jumped into the world with relish and we exploded and then people said 'Keep exploding, keep exploding', but we were like 'Fuck off with your "keep exploding", we want this to last.'

Warners of course were over the moon about the idea of a change in direction – Rob Dickins probably thought he had talked us into making a record with less feedback on – so we were getting a lot of attention from the record company at that time.

Jim

Rob wanted us to work with all these (as he called them) 'world-class producers', so at his insistence we spent a week in Bath with Ian Stanley who was the keyboard player out of Tears for Fears, and Chris Hughes who was their producer and had a studio in his home. It took a week to do one fucking demo – of the song 'Darklands' – and we were utterly depressed by the whole thing because we knew this was never going to work. But we had made a commitment to do it, so we stuck it out.

On the last night we were thinking 'Thank fuck we get to go home tomorrow and think of a reason why this is not going to happen', but for some reason Ian and Chris were totally gung-ho and really getting into it. By the time it got to about ten o'clock at night we were losing the will to live, so we just said 'Right, we're going to bed now' and they were just going to fiddle around with a few more things to finish up. We came down in the morning with all our bags packed, thinking 'At last, let's get out of here', but they were all excited – 'C'mon, listen to what we've been doing!' They'd been up all night putting a fucking double bass on it. I was sitting in this chair thinking 'Don't look at William', because I knew if I did I wouldn't be able to stop laughing. But then unfortunately I did look at him and kind of fell out of the chair because we were both pishing ourselves. Chris was looking at me, going 'For fuck's sake show some respect, we've been up all night doing this', blah blah blah. By the time we got back to London, word of what had happened reached Rob Dickins and he had a massive go at us – 'You fucking losers . . . you FUCKING LOSERS! I got you world-class producers and what do you do? You fucking laugh at them.' We were saying 'Sorry Rob, it just wasn't going to happen.'

William

My favourite place for writing, where I came up with my best songs, was the kitchen in our house in East Kilbride. That was the one place you could open the door to get some fresh air when everybody in the older generations was smoking. It was tiny, and ugly as fuck, with the style of decor you could call 'early-eighties working-class tack', and people would constantly be coming in to put the the kettle on or because they wanted a bit of toast. But for some reason those distractions wouldn't put me off, and later on, when we were out on the road a lot and it was hard to keep my head straight, I would think back to that kitchen and what it felt like to be working on songs in there.

Our granny on my ma's side – Granny McLeish, which is Jim's middle name – died in 1986. For her last year or so she was a bit doolally, so I don't think she could quite get her head round how well things were going for us. I wasn't there when she watched us on TV but I heard she responded with some bewilderment – 'What are those two cunts doin' on the telly?' It was a good question. I guess because it was on the screen it didn't seem like reality to her, and sometimes we felt the same way.

Do you know the old Glasgow song 'You cannae shove your granny aff the bus?' We used to sing that about her. It's sung to the tune of 'She'll be coming round the mountain' and the reason given is "Cos she's your daddy's [or mammy's, delete according to the side of the family] mammy', so you can't argue with the logic of it.

Jim

When the band started to become successful, our parents were quite happy to be proved wrong about the Mary Chain's viability. I think they'd just been worried about what was going to happen to us, so they were surprised and delighted when our plans actually worked out. At that point they realised that we weren't just a couple of weirdos – well, we were, but we were weirdos with a licence because we had a bit of money, and in working-class Scotland, if you've made a bit of money, anything goes. From that point on, my mum and dad became our biggest fans. They were huge supporters of everything we did, even the elements you might not expect parents to approve of. So at the height of our tabloid notoriety, if one of their neighbours had said 'Your boys are a disgrace' (which never happened as far as I know, but it easily could have done), my mum's response would have been 'You're just jealous.' After those uncomfortable years in such close proximity before the band got going, it was like a massive boil had been lanced and now we could just concentrate on what was important, which was that we could all still be there for each other.

My dad had a really tough time in the years after he was made redundant. It was crushing for his confidence not being able to get another job, even though this was no reflection on his abilities and merely the reflection of a wider social problem – men of his age who'd been out of work for a period of time were pretty much unemployable in the late eighties. He'd been excluded from everything he'd been told was important and that was very hard to cope with. But in that context the band's success was something he could feel good about – it was his money that bought us the Portastudio after all – and I think maybe it helped him feel happier in his own skin.

When we were living down in London and the band was doing well, I actually used to enjoy going home and taking my dad to the pub for a pint with me. I'd never been able to do that when I lived at home. And I knew that now in a way I was trying to be the son he'd always wanted, but there didn't seem to be any harm in that. It kind of worked and it was nice that we could develop more of a bond.

William

My da was listening to John Peel so much to see if he would play our records that he became a fan of other people he'd heard on the show. It was funny. Billy Bragg would come on the telly and my da would say 'Oh, this is a good one.' Me and Jim would be looking at each other in astonishment and my da would explain 'He's on John Peel a lot.' 'You listen to John Peel?' 'Yeah I listen a couple of times a week to see if he plays youse.' My ma loved us to death but I don't think she thought we were real musicians playing real songs – her idea of what that would be was some-one playing the violin or the piano, or maybe Frank Sinatra. My da was a bit more savvy about our music – even liking some of it.

Jim

In terms of the direction we wanted the sound of the band to move in, we'd started to realise that the stand-up drumming thing had had its time. We also thought it would make our sound bigger if we had a rhythm guitar, and knowing that John was a guitarist rather than a drummer and wouldn't know what to do with a full-size drum kit if he fell over one, it made sense to get him to swap. This worked well, while also initiating a phase where drummers in the Mary Chain were about as disposable as the ones in *Spinal Tap*. We even toured America with a drum machine, which is not an option I would recommend to anyone in a rock band that wants to be liked. The Cocteau Twins told us not to do that, and they were probably right. And the problem of finding a producer who was acceptable to us as well as to Rob Dickins still had to be solved. In a moment worthy of an unsuitable date in an eighties romcom, Warners even tried to put us in a room with Daniel Lanois, but that union was never written in the stars.

William

The guy we really wanted to produce *Darklands* was Ian Broudie, because he'd done the Bunnymen and we loved their records. Rob Dickins was a combative character who liked getting his own way, but I think this was the only thing he ever really dug his heels in about. We never quite understood why – well not until we found out years later that it was because Ian Broudie had punched him in the face once during an argument.

In the meantime, Rob's allergic reaction to Ian Broudie left us with a tricky decision to make. Even though we thought Ian was a great producer, we couldn't be certain it would work out between us, and we weren't sure if this was the hill we wanted to die on as far as Rob Dickins was concerned, so we compromised on Bill Price, who was a fair bit older than we were but had produced *Never Mind the Bollocks* so he was all right with us. When we first met him, Bill told us 'You won't walk away with my record, it'll be your record', and ultimately he kept his word. We were getting paranoid at that time about the level of intervention Warners might be contemplating – it's scary when you realise 'These people have a lot of control over us, and we're not that important to them. They'll not tell Madonna what to do, but they might tell us.'

Jim

Our general vibe at the time was one of anxiety bordering on panic. We knew we weren't going to just make *Psychocandy* Mk 2, even though we probably could have got away with it because a lot of people seemed to want the obvious follow-up. It seemed like the more interesting thing to do was to make a record that was basically the opposite, with no feedback and everything stripped down to the bone. The question we kept asking ourselves was 'What if it's no good and we can't actually do it?' There was always a feeling of everything hanging in the balance, as if we only had to make one false move and then we'd be standing there flipping burgers in McDonald's hats, but ultimately we thought 'Fuck it, if it doesn't work, at least we'll know we made the record we wanted', and that instinct served us well, because we stuck to our guns and it worked.

William

Soon after 'April Skies' was released, in the spring of 1987, I was on this incredible bus ride from Archway to Victoria. The route down from Archway and into the middle of the city was amazing, especially if you love London, as I do. I used to love being on the bus with my headphones on, watching the world moving past – something I was getting very used to doing on American tour buses too. I wasn't smoking anything at the time, I was just high on life.

'April Skies' was our first top 10 single. We were on lots of magazine covers, including *Smash Hits*, which was the big one, and we'd just been on *Top of the Pops* for the first time (which as it turned out would also be the last, as we somehow, without ever quite knowing how or why, managed to piss off the production team to the point where they never asked us back), so this was a point of maximum public visibility in our career.

I'd been on this great bus ride and was feeling pretty good about everything until I lost my footing as I stepped off the open-backed Routemaster and was dragged along the road by the bus for about the length of a football pitch. I was like Frank Spencer in *Some Mothers Do 'Ave 'Em*. Everyone was screaming at the driver to stop but he didn't hear and by the time someone finally managed to drag me back on, my fucking trousers had huge holes ripped in their knees and I was a bloody mess. It was the most humiliating thing that had happened in my life and the fact that I'd just been on *Top of the Pops* and was now officially a cool rock star living my dream made the whole thing worse. People were very nice, asking if I was OK, but I just ran and stumbled away because it was all so embarrassing.

Jim

The fact that 'April Skies' did so well when it came out as a single proved very helpful to us in attracting the new management The Jesus and Mary Chain desperately needed. After Alan it had been kind of a free-for-all for a while, and me (with help from Laurence) being the closest thing we had to a manager turned into a bit of a nightmare. I was having a mini nervous breakdown 'cos my phone wouldn't stop ringing but when I unplugged it Geoff and Rob Dickins got together to tell me this was unacceptable. It was at this point that an American called Jerry Jaffe – a big character who we got on really well with – and ex-Thin Lizzy manager Chris Morrison (who was more of a businessman) came on board.

Jerry was a star from the first day we met him and we're still friends with him now. He was an old-style American music biz manager with thousands of stories to tell us. He'd been quite a bigwig at Polygram where he'd signed Bon Jovi. They even played at his wedding – he showed us the video and everything – then he'd had some kind of fall from corporate grace which was never really explained, before going into management with Chris. He used to say the most absurd things which were very entertaining. He knew we loved The Velvet Underground, and I remember him telling us 'Yeah, the Velvets, I used to go and see them and they were fucking shit.' We'd only just signed up with him and already he was going the right way about getting fired.

We definitely needed a buffer between us and the world. Even though the largely feedback-free *Darklands* was musically a much less abrasive proposition than *Psychocandy*, that didn't seem to stop us getting people's backs up every time we went on TV. There was one show called *The Roxy* which ran for about ten minutes in the 1980s before it was cancelled – and on the evidence of how they treated us, it was easy to see why. The studio was in Newcastle and they'd asked us to travel up there from London to perform 'Happy When It Rains'. As soon as we got there, we could tell that these people fucking hated us. And this wasn't one of those TV shows where we were off our tits – we were atypically totally on it and together. As we were doing the run-throughs, the floor manager said 'We're just doing camera angles, you don't have to mime to this', but then one of the guys, instead of saying

'Roll the track', he said 'Roll the crap.' It was a Freudian slip and we all fell about laughing. It was one of those things where everyone gets a bit giggly and it's hard to stop joking around after that, but we were still getting on with what we were meant to be doing in a perfectly professional manner, until someone from the production crew came down and said 'Fuck off out of the back door – we're not having this.' We asked what the fuck they were on about, and the reason they gave was that we 'weren't even trying to mime'. We said 'But the guy said we didn't have to, 'cos you were only doing it for the camera angles', but to no avail. We were unceremoniously chucked out of the building and the once-in-a-career opportunity for me to be seen on TV sober was lost. We couldn't believe we'd travelled all that way to have that experience, but at least we had the perfect illustration of how easy it was to put media professionals' noses out of joint in the eighties. Something very similar had happened on *Top of the Pops* where I was deemed to be too animated in performance as compared with a more restrained rehearsal. Didn't these people know anything about the magic of showbiz?

A short history of Mary Chain TV appearances would have to be subtitled 'How to Lose Friends and Alienate People'. It would include Paul Weller turning round to give us the finger as we walked through the *Top of the Pops* studios, and stretch back as far as Pink Floyd's Dave Gilmour being shocked by William painting his Gretsch Tenneseean black on the stage of *The Tube* in 1985.

William

I know that sounds like something you'd make up, but when Dave Gilmour walked by he was absolutely disgusted. I understand what he meant – he thought I was being disrespectful to the guitar, but I wasn't, I was being disrespectful to the way it looked.

It was like a coffee table. I was all dressed in black at the time and I didn't want to wear a big piece of wood spoiling my outfit!

John Squire of The Stone Roses was much more impressed by Jim's borrowing from Jackson Pollock. Jim had a guitar he'd spattered paint on in a Pollock style which I thought looked quite fine, and subsequent developments suggested John agreed . . .

Jim

We'd never had a problem with giving credit to people whose music had influenced us, so we weren't going to complain about other bands seeing and hearing what we did and taking it in their own direction. But in the late eighties there were a series of musical developments in which we felt we'd had at least a supporting role, but for some reason – possibly connected to our isolated position at Warners, or maybe a lack of support in the music press – we never seemed to get a credit.

In the course of *Darklands'* lengthy gestation, Warners' attitude towards us changed. By the time the record was done it was clear we had gone from potential cash cow to the donkey that's allowed to live in the field. There was one particularly painful marketing meeting not long before the album came out where we had to try and persuade them that advertising it might be a good idea.

'What were you thinking?' 'Well, could we have a full-page ad for *Darklands* in the *NME* or whatever?' 'We weren't really thinking we were gonna do that. We'd rather use the money for a new Armani suit.'

William

When you're on Warners, unless you're selling millions of albums, nobody takes you seriously . . . At least, not if you're The Jesus and Mary Chain. I remember once we were up there in some-one's office looking through a bunch of promo LPs – jazz records and classical records – I lifted them up and they were heavy as fuck, so I asked the guy 'Why aren't our records on heavy vinyl like this?' And he said 'Because that's for serious music.' The idea was so deeply ingrained that I don't think he even realised how insulting he was being. (Pick up an original copy of our B-sides compilation *Barbed Wire Kisses* if you've got one in the house – it's pressed on the lightest vinyl known to man.)

If you were jazz or classical you didn't need to sell a lot, but they saw us as 'pop', which meant that even though we were kinda successful, because we weren't competing with Madonna or Rod Stewart no one really gave us the respect that I wouldn't want to be so arrogant as to say we deserved, but we were certainly trying to earn by doing good work. By this point it had definitely occurred to us that if we'd gone with a big independent we'd have been a big fish instead of this tiny fish in a huge fucking pond. But I guess one advantage of them not caring too much about you is that they don't care that much about you, so you can just go away and make your records without interference.

Jim

Once *Darklands* had come out – to excellent reviews and strong sales, but nothing that suggested we were gonna be playing Wembley Stadium any time soon – Warners did basically leave us alone to do our own little thing in the corner. They weren't going to get rid of us, because it was kind of cool for them to have us on the label, as it made them look more in tune with certain types of music than they actually were and ensured upcoming bands in that area would consider them, but I think the basic equation was 'There's a bunch of people out there who like this band already, so if we just do the bare minimum they'll still sell enough records for us to make a profit.' Our resistance to world-class producers ensured that our growth rate was never going to be something that would interest them.

The irony was that while Warners had spent so much time trying to make us into this other band that we never could or would be, the next wave of rock music that was coming through from America from 1986–88 was people like Sonic Youth and Pixies and Dinosaur Jr, all things that weren't sonically a million miles away from what we'd been doing. I'm not saying that generation was necessarily shaped by us, but once Nirvana came along as the next multimillion unit shifters, they certainly had more in common with us than the band Warners tried to make us into. You could say that the bee in the lift shaft had the pollen of grunge on its legs.

Meanwhile, back in Britain, the mantle of 'band the music press thought could do no wrong' was in the process of being handed from The Smiths to Creation's new stars My Bloody Valentine. In one sense this was a great improvement – I'd never really liked The Smiths, but I loved the Valentines. Our fuzz pedal (and it was the exact same one) might have been part of their starter kit, but they took it somewhere completely different. Still, their coronation did leave us feeling like the guy in the middle of the relay who doesn't get a baton.

I could see that Morrissey gave good copy in music press terms, even though I always thought he was a bit dodgy, but My Bloody Valentine's enigmatic reputation was based on not really saying anything. It seemed like the Mary Chain couldn't win. Yes, we'd get the occasional cover of the *NME*, but there would always be a lot of digs in there. It sounds kind of paranoid, but it felt like people – by which I mean music journalists – were just waiting for us to fuck up.

We always seemed to be either just missing the bus, or getting on it too soon. I wouldn't go as far as saying we were very into hip-hop, but we'd been listening to a lot of early Def Jam around the time of *Darklands*, and our next release, 'Sidewalking', would be a one-off single with sampled drums borrowed from New York rapper Roxanne Shante. We weren't going to start rapping on it, because that would be ridiculous – we'd have sounded like a hip-hop version of The Proclaimers – but we did think 'Let's take these rhythms and try to get a bit of a groove going.' Geoff Travis was into that but Warners weren't terribly excited, certainly not excited enough to do very much promotion.

On its eventual release, in the spring of 1988, one of our catchiest singles would limp into the top 30 at number 30. Our gift for seizing the moment had led us to put out our New York hip-hop single at a time when Britain was gearing up for Acid House and Madchester's second Summer of Love. The time when hip-hop or house was actually seen by some people (at least a certain kind of rapper) as a choice seems a long time ago now, but in commercial terms at least, we had backed the wrong horse.

When it came to The Jesus and Mary Chain's place in musical history, we were probably our own worst enemies. I remember when we were still living at home, a few nights before we went down to London to record 'Upside Down', me and my friend Stuart went to see George Melly in East Kilbride (on reflection it may even have been there I got the throat infection). William and I had really loved his books and just the whole idea of his louche and urbane persona and his very sociable existence. We got up the courage to get a book signed and told him we were going to go to London to make a record and he wished us good luck. I think at that point we imagined that the minute someone becomes a bit famous they all start speaking the same language which means they can all hang out together. This seems to be true for some people, but it never was for us.

We assumed that when your band got to a certain level of being known you would receive some kind of pass code which would automatically give you access to a charmed circle of celebrity interaction, but ours must have got lost in the spam filter, because for me it was quite the reverse. One of the things I most wanted to talk about in this book was (and is) some of the terrible experiences we had when we got the chance to meet our heroes. We would find ourselves in these amazing situations and just totally not be able to cope with them. The Ramones on the American *Darklands* tour in 1987 was the first of these incidents that really stuck in my mind. They came to see us somewhere on the West Coast – probably in San Francisco – there was a big aftershow, a couple of the Ramones stayed behind to say hello to us, and I just sat in the corner staring at them thinking 'I can't do this, I can't talk to these people.'

Years later, once me and Alan were talking again (the burger bar sacking took a while to get over, but it wasn't the end of the Mary Chain's long and tortuous relationship with McGee; there were several more exciting instalments still to come) and he was into his vanity project phase, Alan did an album with Joey Ramone and Ronnie Spector, in the course of which the former said 'Oh, the Mary Chain fucking hate the Ramones – they didn't say a word to us.' I felt hideous when I found out that these people who were as responsible as anyone for me and William thinking we could make music in the first place thought we didn't even rate them. If you could only relive these moments, it would be less embarrassing for me to run up to Joey at that party and just blurt out 'I love you' before getting dragged away by security.

We didn't do much better with The Cramps. We went on a short radio promo tour with them in America where we'd both have to do these little shows at radio stations. Sometimes we'd have to share a dressing room and it was a bit awkward 'cos they didn't have much to say for themselves either, and we'd end up sitting in opposite corners in uncomfortable silence with us thinking 'Oh my God, that's The Cramps over there.' I don't think they were thinking the same thing about us – I don't think they gave a fuck – but I so wanted to be able to walk over there and say 'You're a big part of the reason why we're here', and yet I just could not fucking do it.

Once I'd started to experience the pain of strangers trying to talk to me while I was in Marks & Spencer buying a six-pack of pants, that made me all the more tongue-tied and self-conscious around people I was, for want of a better word, a 'fan' of, because I didn't want to put them through the same awkwardness I felt. If it's the audience after a show, I'm totally up for that, and I'm generally OK with people talking to me about the band, but I've never been very good at dealing with compliments and I tend to get quite agitated when people recognise me. Either way, I'm the one sat in the corner with my head in my hands, thinking 'I don't know what to say, I don't know what to do, I'm leaving.' My only way of dealing with meeting my heroes was not dealing with it. William was a bit better, in fact, so long as he was a bit drunk or stoned, he was kind of OK. But my inability to communicate with people I looked up to was one of my biggest regrets.

The one role model I did manage to communicate with would not look back upon that experience with fondness. And this wasn't just a common or garden role model, this was probably the single person I'd derived the most of what might laughably be termed my stage persona from – Iggy Pop. That kind of laid-back, don't give a fuck, it's all on our terms vibe that Iggy and the Stooges had was the one I was going for. I wanted to be Iggy but it wasn't that easy. There were no shortcuts. You couldn't just look at Iggy and decide 'I'll do that', you had to kind of invent a little stage persona for yourself. I wrestled with that for many years – trying to be Iggy. Basically the key to it was ingesting exactly the right amount of drink and/or drugs to put yourself in that place, and I'd say I managed it maybe one time in ten. So when the opportunity came for us to tour with him in America, we just thought 'Wow, playing with Iggy.' We were kind of on the up in America at the time whereas he wasn't really, so the tour was billed as a 'co-headline'. They always do that bullshit – 'Who's going on last?' 'Well, Iggy of course' – but we decided to say yes anyway because we were honoured to be asked.

Unfortunately, from the minute we got to the first show we were being treated like shit. We went to do a soundcheck and Iggy was soundchecking so we walked out to the front of the building to watch, but the crew said we weren't allowed to do that – which I can kind of get, as I hate people watching me soundcheck. Even though I'd never tell anyone that they couldn't, it is kind of private, so it's a bit like someone asking to watch you take a shit . . .

William

Iggy's whole crew and especially his tour manager were a bunch of aggressive bastards and instead of taking forty-five minutes for his soundcheck he took an hour and a half, so we had to take ours fifteen minutes before the doors opened. As we walked out to do it, Iggy's rugs that he writhes around on were still onstage, so because he was my hero and he was fucking us over and I didn't know how to retaliate, I hawked up a big green gobbet of phlegm from the back of my throat and spat it out on his fucking carpet. All his roadies ran over to try and kill me and all our crew ran to my defence – it was brilliant.

Jim

We were sitting in the dressing room trying to process what had just happened when Iggy walked in. This guy is my idol and he was clearly trying to smooth it over because his tour manager had told him 'There's a problem but if you go in there and see them they'll probably just melt', so Iggy came in and said – and you've got to do this in an Iggy voice if it's really gonna work – 'Hey, is there anything I can get you guys?' I didn't know what to say because I felt shat on by someone I adored, but then after a long pause the words finally came to me and the words were 'How about a soundcheck?' He looked at us both with a shocked expression and 'Fuck, I was really looking forward to meeting you guys', then stormed out. I was devastated. This was not a real cool time.

William

It was actually pretty strong of Jim to call Iggy out like that, because I was too upset to say anything.

Jim

By the time we went onstage to play the actual show, we were fucking furious and I trashed the backline, kicked all of the monitors into the stage pit at the front and generally did as much damage as I could. As we got to the last song, which was when the main bit of amp trashing went on, Scott Rodger, our tour manager – incidentally he manages Paul McCartney now, so he probably has to deal with this kind of situation all the time – was standing at the stage with the fire doors open, signalling to me not to go into the dressing room but to run straight offstage into the waiting van and fuck off because otherwise Iggy's crew were going to kill us. So that was exactly what we did, and by the time we came to the next gig the tour managers had somehow sorted it all out between them, so his crew treated us much better for the remaining dates. You could see that as a happy ending but the whole incident was pretty much the textbook illustration of 'Don't meet your heroes.'

William

It was so sad, because I loved The Stooges and I loved Iggy . . . and I do again now, but it took both me and Jim two or three years before we could listen to them again. I do remember playing brilliantly on the last night of that tour on account of being so acutely in two minds – 'Our enemy here is Iggy Pop, and yet . . . our enemy here is *Iggy Pop*!?'

Jim

We never really worked out how much Iggy knew about what was really going on behind the scenes. Much as we wanted him to be completely oblivious, it was hard to avoid the suspicion that a performer of his experience must've had some idea. Those were the kinds of things me and William would brood on in a way that was definitely not healthy for us and probably not much fun for the people around us.

If you're thinking 'These guys needed ecstasy to lighten them up a bit', you've got a point in one way, but not in another. Because on the one hand ecstasy did bring me and William a lot of good times, but on the other I would say that it was the first drug we ultimately had a problem with, in that it changed our brain chemistry in a negative way.

Towards the end of the eighties, in the music scene in general but especially for anyone around Creation Records, it was all about ecstasy, and William and I were no exceptions. There was one of those raves – I didn't even know where it was, because I was just sitting in the back of the car, off my tits, basically – but it was somewhere by a lake in the countryside and there were about two or three thousand people totally out of it, in a field, by a lake, in the middle of the fucking night, somewhere in England. It was amazing and it felt like we were getting away with something, but we didn't get away with it for long

As people who hadn't always found socialising easy, you can see how it would've worked for us. I remember hugging complete strangers at raves and feeling a sense of empathy with everyone.

At the moment this was happening it felt like all the bad elements of your personality had been stripped away and all that was left was the bit where you actually gave a shit about stuff, but as time went on we started to realise that if it's something that you pay £15 for and it only lasts a couple of hours, that hardly amounts to a revolutionary shift in human consciousness. In fact, it's ultimately quite meaningless,

Unfortunately, in the time it took for that to dawn on us, William and I took too many of those fucking pills. I wouldn't usually presume to speak for him, but in this case it's something we've talked about and we both agreed that it burnt something out in our brains to the point where we didn't experience joy or even just happiness in quite the same way after it as we had done before. At first it was purely recreational and a bit of fun, but pretty soon it started to feel like if you went out and nobody could hook you up with any ecstasy then the evening was a failure. You'd end up just going home thinking 'Fuck, it never used to be like this – the point of going out used to be to hang out together or see a band or whatever.' That's not the point at which the alarm bells should be ringing, it's the point at which they've been ringing for ages and you've not been hearing them.

William

Music sounds good for a few minutes on LSD before it goes warped – 'Oh, this is fantastic . . . oh my God, the record's melting.' Mushrooms are a wee bit better, in that you can listen for maybe an hour before it all gets too fluid and s-l-o-w-e-d down, but ecstasy is probably the best drug in terms of being complementary to music, in that it just pounds the songs into your fucking brain. I've never felt anything like that feeling you'd get after a couple of pills when the music would just go inside you. A lot of the early rave music was like punk in that it was made as cheaply as fuck, but it was amazingly powerful. It didn't even have to be music you would normally like – I remember me and Jim going to a club after we'd played the Brixton Academy and this track came on by Yello, who I'm not normally a big fan of, but I was coming up on the ecstasy and everything in the music was so present it was almost like it had an extra physical dimension: you could touch it. This was one of the greatest experiences I've ever had in my life, but one of those ones you can't tell your grandchildren about.

Years later, me and my ex wife had this talk to our kids where we both said 'Hey listen, if you're gonna take anything, try and find out where it comes from, but please just don't take ecstasy . . .' I told them I used to be a really happy-go-lucky guy who had depression for maybe one week a year, but I always thought it would go away and it did. Then I took ecstasy for a couple of years and after that I had the same feelings of really horrible sadness – weird dreams that were violent – and they lasted for months. It's a sadness that sticks to you and imbues everything with a sense of regret, the same kind of regret you feel when you wake up the morning after being drunk – not so much because of anything you've done, but because you're dehydrated and you've no minerals and your brain is in a bit of a stew. It's basically that, but magnified and over an extended period of time. I think ecstasy kills a lot of the brain cells associated with our ability to experience pleasure in normal things. I know science has told us it's impossible to use up your endorphins because they're created in your body, but surely you could mess up the mechanism for making endorphins so it doesn't work properly? It wasn't just me and Jim that were feeling this way, a lot of our friends were having these weird depressions that lasted weeks.

Jim

I've tried to warn my kids – Simone, who is nineteen at the time of writing, and Candice, who is fifteen – about the bad impact ecstasy had on us, too. I didn't want to lecture them, 'cos I remember how it used to sound when adults would say 'Don't do drugs, kids.' I used to think 'Are you kidding? You stupid old cunt, you've got no idea.' Whereas my kids know that I've taken drugs, and shitloads of them, so I couldn't really blame them for thinking 'You've had your fun and now you don't want me to have any.'

In terms of what was happening musically at that time, the Manchester baggy scene of Happy Mondays and The Stone Roses was interesting to us, but when it came down to the house and techno that had inspired them, there were elements of that music that I liked, but at the end of the day I'm into songs. Often when I would hear one of those dance tunes I would think 'Oh right, good intro', but then ten minutes later the good intro would still be doing what it was doing and I'd be thinking 'Oh, it wasn't just an intro'. The Mary Chain would've sounded ridiculous if we'd tried to jump on that bandwagon by releasing records with house beats. There would be no baggy remix for us, but when we worked with Alan Moulder on *Automatic,* we did experiment a lot more with electronic rhythms.

Alan had asked to be the tape operator on the 'Some Candy Talking' EP because he was really into us, and because we'd hit it off so well with him when we were working with Flood, Alan was the obvious next port of call when Flood got too in demand for us to get hold of. Not only was he a great engineer and producer, he was easy company and very good at taking some of the stress out of the recording situation. That's probably why he in turn ended up doing such a good job with Nine Inch Nails, once they'd taken the obvious next step up to megastardom by supporting us on tour in America.

Now *Darklands* had established the principle that a new Mary Chain album didn't have to sound like the last one, it was much easier for us to go in whichever direction we wanted. When we tried to figure out where we fitted into the whole scheme of things, the realisation we came to was that we didn't fit in and we were never going to, so we might as well just make another Mary Chain record. Hence, *Automatic.* The single 'Head On' got to be on the heaviest rotation on MTV that we'd ever managed, and for a brief period when we checked into hotels the guy on the desk would recognise us – 'Hey, you're that guy on MTV' – and we'd get treated with a little bit of extra respect rather than them looking at you like they'd have to hide the silver. It was a blip, but it was enjoyable while it lasted.

Back home, our stubborn refusal to put on baggy clothes and say we were mad for it did not go down so well with the *Melody Maker,* who put us on their front cover with the legend 'Mary Chain RIP?' I suppose we should've been grateful there was a question mark at the end of it, but it was hard to understand why they'd use that kind of headline for a band they were supposed to be getting behind. That these people would use the advent of another musical movement to try to make us look irrelevant seemed to validate our sense that they were waiting for an opportunity to fuck us over. Just because we were paranoid, it didn't mean they weren't after us.

On the upside, this was also the point at which 'The Erasure Thing' happened. The fact that it happened is the most interesting thing, but the story of how it came to be is mind-numbingly dull. We were mixing *Automatic* and we didn't know Erasure were recording in the studio upstairs. Their producer knew Alan Moulder and I think he thought it would be funny to have the Mary Chain in any way connected to an Erasure song, so he came down and told us he was looking for people to shout the word 'Guilty!' on the chorus of this track, and asked if we'd be willing to join them. I think he expected us to say 'No, sorry, that's not us, man' like we thought we were too cool for it, so when we just said 'Yeah, let's do it', he looked quite surprised. But not as surprised as Andy Bell was when me and William walked into the studio.

It was quite fun all shouting 'Guilty!' when it got to the chorus, but it wasn't any big deal. It could've been anyone and you can't really hear it's us. The only shame of it was that Vince Clarke wasn't there, because I quite like his music. My favourite Depeche Mode songs are the ones he wrote – to this day I still play 'Dreaming of Me' and 'Just Can't Get Enough' on compilations at home. And I've got a couple of Erasure singles and Yazoo's *Upstairs at Eric's* – 'In My Room', the last track on that album, is like Cabaret Voltaire, but with an eye on the charts.

William

As far as the band's long term future was concerned, there was one big upside to how little of a priority we now were at Warners, which was that they forgot to renew our shitty publishing deal. This might not sound like good news, but it really was. One day in 1990, our co-manager Chris Morrison called us up to say he'd not had the courtesy call a major record label usually gives you in advance of renewal and there were only four days left till it was up. Then he rang the next day, and the next, and the next, finally calling to congratulate us: 'Hey, you're rich.'

It was all a mystery to us, and it shows how chaotic these big organisations can be, but because Warners had forgotten to renew the not very good deal we'd had from the start of our career, and now we had a catalogue behind us and were starting to make inroads in America, that deal could now be renegotiated on much more favourable terms, to the point where I was able to buy my house with it. Meanwhile, the gruelling tour schedule we'd committed to in the hope of building on our success in America was starting to take its toll on my relationship with Jim. And after an extra Tokyo show tacked onto a long US tour, the music press prediction of our imminent demise all but came true.

Previous accounts have left an element of mystery around the exact cause of the argument which nearly brought The Jesus and Mary Chain's story to a premature conclusion in the autumn of 1990, but I can reveal now that we almost broke up over a bowl of macadamia nuts. Obviously it was ridiculous to fall out over something so small – and it wasn't even me and Jim that had the row, it was me and Jim's girlfriend, Laurence – but one of the things you find as the pressures build up in a band situation is that small things begin to assume huge importance. Everything seems like it's in code and slights delivered by – and to – third parties can be just as important, sometimes more important, than things that are said directly.

Jim and Laurence were together for a long time (incidentally you've got to pronounce it the French way, so it rhymes with 'Provence' – that way you know she's a woman even if you haven't met her) and I got on very well with her, except when I didn't. I really liked Laurence, and she really liked me, but sometimes she would say or do things that I disagreed with. At that point most people would just shut up, but I wouldn't, and it was always friendly, until this one time in Tokyo when it wasn't.

The problem wasn't really with me and Laurence, it was with me and Jim. We'd been fighting about something or other, and I just hated him at that point, so I kicked off about some nuts. I can't eat them any more these days because of my stomach problems – I've got diverticulitis – but I used to love macadamias, those expensive nuts that aren't peanuts. Of course I would never buy that sort of thing for myself, I would just think 'I will go on tour and eat them in dressing rooms' – which was very working-class of me!

So we were in Tokyo playing this really weird gig where people didn't mosh or stage-dive – they just stood still. Backstage I was getting pissed off because Laurence was eating all the macadamia nuts, so I just took a big handful out of the bowl and finished them. The whole thing was so pathetic on my part that Laurence complained – I am not mocking her accent here, because her English is a lot better than my French, but it did add an extra element of comedy – 'You took ze last of zose nuts!'

I was adamant – 'They're my nuts!' But she was insisting 'No, zey are everybody's nuts and you ate half of zem!' Then there was this huge fucking fight, which should have ended there – and it did, between me and Laurence – but after that me and Jim didn't speak for about three months. To the point where we, and people close to us, thought the band was done. It was awful, and it was a taste of what was to come.

iii. The Endgame

William

On the face of it, the Australian guitarist Ben Lurie joining The Jesus and Mary Chain in 1990 was the beginning of the end for Douglas – not for any specific reason, just because it changed the dynamic of the band in a way which made his diminishing commitment to us hard to ignore (and also because Ben switched to bass to replace him after Douglas had gone). It wasn't that Douglas was a terrible bass player, it was just that he had no discipline about learning the songs. We'd arrive for the first night of an American tour and he'd be playing completely the wrong bass lines. All he seemed to want to do was get wasted, which was something we all liked to do, but by this time me and Jim had got to thinking 'If you're going to do something, you might at least do it as well as you can.' Douglas hadn't got to that point yet (at least, not as far as the band was concerned – he was very conscientious in his new career, making videos).

To be honest I'd say the seeds of his ultimate departure from the band were planted a lot earlier, when we were making demos while we were unemployed and everything we had was going to fix the four-track which kept breaking down. Meanwhile Douglas was travelling all over Scotland following The Cramps – staying in hotels and buying big leather biker boots 'cos his ma adores him and he's the baby of the family. I remember us thinking 'How much did those boots cost? Couldn't you have given us that to help fix the Portastudio?' And if I'm honest the memory of that probably sprang into my mind when we were considering his future. Plus there's the fact that he's a very handsome man – he's only put on about half a pound in the last forty years and he's still got quite a chiselled face now, the bastard . . .

Jim

Sacking Douglas was difficult but not too big a deal, as he had a lot of other stuff going on – both professionally and with his busy social life – and we've still got a good relationship with him today. The situation had just progressed from him not really learning the demos and me thinking 'I might as well just do it rather than have him do a bad version', to us no longer asking him to come to the studio and him not seeming to be that bothered. After a couple of years of that we'd thought 'Fuck it, let's ask someone who can actually play.'

Sadly we never found our Mani or our Peter Hook, so from that point on it was more a case of rhythm sections coming and going. Hopefully no one felt fucked over by us, though we did have so many drummers I can't really remember them all. If someone asks 'Who was that guy who was drumming with you at that point?', I have to say 'Give me something to go on, what did he look like? . . . It's so hard to put names to faces.' People used to say it was like the bizarre gardening accidents in *Spinal Tap*, but at least our drummers were alive when they left.

Douglas had been a big part of the whole experience of the band so it was good we were able to part on friendly terms. The other break-up I went through that year was a lot less straightforward. Laurence had started working for McGee as a press officer by that point. Although I'd made it up with Alan by then, Creation were riding very high at that time, and – although it sounds a bit dramatic to put it this way – I was having something of a mini nervous breakdown, which made her professional involvement in all that quite hard to take. All the new 'shoegazing' bands seemed to be getting all the attention, without anyone feeling the need to acknowledge how big an influence we'd been on that sound.

There was a little bit of jealousy from me, when I look back on it.

At a time when (at least in critical terms) it seemed like we were the dog in the corner that everybody just booted, Laurence was out there getting *NME* covers for 18 Wheeler. We argued a lot and it was mostly me being a bit of a cock, to be honest. I didn't even care about the other bands, I was just feeling a bit sorry for myself and I picked fights to push her into leaving, which she eventually did. It was unfair because it was nothing to do with Laurence, but the minute she left, everything was fine, because I had to sort myself out and she didn't have to put up with me blaming her for everything.

William

I was still with Rona at the time, but when she went away to go to college and took the car with her, it was an incentive for me to do one of the best things I'd ever done, which was learn to drive. We were living in Muswell Hill by then. The worst thing about living in Muswell Hill, which is that it doesn't have a tube station, is also the best thing about it, because it's like living in the countryside. But better than the countryside, because it's full of soap stars. They were everywhere – I'd be sitting next to Fred the butcher from *Coronation Street* in the local diner. I'd liked it when Rona was the driver and would give me lifts everywhere, but I liked it even better when I acquired the skills to do it myself. I was into my thirties by then – in 1991 – so I learnt pretty late, but I was pretty good at driving and passed my test first time, which was brilliant. I used to trundle around north London thinking 'I can't believe I've never done this before – this is the most fun I've ever had in my life!' If for some reason I couldn't have been a musician any more, I'd have definitely opted to be a delivery driver at that point, or better still get an HGV licence.

By the time I was picking up Jim (who hadn't learnt to drive himself yet) to head down from Muswell Hill to our own studio just south of the river – because we'd realised it made much more sense to channel some of Warners' money into getting a place of our own – I was really living the dream. Having your own studio meant you could record at your own pace. It also gave us a base independent of the record label, so it was a win–win, or at least it seemed that way at first.

Jim

When we went to Warners and said we wanted to take the budget for *Honey's Dead* – which was somewhere around a hundred grand – and use it to buy a studio, there was a big argument. 'Absolutely not.' 'Why not?' 'Because you're saying it and we disagree with everything you say.' You could see their point, in that getting a studio of our own gave us more power to call the shots away from Warners' influence, which was the last thing they wanted. But somehow we persuaded them to agree that it could come out of the recording budget, and we ended up with The Drugstore, which was in Amelia Street in Elephant and Castle, just around the corner from what was then the Labour Party HQ in Walworth Road.

We had no connections to the neighbourhood and it was nowhere near where any of us lived, but it was a great studio and we made really good records there. *Honey's Dead* was our last sober album, in that we kept up the discipline we'd always maintained (excepting the odd line of speed in the *Psychocandy* era) of not getting drunk or high when we were recording. We gave the record that title because we were very aware that the earlier version of the band didn't exist any more and we were leaving a lot of baggage behind (not to characterise Douglas as baggage). And yet, when the album eventually came out, the critical response was 'How can they use "honey" in the title again? They've run out of ideas.' It was very frustrating when the whole point of it was that we were moving into a new phase of our history. At least 'Reverence' shook things up a bit . . .

William

Being blasphemous means to show disrespect – even hatred – towards God, which that song doesn't do. At least, I don't think if does. I wasn't trying to be disrespectful, I was trying to make something which was pop art. When you use iconic names like Jesus Christ or JFK in that way, it's more of a compliment . . .

Jim

We were glad that no one tried to assassinate us as a tribute. There was a Travis Bickle-looking guy in the front row of a New York show once who I didn't like the look of, and when we took t-shirts bearing the slogan 'Jesus Fuck' to America, there was a promoter somewhere in Texas who was so outraged by them he wanted to put a bit of tape over the word on the one that was pinned up on the merch stand. I thought 'OK, if you must.' We thought he was going to cover the word 'Fuck', but instead he taped over the word 'Jesus'.

The Pixies covering our song 'Head On' in 1991 was a nice tip of the hat from America, but by the early nineties it was clear that if we wanted a musical community that we could fit in with, we were going to have to create it for ourselves. That was where the idea for the Rollercoaster tour came in. In my mind it happened after Lollapalooza, though it was actually before, so I guess Chris Morrison must've got the idea after we were initially booked for the American alternative rock circus. The plan for Rollercoaster was to be more of a stripped-down affair, like the original punk tours where you'd pay to see The Clash and get Buzzcocks and The Jam as well.

The bands got to play in bigger venues than they otherwise would have, and fans got great value for money as tickets were only £12 a pop. We put together a really good bill with all the different areas of our musical hinterland being represented – Dinosaur Jr from the American guitar upsurge which at that point was solidifying into grunge, Blur for the indie/baggy pop crossover contingent no one was quite calling Britpop yet, and My Bloody Valentine from the Shin-ei fuzz pedal fan community. We headlined every night with the other bands in rotation but with everyone getting the same time on the stage and being treated equally off it. We weren't just paying lip service to this ideal, we actually followed through with it.

They were great shows and the bill clearly demonstrated the part we'd played in influencing a number of different scenes. Posterity didn't really see it that way, though, as everyone else's reputation was enhanced – especially Blur's, as they couldn't really get arrested before that tour, to the point where we actually got a fair amount of stick for including them in the line-up, but after it they went from strength to strength (with the help of our manager Chris Morrison, who had been recommended to them by Laurence), so it was kind of the turning point for them – whereas the critical response to our participation was more along the lines of 'Oh, the Mary Chain . . . are you still here?' As Blur's star rose over the next few years while ours sank into the mire, we would sometimes idly wonder if some kind of reciprocal gesture might be forthcoming from them in our hour of need, but nothing like that ever happened.

Pretty much all the things that had been good about Rollercoaster were bad about Lollapalooza. It was one of the hottest tickets going in 1992 and it was sold to us as a travelling festival that was a complete democracy. No matter who closed the show everybody got the same deal – obviously not when it came to money, so that was bullshit for a start. And when we asked if we could bring in extra PA to beef the sound up like the Red Hot Chili Peppers had done, it turned out it was fine for them to do that, but not for us.

I must admit it did dent our ego a little bit that we were on in broad daylight at two in the afternoon. Had we just gone out and done what the Mary Chain do with a 'Fuck you' attitude it would have been a lot better, but I think we were a bit spooked to be playing in sunshine while loads of little Beavis and Buttheads wearing Chili Peppers t-shirts ate hot dogs and looked at us with complete indifference. We didn't have our baseball caps on backwards so what could we possibly have to offer them? It was kind of hard to take . . . that was day one and day two, and then we thought 'Fuck, there's ten weeks of this.' We tried to pull out but they threatened to sue and so there was no option but to knuckle down and try to get through it.

My strategy was to do a mountain of the cocaine that was everywhere on that tour in the hope of numbing myself to how grim it was. That was just one strand of my self-care strategy. I would also get legless before the show because I couldn't bear to face that crowd in daylight otherwise, then I would crash out for a couple of hours afterwards and wake up at about 5pm feeling disgruntled and somewhat sobered up. At this point I would go out hunting for cocaine and I didn't have to look far. So I ended up getting wasted twice a day for ten weeks. It wasn't healthy.

Another thing that made Lollapalooza really hard to deal with was that everyone seemed to get on with everyone else except the Mary Chain. The Chili Peppers were slightly aloof but only because they thought they were bigger than everybody else (which I suppose they were). Soundgarden and Pearl Jam was one big love-in 'cos they'd come up together in Seattle, but even the people that had only just met were acting like they'd known each other their whole lives. Everybody else seemed to be having a great time while we were miserable, but there was a kind of phoniness about the whole thing that meant we wouldn't have wanted to be part of it even if that had been an option.

Ministry and Lush were the only other bands we could even halfway relate to on that tour. William nearly got in a fight with

Ice Cube's entourage after they were messing about with water pistols and Rona got soaked. The only thing that kept me slightly sane was walking around the downtown areas of US cities that I hadn't visited before when we got stuck in hotels while the endless sea of tour buses disgorged their heavily branded cargo. People said it was dangerous but it wasn't as dangerous as having to get in a lift with some guy in shorts going 'Hey buddy, what's up?' I never knew how to respond to that because it seemed that once I started I might not be able to stop.

The pretend positivism of Americans started to really grate on me, and even though it's a terrible thing to say, the whole experience of Lollapalooza left me with a better understanding of the people who shoot up shopping malls. Whether we were scouring junk shops looking for underpriced semi-acoustic guitars, photographing diners or fifties cars, or going to look for what remained of the places in New York where The Velvet Underground used to play, a lot of the stuff we did when we toured America had always had a nostalgic component, but I think the disillusionment of Lollapalooza was probably the moment I finally realised that the USA I loved was a place that now only really existed in my mind. The actuality of what the place had become – as represented by and in that festival – was much harder to love, although I guess William must have felt differently, otherwise he wouldn't have ended up moving there.

William

With a lot of the successful musicians I've met – especially Americans – I've got this huge vibe of 'Yeah, the school bully really did a number on you, but now you're winning.'

It was the same with a lot of the other people on Lollapalooza. American high schools – like any others – can be cruel places for people who seem a bit strange. Jim and I had done a pretty good job of staying out of the way of that kind of pressure growing up, but we could still see the impact of it on others. And I think that's the root cause of a lot of the very conspicuous health kicks a lot of those musicians were on – they were still trying to shake off childhood trauma.

Jim

As far as the ongoing social ordeal of Lollapalooza was concerned, I was grateful for the extra confidence cocaine gave me, because I don't think I could've got through it otherwise. On all of those early tours where we'd been burning the candle at both ends, as soon as I got back home I'd think 'I don't need to do that for a while', and then I'd go for months without touching a drink or doing a line. I'd be happy that I didn't have to get shit-faced every night to do my job. 'Slippers on, cup of tea, read the papers – this is great.' At that time – although professionals in the field might disagree – I'd say I didn't really have a drinking problem.

At first when I got back from Lollapalooza, things went more or less as they had done before. I sank gratefully into the arse-shaped dent in the sofa and contemplated a spell of sobriety with total equanimity. Touring had almost been like aversion therapy as far as drinking was concerned, but this was the point where the aversion therapy started to stop working. It wasn't long before I started to notice myself editing experiences which didn't involve drinking or taking drugs out of my life. Next thing I knew, I was drinking, on my own, in the day time, in my living room, and even as I was thinking 'Hmmm, I'm not sure about this', I was also realising that even if I'd wanted to, I couldn't stop. Then daylight-hours drinking went all too smoothly from something that happened one day to something that was happening every day, and the louder the alarm bells rang, the clearer was my realisation that I was powerless to do anything to turn them off.

What I hadn't yet realised was the extent to which cocaine had also become a problem for me. In early 1994 we were in LA making the video for 'Sometimes Always' with Hope Sandoval, when Alan McGee – who I was fully friends with again by that time, although there was always some reserve between him and William – had his famous drink- and drug-induced meltdown where he got off the plane and had to be hospitalised straight from the airport. We were staying at the Mondrian, which is one of the big rock 'n' roll hotels, and we'd asked Alan to come down and see us. I definitely wasn't good company for someone in his vulnerable condition at that time because I offered him a line of coke and he had a kind of panic attack. He never fully explained what had happened, but as far as I was concerned it was all water under the bridge – 'Taken away in an ambulance, nearly died, blah blah blah' – so when I saw him in the restaurant later I asked him a second time if he fancied doing a couple of lines and he freaked out again. I can see now that the offer of more drugs probably wasn't really what he was needing, but he looked all right to me, and at the time 'Have another line of coke, you'll feel better' was the outer limit of my capacity for human sympathy.

While we were making Stoned & Dethroned, I'd walk past the Labour HQ and see the party's then leader John Smith giving interviews on the steps. He'd be doing his level best to bring a long-overdue end to the Tory rule which had divided the country since 1979, while I'd be on my way to some debauched recording session involving high levels of drink and drug use and all manner of strange characters, the strange characters being the rest of the band.

One unforeseen consequence of not being on the clock in the studio was that it was only a matter of time before someone suggested we might make a better album if we got fucked up. This was not a good idea. As it turned out, we didn't make a better album – or a worse album – it just took much longer. You make records in a different way when you're under the influence because you're looser and you'll try things. But when you're drunk or stoned in the studio, everything sounds great, so then you listen back when you've sobered up and you realise 'Ah fuck, we've really got to do that again.' The idiotic thing is at that point you quite often start drinking again because you're so pissed off with how badly the recording turned out.

I don't suppose *Exile on Main St.* would've sounded the way it does if the Stones had been on nothing stronger than a cup of tea when they made it, and *Stoned & Dethroned* ultimately turned out to be a perfect reflection of the circumstances in which we made it. The Drugstore was over the road from a horrible sleazy pub where we ended up spending way too much of our time in the mid nineties. We went in there for a pint at the start of the recording process and the pint lasted about two fucking months. 'What are we doing here again? Oh right, we're making a record.' You could see that place out of the studio's live room window and it would kind of beckon to us, even though it was very rare that any good came out of going in there. Let's just say it had a strong Irvine Welsh vibe – we got in a fight in there once when someone randomly headbutted William.

The album we were trying to make was initially a fully acoustic record. This was a plan which had been on the back burner for several years. We'd both loved that Johnny Thunders acoustic album, *Hurt Me* – it was rarely off our turntables in 1985–86, around the time we were doing that first acoustic Peel session – and when we'd told everyone we were going to make our own version of that record they kind of wouldn't let us forget it, so we thought we might as well give it a go. The problem was we needed things to hide behind so people couldn't find out how limited we were as musicians. We'd got away with it with the Peel session because there were only four tracks and we'd whacked the reverb up so much they might as well not have been acoustic. So we decided on a compromise – which ultimately worked really well – which was not to be too rigid about just using acoustic guitars, but also to take the foot off the gas a bit and let the album evolve at its own pace.

An important part of that slowing-down process was doing a track with Shane MacGowan . . .

William

I remember seeing The Pogues on *The Tube* and just thinking they were brilliant. The reason I never went to see them in the early days was because we were coming up around the same time, and we were always so busy. There was a time when we lived in Fulham and they were playing regularly at The Greyhound down the road, and I was always saying to Rona and Jim, 'Let's go and see The Pogues before they get too big' – we'd have had so many stories to tell, but unfortunately we didn't go.

Over the years we'd bump into Shane around town and every time we met him he'd always mistake me for Jim. It didn't matter how many times I'd say 'I'm William', he'd still say 'Jim, you're a fucking genius', until eventually I just decided to go with it. He'd always tell us how much he loved The Jesus and Mary Chain so we'd thought about maybe getting him to do something. When we were doing *Stoned & Dethroned*, I'd written a song called 'God Help Me' which I'd tried to sing but I didn't like my vocal. Jim had a go, too, but his version didn't sound right either, so I said, 'Why don't we ask Shane MacGowan?'

Because Jim's the spokesman or the ambassador of the band, he was the one who ended up speaking to Shane, and he ended up doing that a lot, because even though Shane had agreed to do it and we'd been told he'd be coming down on a Monday, he never turned up. Every week for several weeks Jim would ring him up: 'Hey Shane, what's going on?', 'Who's this?', 'It's Jim Reid, you said you were gonna come and sing on our record', 'What? When?', 'Last week.'

Every time Jim called him, he'd forgotten all the previous conversations. Until he finally remembered, and when he came down to The Drugstore, it was very interesting. Shane turned up drunk, which was fine, and did one pretty decent take, then another take that was not so good. I think we got four takes out of him altogether, which got progressively worse until Alan Moulder went away and performed a miracle, shaping the four vocals into one absolutely brilliant one, which to this day nobody would say was a compilation because it's so beautiful.

Jim

Shane always used to call me William, so at least he was consistent. I'd never actually tried a vocal on 'God Help Me', but we'd had an earlier plan to do a tune with Lee Hazelwood – which Lee was quite up for, until he came to meet us at Lollapalooza in LA and the security were rude to him and wouldn't let him backstage – so we were really happy to get Shane involved, as we both saw him as one of the greats. It wasn't just four takes Shane did, it was many more than that. Because he had no idea what song he was doing – I think he thought we were going to do one of his. He had to learn 'God Help Me' virtually line by line, then Alan had to cobble it together literally one word at a time.

The interesting thing was that even though we'd spent ages getting that version together, when we finally listened back to it, Shane's delivery just seemed too aggressive – it was done with too much gusto. So we told him, 'This song is about a man at his lowest ebb, sing it like you're just about to top yourself and you need to talk to somebody, but there's no one around.' Shane did it like that, with the vocal almost a whisper, and that was the version we put on the album. The more upbeat, Poguesy take got released as a bonus track on one of the compilations years later.

We'd also done a cover of a Pogues song, 'Ghost of a Smile', as a B-side, so when the time came for the album launch and we were playing at Madame Jo Jo's – just a little club gig to get a bit of a buzz going – we asked Shane down to sing both tunes, and I think we also did 'Sunny Side of the Street'. The funny thing was that after our earlier experience with him, this time he turned up totally sober. Everyone else in the band was falling over the place drunk and he was glaring at us as if to say, 'You fucking amateurs.' At one point William and Ben even played the wrong part of his song and Shane turned around and looked daggers at me – 'I didn't fucking do it, it was them two!'

William

It was Jim and Ben who started the drinking in the studio. I walked in one day and they'd installed one of those things you press and it gives you a shot of whiskey – an optic. I didn't complain and I would sometimes join them in a glass of Jack Daniels' (I wasn't on the vodka yet), but I was more the person who takes a drink of milk from the udders of a stray cow than the one who bought the cow. Do you see the difference?

Tensions between us had started to rise by then, and when he was drinking Jim would sometimes attack me in a weird coded way where no one else noticed but I knew exactly what he was doing. A mild example would be something like him saying 'Aren't people with small toes just weird? They're the worst – almost prehistoric . . .' This could build up through the course of a day or an evening with him saying little things like that to hurt me (because I have small toes) until I'd explode: 'You know what, Jim, you're a fucking prick!' And everyone else who hadn't realised what had been going on would think 'Oh William, he's so out of control.'

Jim

The whole 'feuding brothers in bands' thing always comes down to territory. It's natural for siblings to compete anyway, and in the unnaturally close proximity of a band – where you're sharing the same creative space in the cramped physical surroundings of a rehearsal room or a tour bus – there is bound to be friction. Right from the start of the Mary Chain, when we were on the same page about pretty much everything, William and I could still scream at each other for half an hour, to the point where other people would feel uncomfortable enough to have to leave the room. Because you know each other so well, you know exactly the right buttons to press. So even when we were getting on perfectly well, we would still have arguments where people would be thinking 'Oh my God, did he really just say that?'

They'd be astonished to find us laughing and joking together again ten minutes later, but because you're brothers, you know you can say unthinkable things to each other and it will be swiftly forgotten. You almost get a kick out of how amazed people are to see you sharing tea and biscuits moments after an apocalyptic row. 'But you said . . .?' 'But he said . . .?' And then suddenly something changes, and the no-holds-barred stuff starts to leave scars.

If you plotted our relationship as a graph, in the early stages of the band the two lines of our interests almost coincided, we virtually thought the same thoughts, but as the nineties went on – for a variety of reasons which at this point in the book we're probably going to have to go into – the lines started to diverge, so that we moved gradually from a place where nothing was taken personally, to a place where everything was. This trajectory is common to pretty much all bands, I think, but it's more deeply felt in bands with brothers in (and presumably sisters as well – I bet The Shangri-Las had some arguments) because that relationship is so important in terms of the whole of your life.

William

Me and Jim used to fight all the time back when we were younger, but the thing we would never fight about was anything in the artistic realm – whether it was music or films or sculpture – because when we were talking about that there was no bullshit and no ego . . . Have I mentioned that Jim's a little prick? Sometimes he can be, let me tell you. I love that little prick, but anyway, the reason I would never call Jim out when it came to an opinion on the arts was because – and I'm talking about the time before we'd had any kind of success or even properly started the band here – me and Jim were the elite, at least in our own minds. In the eighties, we used to feel like our joint opinion was the best opinion in the world, and sometimes we were right.

Other times it was almost a wee bit embarrassing, the extent to which we would be in agreement over things. You don't want a timeshare personality, do you? You want a whole one of your own. And there were times when it was a weird situation. Imagine you had a brother who was three years younger than you, and you were in this band together, and you started to have some success, but because your brother was the singer, everyone thought he was the leader of the band, even though a lot of the songs he was singing were words you'd put in his mouth.

It wasn't him singing the songs in itself that I found frustrating, it was the fact that he didn't correct people when they thought he was responsible for songs I had actually written. I first noticed this happening in the eighties, when everyone was walking up to to Jim and congratulating him on 'Some Candy Talking', and I'd be like 'What the fuck? That was me! That was me!' But I didn't actually mind too much at that point. We'd made the decision right from the beginning – which I stood by – that the songwriting would be 50/50 Reid/Reid, straight down the middle, so no one knew who'd written what.

I'm not saying that my songs were necessarily better than Jim's – he wrote 'Upside Down' and 'Never Understand' for a start, which are two of the defining Mary Chain songs which are also my favourites – but I did tend to write more than him, and as time went on we did start to fall out over the times when people would be fawning over him, like 'Oh yeah great, Jim, "Reverence" is amazing, dude!' And I'd be looking at Jim waiting for him to put them right, but it seemed like he never did. This definitely got worse as the nineties went on – I guess whatever else you say about cocaine, it's not a drug that makes people more inclined to share the credit.

'Sometimes Always' ended up being the perfect visual representation of that, because it was my song, and at the time Hope was my girlfriend, but it was quite a complex situation because I had only just split up with Rona, and you can just about see me in the background of the video while Jim and Hope sing away to each other.

Jim

I felt bad afterwards that maybe I was a bit judgmental of Hope in the time she and William were together, implying she was a bit of a diva, when looking back I don't really think she did anything wrong . . . certainly nothing worse than the kinds of things I was doing at the time.

William

What's the male version of the word diva? This is what I've seen in the world: when a man walks into a place and says 'Do this, do that, shut up, blah blah blah', do you know what people say? 'What a good, strong man.' But when a woman does it, they just call her a diva or worse – it's not fair. It was complicated when I was in that relationship with Hope, though, because I was, and still am, a big fan of Mazzy Star, and I did feel that David Roback was probably the love of Hope's life. So everyone else was . . . what is it the kids call it these days? An NPC, or Non-Player Character – the people who made the game spent a lot of money on the hero and he can walk good, but the NPCs just look like robots. That's how I felt.

On top of that, I really liked David, and you know how I spoke about Jim not being comfortable jamming? Well there's not been a lot of guitar players that I could relax with the way I relaxed when I was playing with David. When you're jamming with someone, it's a kind of musical intimacy – you look in their eyes trying to guess what comes next, it's kind of the opposite of shoegaze – and because Jim is very reserved emotionally, I think that sort of thing makes him a bit uncomfortable. Whereas me and David used to get totally wasted and have these great fun jams together, a couple of stoned guys just laughing and playing. He's one of the few other guitar players I've ever had that sort of real connection with. There's a lot of trust in it, because when you fuck up you're not judged, in fact your playing partner might even run with it.

Either way, it's a great thing and I wish I'd had more inter-actions with musicians like that. But the fact that I had that musical bond with David, and Hope had that emotional and musical bond with him, meant it always felt like there were three of us in the relationship. It was quite overwhelming enough, even before Neil Young got involved . . .

One time when we were touring America with Mazzy Star, Hope told me she was going for dinner with Neil Young the next day in San Francisco. I just thought it was funny but while I was thinking about it I went away and got really stoned, then I was panicking because we had to go on in half an hour and I was all stoned and I was thinking 'Fuck, what have I done? I can play a bit stoned but not fully stoned' – you don't want to be on another planet when you've got to pick out some chords. The fact that I was also drunk out of my fucking noggin' only made it more of a huge mistake.

At this point I walked into Hope's dressing room and Neil Young was standing there – it was the last thing I needed. Before I was stoned but now it was like I was on acid. Neil Young was shaking my hand and I saw him as a giant – it was like he was nine feet tall, and as I went off to play the gig, off my fucking tits, I had to keep telling myself 'No, no, no, he is a tall man, but he's not a giant.' I'm talking in physical terms there, because obviously in artistic terms he *is* a giant.

Jim

I think we've covered the 'Stoned' element of that album's title pretty well by now, but the 'Dethroned' part was a reflection of how we felt at the time that also ended up becoming quite prophetic, because the process of us recording the album aligned with Britpop starting to happen. The Mary Chain had always felt like outsiders, but by the time that album came out it was like there was double glazing on the patio and they'd thrown away the key.

What made it even harder was that I kind of liked a lot of what was happening. Britpop bands wanted to be on *Top of the Pops* but kind of underground as well, just like we always had. The only differences were that they got asked back to play the show more than once, and no one thought of them as a sell-out indie band once they were signed to majors (as Oasis were, once Creation inked the deal with Sony which saved Alan's financial bacon).

I liked Oasis and I liked Pulp, who were actually our contemporaries – they'd just been going a long time before they achieved any success. Blur got a bit too middle of the road for me in the 'Country House' era, but they came back with some good records afterwards. My problem was that I couldn't see why we were excluded. Why couldn't we be a part of this thing? I used to think 'Fuck, what about us?'

Now I look back on it with more perspective I can understand how we fell through the cracks. The fact that we said we wanted to be pop stars and did interviews with magazines like *Smash Hits* and *Number One* had put the music press's nose out of joint at the time when that early-eighties thing where all sorts of experimental post-punk people were suddenly having number one pop albums had kind of ground to a halt. Meanwhile the new idea of what 'indie' was meant to be was coagulating around The Smiths, so we were left out of that as well. And then by the time baggy and shoegaze and grunge had come and gone and Britpop had taken over, it didn't matter how good the music we made was – and I honestly think *Stoned & Dethroned* and the next album *Munki* are as good as, if not better than, anything else we ever did – we were destined to be a back number.

The other part of it was that we were absolutely terrible at playing the game – something Blur and Oasis and Pulp in their own different ways were all very good at. You've kind of got to hang around with music journalists and buy them pints of beer and pretend that you're their friend, but we would never do that. If someone appeared to us to be a bit of a dick, we would let them know it, and the sad fact about music journalists is a lot of them *are* dicks.

I know this is a cliché, but with a lot of the people we met who were journalists you could see that they were frustrated musicians. They wanted to be you but they couldn't be, then the next best thing was to be your best mate, and if you weren't having that, then they hated you and were waiting for you to fail. Even at the height of their huge fame, Oasis and Blur still managed to give the people who were writing about them the feeling that they were part of the entourage – an impression that we never managed (or in fact even wanted) to give to people from our much lower level of renown. That's why there were journalists who liked us and appreciated what we were doing, but we didn't really have any champions – there was no Paolo Hewitt to our Paul Weller. When it came to making the case for us being relevant to some new scene, there was no one to do it because nobody really gave a fuck.

William's song 'I Hate Rock 'n' Roll' with its heartwarming final chorus of 'Rock 'n' roll hates me' was a pretty fair reflection of where The Jesus and Mary Chain stood by 1995. In the long term I think that's worked out well for us, because it's meant our music has survived and ultimately thrived on its own terms, not being tied to any particular time or any particular movement, but in the nineties it was fucking hard work. It always felt like we were swimming against the tide, and ultimately the tide overwhelmed us.

William

When Oasis were really happening it was like Liam and Noel were the big Hollywood remake of our little indie film of a brotherly rivalry which maybe did OK at Sundance. I remember seeing an interview with Noel years ago where he basically said 'We go on tour and after the gig everybody goes to a club and I go back to my hotel room and write the new album.' I was like, fuck, that was my life in the nineties! The older mousier one is upstairs working on the songs and the younger handsomer one is down in the bar going 'Yeah, baby, I'm the singer, c'mon.' Then the next morning everybody is asking 'Why weren't you there last night?' 'Because I was in the hotel room playing my guitar and trying to work out the difference between an A7 and an A7 diminished.' I'd sit there smoking a joint for four hours working that out . . .

What really broke us apart over the last two or three years of the first period of the band's life was that the self-fixing mechanism we'd had in the earlier years stopping working. So where in the beginning an argument would be forgotten in minutes, now it would fester for weeks. Jim would feel slighted about something where even though I didn't think I meant it that way, maybe at some level I did. Then that would become a chip on his shoulder and because we were getting drunk all the time and he was doing coke and I was stoned, there was no way of us really reaching out to each other. Everything was broken.

Jim

By the time we were making the album that became *Munki*, we were spending more time in that awful sleazy pub over the road than we were in the studio. That place just seemed to attract the dregs of humanity – I suppose that was why we felt at home there. The barman used to sell drugs in the toilet and when he just disappeared overnight we seriously suspected he'd been killed, because no one knew what happened to him and he was one of those guys who just tended to blether about all sorts when it seemed like it would be safer for him to keep his mouth shut.

That was sort of how it felt making *Munki*. It had become quite a soul-destroying ritual delivering what we considered to be great records to a company that just wanted to chuck them in the bin, and by this time me and William had started to lose that sense of a common cause that had been the only thing that made life at Warners bearable. We weren't dropping obscure reference points we knew they wouldn't have heard of at meetings any more just to have a laugh afterwards about the tumbleweeds crossing the room. The record company had always hated us, and now the media and the general public seemed to be coming round to their way of thinking. In the meantime things between me and William were going from bad to worse. At the time I couldn't put my finger on why, but we just seemed to be arguing all the time – we'd gone from agreeing on almost everything to agreeing on almost nothing, to the point where we made *Munki* on something closer to the dual template we'd initially imagined in our late-night planning meetings in East Kilbride in the early eighties.

In the context of those fractured and difficult circumstances, I think it turned out pretty fucking well. I guess the fact that I wrote a song called 'I Love Rock 'n' Roll' as a more positive counterpart to William's earlier burst of negative energy was a sign of the way the band was now embodying alternative perspectives. We weren't actually twins, but the egg had certainly divided.

William

It really annoyed me when Jim wrote that song. I didn't feel that 'I Hate Rock 'n' Roll' needed any further qualification – the love part was in there already.

Jim

One of the few upbeat elements in our situation when we were making *Munki* was the involvement of our younger sister Linda. She'd got credits on a couple of earlier records for contributing design ideas but this time around she actually gave us the title, which came from the Japanese anime cartoons that Linda really liked. After a series of album titles which had expressed where we were coming from at the time very precisely but no one seemed to like, we decided to opt for one that seemed to have no connection with the Mary Chain whatsoever – even we were bored of ourselves.

Because there'd been such a big age gap, in the early eighties Linda had been into things like Madness so we just kind of let it be. But as she got older we could talk to her about music and she got into all the stuff we were into. Linda was around at The Drugstore when we were recording so we decided to ask her to sing on a track, in the spirit of Karen Parker singing backing vocals or drumming at the Haçienda. She said OK and we liked the way her voice sounded like Moe Tucker from The Velvet Underground. It was actually a song about taking cocaine – the original title was 'Suck My Coke', which would've taken a bit of explaining to my mum once her daughter was singing on it – so at Linda's suggestion we changed the title to 'Moe Tucker', which worked just fine.

William

It was a sign of how far we'd drifted apart that I don't think Jim realised this at the time, but what happened with that song was a big factor in the band eventually splitting up. Not because of Linda's contribution – which I really liked – but because I wasn't allowed to play on it. I went away to America with Hope for a couple of weeks in the middle of the recording process, but all the time I was away I was thinking about what I was gonna play on that song. It was important to me because it was the first one that Linda had appeared on. But then when I got back and went into the studio, the engineer Dick Meany lived up to his name (though I realise this wasn't his fault as he was only obeying orders, and it was all Chinese whispers and ego problems between me and Jim by this stage) by telling me it was already mixed and 'sounded good'. I phoned up Jim and told him I wanted to play on that song and he – all coked up or whatever he was – said 'No need, it's perfect.' I didn't think it was perfect then and I don't think it's perfect now – it's pretty good, but it could've sounded a lot better if I was on it, because I'm the guitarist in the band – but I didn't push back hard enough, and this became something I really brooded on.

The problem was that the different drugs Jim and I had got addicted to – he was hooked on coke and I was addicted to weed (I know people say weed is not addictive but I am living proof that it is) – were taking our brain chemistry in different directions. Cocaine tells you 'Go ahead, you're the best, you can get the better of him, keep attacking . . .', where what weed does is make you reflect too much to the point of being paranoid, so you won't fight back because you've got too many thoughts in your head.

Years later, when we were trying to talk through where things had gone wrong between us, I told Jim 'I know I'm no angel, but I would never have done that to you. If you'd said you wanted to add something to my song, I would never have said no, because the whole point of being in a band together is you don't say no, you say yes – you take on ideas. That's why Fleetwood Mac have sold a hundred million records, because they all flowed towards each other musically even when they were all getting divorced.' I still don't think he really gets it, though.

Jim

As far as I remember – and this is within the confines of my memory not having a lot of clarity because I was pretty out of it at the time – William was in the studio with us when we were recording 'Moe Tucker', and the two of us just hated each other at the time so we were glaring at each other across the whole room. I don't know whether I actually asked him to come up with a solo, or maybe I was just waiting for him to do it because that was what he was supposed to do, but either way he wouldn't do it, and I knew I couldn't do it because I'm not a lead guitar player, so in sheer desperation I just picked up the little Oscar synth that was sitting in the corner and started making mental little noises with it. I only did this out of utter desperation to try and fill the space I'd left for the guitar solo, but then when I listened back I thought 'That actually sounds really good, so William can fuck off' – which not too much later he actually did do.

I was going to say that if William remembers all this differently from me, then so be it, but on reflection I think the two different versions of the story are actually quite compatible. Although I don't know why he'd have thought of nothing else but this solo he was going to play for the whole two weeks he was on holiday with Hope in America, because he was there when I picked up the synth and made that noise, so he must've known there was no space left.

Either way, as the good ship Mary Chain ploughed on through ever more turbulent waters, an iceberg was heading towards us. Jeannette Lee – Geoff Travis's partner in running Rough Trade management at that time – had come down to the studio while we were working on the final mixes and she had raved about them. It was a real morale boost, thinking she and Geoff were really on board, as we geared up for the painful experience of playing the new record to Warners. Then, a couple of days later, we got a call from Geoff telling us that *Munki* wasn't up to our usual standard, in fact it was the worst record he'd ever heard. He went through the album trashing it track by track and then told us he didn't want to work with us any more. We were devastated, and twenty-five years later I still don't know what caused him to have such a drastic change of heart. We knew he had a reputation as quite a ruthless operator, but we hadn't really seen his dark side before. Given where our band stood at the time, maybe he just didn't think we had a future. Looking at it in narrow commercial terms – which is something Geoff doesn't get as much credit for doing as he possibly should do – he might've had a point.

After a final one of those chess match-like encounters with the eternally forthright Rob Dickins – who told us he would put out the album if we wanted him to, but since neither he nor anyone else in the Warners building gave a shit about it, we might be better off trying to find someone who did – we were fully out in the cold. No record deal, no management. Happy Fucking Christmas (figuratively speaking – it wasn't actually Christmas).

Part 5
Creation (1998)

'I think I'm going out of style,
I think I've known it for a while'

– 'Never Understood', The Jesus and Mary Chain
(William Reid)

Jim

We'd left Creation in 1984 because we'd got too big for them,
but by the time we went back there, fourteen years later, the whole
thing had gone champagne supernova to a point that wasn't really
sustainable for anybody. It wasn't like that should've been a surprise
to me either, as I'd seen the inner workings of the operation from
the extreme comfort of Alan McGee's VIP box at Chelsea.

Once me and Alan became friends again, I started to go along
to Stamford Bridge to watch the game I had disdained as a small
child. The kits were a slightly different shade of blue to Rangers',
but the executive experience was on another planet – this was a
kind of football I could relate to. If I'm going to be watching sport
I'd rather be sitting in the lap of luxury, quaffing champagne and
eating steak and chips – the masochism of the 'authentic' version
never appealed to me the way it did to William.

My dad had always wanted me to be going along to the
match with him, so when I told him I'd been getting into the five-
star freeloader's version, he'd say 'Really, can I come?' But sadly
he never seemed to be down in London at the right time, and I
don't think he would have fitted in anyway, because there was a
lot of sucking up going on.

They used to spoil you rotten in that box. Someone would come
in and ask 'Does anyone want any food or drink?' Because Alan
was on the wagon and all his minions were scared of him, booz-
ing wasn't considered to be the done thing among his immediate

entourage. Everyone would be primly asking 'Oh, could I have a cucumber sandwich and a Perrier?' Whereas I'd go 'Fuck yes, I'll have a crate of beer and a burger, please.' They'd be waiting to see his reaction but I don't think he begrudged me a bit of payback. In fact, given us having sacked him as our manager all those years before, he was probably quite happy to have me joining the ranks of his hangers-on.

You did have a sense of it being a bit of a circus in terms of Alan's desire to be the star of the show, but fair play to him, he'd put a shift in and now he was in the position he'd always wanted – up there with Malcolm McLaren and Tony Wilson. I never understood why people talked about Tony like he was some kind of prophet, where in Factory's whole history he had signed Joy Division and the Happy Mondays, that's two fucking bands that were any good – what about the other 250 that nobody gave a shit about? I'm not saying these guys didn't make a contribution, but people talk about them as if they had access to some kind of wisdom the rest of us don't have and it's just not true. They weren't a higher order of being. What they did have – and this was especially true of McGee – is drive. They'd have to be out there hawking their wares on the street corner even though the last fifty people to walk past had all punched them in the face, and Alan in particular was very ready to do that.

I guess they're a little like politicians in a way, which is one reason why the whole Creation/Tony Blair overlap made so much sense. It was sad when John Smith died not long after I saw him doing interviews on the Labour Party's front doorstep, but Smith had made it pretty clear that he would've taken the party in the same direction as Blair did had he lived. And I kind of understood 'New Labour', to be honest. It almost felt like it had to be that way to get rid of those cunts that had been running the country for a decade or more. It felt like Labour were just trying to be realistic and they were still pumping loads of money into the NHS and getting a fair bit of good stuff done. Tony Blair's gift was that he knew how to handle the media – he was a used-car salesman who could talk anybody into anything. The seventies had gone (and the eighties), this was what Labour had become, and I didn't even mind Blair too much until the Iraq war a few years later – that's where it crumbled with him for me.

In the meantime, McGee and Noel Gallagher going to that party at number 10 after Labour won the 1997 election was just everyone feeding off everyone else. There was no real harm in it, but there didn't seem to be very much sincerity in it either – it was just people grabbing hold of a little bit of something that would flatter their own sense of self-importance. McGee was proving he'd finally become this McLaren character that he'd always wanted to be, and Tony Blair was showing the world how cool he was, at least in his own mind.

You get to that level where you have those kinds of riches and you're surrounded by people nodding their head the whole time and sometimes it can make you very casual in your dealings. Once when I was going to those football matches at Stamford Bridge I was telling McGee what had happened with *Munki* at Warners – how Geoff Travis, who had been our ally, phoned us up one day and said he wasn't interested any more – and Alan just said 'I'll put it out.' The words came out as simply as that, although of course, and this was typical McGee, I had to remind him later to follow up on it.

McGee and I agreed an advance, which wasn't a great amount of money in the scheme of things – maybe fifty grand – and then he said 'I'll give you forty grand on top of that to make a video, and if you want to make it on Super 8 and keep the rest of the money for yourselves, that's up to you.' So of course I said 'Fuck, great, we'll do that', but then when we actually came to do the deal, there was no sign of that provision in the contract.

I explained the situation to Alan's right-hand man Dick Green and he said that was the first he'd heard of it. By the time this went back to McGee, of course he'd conveniently forgotten all about it as well, and basically acted like I'd made the whole thing up. So I was standing there shouting 'Fuck off! You did say this!', while everyone else was going 'Uh-huh', and I was made to feel like I'd been trying to chisel money out of them. What made it worse was McGee just laughing and saying 'Just gi' it to 'em', as if I'd come cap in hand. That was utterly galling.

There wouldn't have been a Creation Records without the Mary Chain, but even now we were technically back in the fold, it still felt like we were on the outside looking in. What could've been a beautiful homecoming turned all too quickly into a reprise of the situation at Warners because no one at Creation cared enough to try and facilitate a better outcome. McGee telling us he'd put *Munki* out turned out to be pretty much the end of his involvement with the record – he had no input into anything that happened afterwards and he didn't get anyone else at the label on board either, so no one there really gave a fuck. At least at Warners we'd had Rob Dickins to be straight with us about the fact that no one in the building had the slightest interest in the record. At Creation no one told us anything until the album came out and died on its arse.

William

Creation at that point didn't really have any connection with the label we'd signed to fourteen years before – it was a bloated distorting mirror of itself. The one upside was that because it was just part of Sony now (and going in there didn't really feel any different to the way Warners had done), that meant if we had to go into the office we could at least take the jazz reissues from the store room . . .

Jim

We went into Sony to do some interviews, they pointed to the room where the journalists were, and I just said 'But where's your cupboard? I want free records and I want them now.' It was one of those 'Bring me the finest wines known to humanity' situations, as that was the time when a lot of the Miles Davis and John Coltrane boxed sets were coming out. I got them home and thought 'I'd better actually play these before I take them to the Record and Tape Exchange, there might be something good on here', and it moved pretty quickly from 'This isn't bad' to 'Actually I really like this.' When I was younger I didn't get jazz at all, I thought it was a bunch of guys who were just winging it – 'If you can play it me once and then play it again the same, then I'll accept it's real.' But as I worked my way through those boxed sets, I thought 'I'm actually ready for this now – this doesn't sound like a bunch of people that are taking the piss, this sounds like a bunch of cool dudes!' So that was one silver lining behind the cloud of the *Munki* era.

I should also own up to the fact – in case anyone hasn't noticed – that we probably weren't the greatest ambassadors for ourselves at this stage. We went to Paris for a three-day press trip – me, William and Ben Lurie – and I didn't sleep or eat at all. Not a single morsel of their delicious French food could tempt me in my cocaine frenzy, not even a croissant. On day one of the press trip I was still making sense, by day three I was bordering on psychotic. All these journalists were lined up to talk to me and I walked into the room and said: 'Look, here's the deal, I'm not going to say a fucking word until someone goes out and brings me some cocaine.'

They were looking at me like 'Is this a fucking joke?' And I was saying 'Do I look like I'm joking? I'm not fucking joking.' The woman from the record label went out and got me some, so I was just sitting there chopping lines out and talking utter nonsense . . . God knows what that must've looked like, but not far off twenty years later, when our long-overdue comeback album *Damage and Joy* finally came out, I went out to do another press trip in Paris and I was telling one of the journalists what had happened – as in 'That's how bad I got, I sent some woman from the record label out to get me some cocaine' – and a voice piped up from the back of the room saying 'That was me.'

I said 'Was it really? Fucking hell, I'm so sorry . . .' But she was very nice and told me not to worry about it.

On that first trip we came back on the Eurostar and I still had a wrap in my pocket. I was basically a wild animal at that point. When we got on the train there were all these policemen with sniffer dogs who came up and sniffed me (the dogs, not the policemen). I was thinking 'This is it', but the fact of me having not had a bath while being in a cocaine sweat for three days must've overloaded the poor animal's nasal apparatus, because it just ran off looking a bit confused.

Rather than appreciating what a narrow escape I'd just had, I stuck with that cokey bravado – 'Oh well that's great, I've still got a couple of lines for the train.' I should've been busted so many times because I was so indiscreet – doing lines in the back of New York taxis or wandering off on dodgy drug deals to meet complete strangers in back streets when I was already too off my tits to recognise any danger signs. I was even snorting lines on internal flights in America which is basically signing the death warrant of your career there if you get caught. Ben Lurie was my accomplice but even he thought that was too chancy. He said 'Fucking hell, something bad is going to happen if you carry on like this', but I knew no fear.

Of course Ben was right – but the bad thing that was going to happen was not a drugs bust, it was our American tour.

Before we get to that, there was one bright spot in the carnage of the live shows we did after *Munki* came out, and that was our sister Linda. After she did the 'Moe Tucker' song on *Munki* she came out on tour with us and was playing festivals in Europe – she would come out and sing that song and the funny thing was she was a total fucking natural. I used to have to have half a pint of whiskey before I could walk onstage but there was one big festival I remember in particular, maybe it was Benicassim, where The Stone Roses and all these other bands she loved were watching us from the side of the stage. I was really nervous she might not be able to go through with it, but when the time came to do 'Moe Tucker' she just walked up to the mic as calm as you like, sang the song and walked off – not a sign of nerves. I was cracking up laughing that she found it so easy – she put the two of us to shame.

Over the years Linda had found herself in the awkward position of becoming the Kofi Annan of the band. She tried to mediate between me and William and got a lot of shit from us in the process. It can't have been fun for her. The two of us would be having these huge rows, and as soon as they were finished I'd be on the phone to Linda saying 'Guess what William just said', and even while I was talking to her I knew he'd be trying to get through to tell her his side of the story. Her call-waiting was red hot and putting that blue UN helmet on to try to deal with our, by that time, almost fratricidal conflict must have been more stressful than she let on. And it was getting to the point where even Linda couldn't talk sense into us . . .

William

Did I mention that when Jim discovered cocaine he became a fucking arsehole? I probably did, because whatever was happening between us we always used to be able to fix things, but then he started taking this cocaine and nothing could be fixed any more. For about a year I couldn't understand why he seemed weird and kept attacking me the whole time – little arrows, little daggers that hurt me even though no one else noticed, because they were all happy getting drunk or stoned.

They'd say 'Oh, Jim is so cool when he's wasted.' And I'd be thinking 'No he's fucking not.' They'd say 'What's your problem? Jim just asked you how you're feeling', and I was the only one who could hear what he really said, which was 'How are you feeling, *big nose*?' Well not exactly that, but your family can get under your skin like nobody else, and I had to go on tour with the bastard.

Jim

While it was all going on, I just used to think 'What the fuck has happened to us?' I never really analysed it at the time the way I can now. The problem was that Reid/Reid as a functioning creative partnership had more or less broken down. If you asked people who wrote which songs on *Psychocandy*, no one would really know. Without getting all tree huggy about it, there was a lot of love between us in those days, whereas by the time we got to *Munki*, there wasn't much love to be seen anywhere, it was all negativity.

I hate revisiting this time and it's hard to describe what it felt like to be so at odds with this person I'd been so close to and worked in such harmony with. From the moment in my late teens when me and William really started to become friends, I'd thought that was it for life, but now something terrible was happening between us and it was hard to get a clear idea of what it was, because we were always so fucked up. And because we were into different drugs, we couldn't even be on the same page when we were off our heads.

We would argue about things, and then I would think 'This isn't him arguing, it's the dope', and I'm sure in the same way William would think 'This isn't him arguing, it's the coke', and he would've been right and I would've been right, but being right wasn't any use to us any more. I think William probably also felt a bit excluded from my friendship with Ben, because we were both a couple of hopeless coke-heads by that time, so we'd bonded over that.

William

I'd totally put myself out there to bring Ben into the band, because Ben is very intelligent and very logical, but once he became Jim's coke buddy I would say sensible things and Jim would disagree, and then suddenly I was dealing with two against one. I found that really disappointing – when Ben started taking Jim's side – and that was another reason why it rankled so much when I was wanting to put a guitar on that track and they were treating me like the guy who had come round to clip the roses.

Jim

At some point during the making of *Munki*, we'd effectively gone from being one band to being two – there was still a band to some degree, in that I played on some of William's songs and he played on some of mine, but towards the end it completely broke down, so he wouldn't be in the studio if I was there and I wouldn't be there if he was. The Mary Chain had become an umbrella that we both stood under, rather than it being the two of us against the world. In a strange way, we'd almost gone back to our original concept of having two separate bands. The even stranger thing was that, as utterly fucked up as everything was between us at the time, musically it really worked. If you listen to songs on *Munki* like 'Cracking Up' and 'Never Understood', William is addressing his (and our) awful situation very directly, and even though it died a death in commercial terms, I think that album is as good a record as we ever made.

When you're making one of your very best records and no one's buying it, it's hard to sit there and think 'At least we're still cool.' It's embarrassing. It's like you've fallen asleep in a pub with eight people in it and you wake up with those words on your lips and someone says 'What was that you said?' 'Nothing, I was just thinking out loud.' 'Well, in that case we're gonna chuck you out of this pub . . .' Some people had been waiting for us to be thrown out of that pub for ages, and when we most needed a united front, me and William were fighting each other on the way down the stairs.

Sadly, there was no one with the authority – or the good sense – to separate us. By that time Chris Morrison was managing loads of other bands as well as Blur and we'd felt like we'd dropped off his radar, so we made the same mistake we'd made with McGee of telling him we were going to get someone else without having anyone in place. We tried a few people but no one worked out, although the management we did have managed to do the one thing that should never have happened, which was book us on a three-month American tour. All me and William really needed was to get away from each other for a while. So where did we find ourselves? On a tour bus in America, which is a claustrophobic environment at the best of times, and this was not the best of times.

The end of the first run of The Jesus and Mary Chain was something that famously happened onstage. I wish it hadn't, but it did and I'm just so fucking grateful that people didn't have camera phones back then because it was messy and brutal and horrible and not something you would really want other people to see, or yourself to be endlessly reminded of.

There was a long period of time where I found what happened too painful even to think about, never mind discuss in public, but I don't mind talking about it now because the wound has kind of scabbed over – and I guess the way things have turned out makes it easier to look back on, because if it had been the end of our story rather than just the conclusion of a difficult chapter, then it would've made it much harder to deal with. Now I've gone over it in so many interviews that it almost doesn't feel real any more. The memory is more like looking at a picture – it's almost as if it's been laminated. Obviously that doesn't preclude the possibility that William's recollections of these events and mine will differ slightly, or even significantly, but either way, it's all sewage water under the bridge at this point.

How I remember it is that the tour manager, Laurie, was driving us back to the hotel after a show in San Diego. Everything was getting worse between us, and William was very drunk and stoned. We got into an argument in the van. I think William had been insisting that he should be allowed to drive, despite being in a state of cosmic inebriation, and I threatened to hit him. I was going to do that too, but as it happened, Ben beat me to the punch. I don't know if he saw that I was about to do it and thought he'd jump in first or whether he came to the decision independently, but it made no difference.

We were in a Transit van, William was in the front row of seats, I was in the middle row, and Ben was in the back, so the funny bit was he had to jump forward into my seat to hit William, William jumped back into my seat to fight back, and the next thing I knew Ben and William were having a fight on top of me. I'm not kidding when I say I think it was me that got hurt the most – punches were going into my ribs and someone else was kneeling on my face. The shit had totally hit the fan.

William

It was just a bunch of drunk people being drunk and then the next day everyone was coming up with a story that made them come out of it a little better. The reality was that me and Jim had a fight and Ben might or might not have joined in – when I say a fight, nobody got a black eye. I know he's an idiot, he knows I'm an idiot, and every now and then we have one of those pushing and shoving fights, what the commentators call 'handbags' in football.

I was in Australia a couple of years ago and there was a thing on TV about the Premier League where they just showed people falling over when no one had hit them. They've gone down like they've been shot when the other player's not even gone near them. That's what me and Jim are like. We get mad at each other and we scream at each other and one of us might feign an injury, but the idea of actually hurting my stupid wee brother? I could never do that. Although the idea of humiliating him because at that moment in the argument he's a fucking fool? Yeah, I'd be totally up for it . . .

Jim

The next day William announced that he was leaving the band, but said he was going to do that night's LA show at the House of Blues as his last one. My response to this was to get incredibly fucked up on alcohol and cocaine. By the time the show was due to start, I was wasted to the point of not knowing who – or where – I was. I remember catching sight of William and thinking 'There's the bastard.' I started yelling at him 'You cunt! You fucking cunt!' Then I turned round and saw all these people looking at us, and realised I was onstage and this was our audience.

I think we'd played a song or two by this time but I wasn't in any condition to understand what was happening, as the combination of alcohol and cocaine turns you into a weird kind of zombie – you've drunk so much you should've passed out a couple of hours before, but the cocaine counteracts the drink so you can still stand up and take the opportunity to make even more of a fool of yourself. There was a vague realisation that the person doing all this was actually me, and at that point the big metaphorical shepherd's crook came on to pull me off. I was duly dragged offstage and deposited in the dressing room with multiple people screaming at me, mostly the promoter who was understandably concerned that he was going to lose his shirt.

All I remember doing at that point was looking at the fridge where the drink had been kept and thinking 'Some cunt's put a padlock on the fridge.' That was my main concern. The next memory I have is of being back at the hotel. Lots of other people were there but I don't know who they were, how they got there or what became of them. Either way, some more cocaine and lots of booze arrived, and the grisly scene flashes forward to me and Ben in an outdoor jacuzzi on the hotel roof at six in the morning having a conversation about what the fuck we were going to do next. If William wasn't certain to leave before, he definitely was now, so the question was did we just cancel the remaining shows? We found out pretty quickly that this was going to be financially crippling, so we made the decision to end the band but complete the last two or three weeks of the tour.

William

I was so mad at Jim for doing that. I couldn't understand why he went on with it. Yes, there was a financial cost to cancelling the tour, but that was the least of our worries at the time. We should've just stopped the band there and then and retained a shred of dignity. For him to do all these gigs without me there, essentially pretending the band hadn't split up when he knew it had, was just terrible.

Jim

I didn't feel angry with William, I didn't feel guilt, I just felt deep sadness and sorrow that this was a big part of my life which had now come to an end. There was a lot of anxiety as well. In the long term I didn't know if I would be able to pay my bills. In the short term we didn't know if we would be able to do a gig without William, because obviously his presence and his guitar were a massive part of what we did.

Of all the shows we could've had to play, the next gig was at a Californian supper club, so we went onstage and there were all these people eating shrimp dinners and surf and turf. We were contracted to do at least sixty minutes but when we went through the possible set list – 'We can't do this one without William, we can't do that one without William' – we cobbled together about fifty-five minutes and did an extra-long version of the last song. It was nightmarish but we just about got away with it. The light show was so bright I'm not sure everyone noticed William wasn't onstage. I certainly don't remember announcing it – all I know is we went out there and played gigs and people didn't boo us off, in fact sometimes we went down quite well. Our state of mind was bad but the actual shows weren't that bad, and as the tour went on we got a bit better.

That didn't matter though, because the whole trip was cursed. Somewhere in Texas the drummer, Nick Sanderson, broke his shoulder. We were playing a show in some middle-of-nowhere place and the hotel the night before was out on the freeway with nothing nearby for miles around. It was the only game in town and it did have a disco, where Nick Sanderson was the textbook mad northerner out on the dance floor shouting 'This is shite music, put on New Order' and trying to balance a bottle of beer on his head. There was also a sheriff with a gun in his belt who was there to keep the peace on the dance floor, and he told me 'You've got to get that guy out of here.' I was telling him 'Nick, Nick, the guy's going to arrest you – he might even shoot you, for fuck's sake', but he wouldn't listen. Eventually I got him back up to my room, but I was essentially babysitting by that stage. Every two or three minutes Nick made another drunken dash for the door to try and get back down to the disco. I was just thinking 'For fuck's sake stop it, you maniac', then on one of the dashes he made for the door – well, I suppose logically it was the last one – he misjudged the point where the room narrowed from the bedroom to the corridor and caught his shoulder on the wall.

At first I was pissing myself laughing – I could see that Nick was in pain, but I was just thinking 'You stupid bastard, you deserve it' – then it was clear that the pain was really bad, so I had to get Ben from across the corridor to help me take him to a hospital. Once we got there, it turned out he'd broken his shoulder and we had to fly in one of our army of standby drummers from the UK to finish the tour at a moment's notice, which Nick was furious about – 'Fucking bastard, he's doing my job.' So in the end we limped over the line two men down.

It was a disastrous tour, everyone was depressed, and those few days around the incident with William went beyond depression into a kind of madness. Our management situation had totally broken down by then so there wasn't must structure left around us, which was probably a symptom of our situation as much as the cause of it. The Jesus and Mary Chain was a ship with a hole in its side. If there'd been crew members that cared enough we could've limped into port, done some running repairs and maybe lived to sail another day, but there was no one left on the bridge. The ship sank, and there was nothing to be salvaged. There were no lawyers involved, we just didn't speak.

Part 6

The Best Part of Breaking Up Is When You're Making Up

i. In a Hole

Jim

Sometimes, when the worst happens, it can actually be a relief. As grim as it was, the break-up of the Mary Chain in 1998 seemed so utterly final that in a strange way it almost took the pressure off – especially once I realised I wasn't going to be sleeping in a cardboard box in a doorway. After all those years of anxiety, of being ground down by the music industry, worrying that every record might be our last, so we could never relax and enjoy it because it always felt like there was a noose around our neck and we were standing on a rickety chair, it was actually quite comforting to tumble into the abyss. And it was a huge weight off my mind to find out that my whole world didn't need to come crashing down around me just because the band was over.

I wasn't loaded by any means, but I could get by. Royalties still trickled in, and I took in lodgers to make ends meet, so I had enough money for pizzas and beer and I could still afford something of a rock 'n' roll lifestyle. Not on the scale I'd had before, but hanging around with the right people and sitting at the right tables, you could get their crumbs. At that point I was free and easy and nobody depended on me and it was a merciful release not to have to think about the band any more.

The last few years of the Mary Chain had been such a shitshow that part of me was glad to be free of it. I'd spent too long dwelling on the negative aspects of our career. It's like you get to the Emerald City and you meet the Wizard of Oz and he's not quite what you expect (no disrespect to Rob Dickins), and then you get behind the scenery and you see it's all held together with bits of string and old rusty nails, but being free of all illusions is actually quite liberating. Now I didn't care what William was doing and I don't think he was bothered what I was up to either. There was a year – maybe two – when we didn't even speak. The unbearable pain of losing this beautiful thing we had created and loved and then watched slowly disintegrate for no very good reason was an emotional landscape I wasn't ready to admit I inhabited.

In the meantime, I more or less completely stopped listening to music – everything seemed to sound like something else, and the joy had gone out of all of it – and with time and space at last available to consider my options, I decided to go for full-spectrum alcohol and cocaine addiction. Part of the problem was the identity of my lodgers. One of them was Ben Lurie, with whom I shared a number of unhealthy enthusiasms, and who would sometimes cut out the middlemen by paying his rent in cocaine. The other one was a young guy who worked for a mate of mine and every weekend twenty of his mates would turn up at the flat with a big bag of ecstasy, or 'disco biscuits' as they called them, which were shit by the way because every now and then I'd take one to check.

They'd be mumbling 'Oh man, I'm on one', and I'd be the older guy in the corner saying 'I hate to tell you this, pal, but the stuff we had at Creation in the late eighties was a whole different ballgame . . .' It was a party house where no one needed a reason to get fucked up, and that was just the way I liked it, because I didn't want to have to think about what my reasons were.

My memories of this period are quite hazy for obvious reasons but I remember feeling quite . . . relaxed. I didn't have to worry about going on another fucking tour or making another fucking record with a brother who didn't even want to fucking know me. Everything might have gone totally to shit, but as far as my short-term objective was concerned – which was not thinking about the Mary Chain – we were golden.

My alcoholism was (and is) definitely linked to my awkward behaviour around people. I had felt painfully shy for as long as I could remember and the only thing that ever helped was drink.

For a while when I first started drinking it seemed like the magic solution, because all of a sudden I could chat with people and make small talk which was something that I could never manage before – 'Why would anyone want to talk about the weather? I don't give a fuck about the weather, talk to somebody else.' Beneath that protective layer of arrogance I'd be squirming inside, thinking 'I can't deal with this, I want to get away.' But get a pint or two or a couple of whiskies inside me and I could natter away like Joe Normal. It was always a high-wire act, though, because a couple of drinks too many and you're a fool, but a couple of drinks too few and you're still the person you were at the beginning. The fear of the second option always takes precedence, so you reach for another drink too soon and then that happens again and then you're stumbling towards option one.

It was always about walking that fine line where I'd have a couple of drinks to feel relaxed, then try to leave it a bit longer before I had the next one so I could stay in that place for as long as possible – I believe Renaissance philosophers called it the golden ratio. My problem was that I could never just have the couple of drinks I needed to be what I always assumed everybody else was like. So if you took a vox pop on a crowded room where I'd spent an evening, you'd get three different responses from people according to which stage of the evening they caught me at – 'Yes, I talked to Jim and he was a nervous wreck', 'Yes, I talked to Jim and he was charming', and last but not least, 'Yes, I talked to Jim and he ended up puking down my trousers.'

Eventually the time came that I started to think 'I can't just sit around at home drinking for the rest of my life – I need a reason to go to America and drink.' At this point the band Freeheat was formed with Ben Lurie, Nick Sanderson (whose shoulder had eventually got better) and Romi Mori, who'd been the bass player in The Gun Club. Instead of sitting in the pub moaning about being excluded from everything and wondering 'Why aren't we famous?' 'Why aren't we adored?', we decided to take that show on the road and did two tours of America that were almost completely built around alcohol.

The amazing thing is I've seen live clips and we were actually playing pretty well – we were a tight little band in every sense. It was fun to make music on a very small scale again – four friends just travelling round and playing for the hell of it, with no pressure or structure of any kind. That was how William and I had started off and it was very enjoyable to do it again, even without him. Unfortunately, with no management, no record label and no agent behind us – we tried to get other people interested but for some reason no one would take us seriously – it could only go on for so long. And when that fell apart, my drinking really went into overdrive.

My life has offered me many illustrations of the wisdom of the saying 'don't meet your heroes', but my two-night run as a guest vocalist with Primal Scream would provide one of the most painful. I'd done a guest vocal on the Primal Scream album *Evil Heat* in 2002 and when Bobby asked me to join them on tour for a couple of dates I really appreciated the gesture. That was a bad period of my life in terms of how heavily I was drinking, but for some reason I broke the habit of a lifetime by doing the warm-up gig stone-cold sober. It went well, even though Primal Scream's music was so heavily sequenced at that point – like ours had been in the early nineties – that it was easy to get tangled up in the gears.

So we headed off to a festival in Belgium, maybe it was in Bruges. I think I was feeling a bit fragile about being on a tour bus that wasn't mine with so many people, some of whom I knew but many of whom I didn't. I got tanked up to calm my nerves on the way over, so I was already pretty far gone at the point where someone produced a big bag of speed. I thought 'Well, that takes me back a bit, have you not got anything else?' But that was all there was, so I was dipping in the bag the whole trip while also continuing to drink.

By the time of the gig I was in really, really bad shape, and as

The Best Part of Breaking Up Is When You're Making Up

I was lying down backstage with the room revolving around me, I could hear someone doing vocal exercises to warm up before going on – all that 'Fa-la-la' stuff. I shouted at them to shut the fuck up because I was trying to sleep. Then I got up to see who the offender was and found myself face to face with a very sober David Bowie. I didn't know what to say, but David Bowie did. He slowly looked me up and down and then said something quite poised and sarcastic like 'Well, it's a look.' I just grunted 'Uh huh.' Then he walked one way and I walked the other and that was it – the time I met David Bowie. It was not my finest moment and worse was to come.

When I walked out to do the song with the Primals, the intro started up and at that point I realised I had no idea what I was doing. I started singing at some random moment then saw the horrified looks on everyone's faces and realised I'd come in at the wrong time. It was a fucking disaster and Primal Scream never asked me to sing with them again, but they were all total gentlemen about it and I'd like to take this opportunity to apologise for letting them down.

So that was David Bowie and Iggy Pop ticked off the bucket list. Thank goodness I'd avoided a full house of the holy trinity of pre-punk by turning down the chance to meet Lou Reed when the agent we shared suggested I should 'Come and say hi to Lou' at a festival we were playing in the nineties. I knew he could shred people, remembered the Iggy Pop experience, and decided 'I will cling to the version of Lou Reed that I already have.' Of course he would probably have been charm personified, but I'll never know now, will I?

It wasn't just on the European festival circuit that my drinking was causing me problems. There were also the driving lessons. Driving round London had always seemed like a nightmare so I'd never got round to learning – I used to get more cabs than I could really afford and justified the expense by thinking about how much buying and running a car would cost, never mind the price of lessons. Towards the end of my several-years-long lost weekend, I did make an ill-advised foray onto the roads. I would turn up for the two or three driving lessons I had (before common sense prevailed) hung-over and reeking of whisky. 'Are you sure you're all right?' 'Yeah, yeah, I haven't had a belt of anything since six o'clock.' 'Last night?' 'No, this morning.' 'But it's only nine now.' 'It has been a few hours – have you got a drink on you?'

The death knell of my capital city driving career was signalled by me smashing into a traffic island in Chalk Farm – 'What the fuck was that? I've not hit someone have I?' 'That was a traffic island, Mr Reid.' Luckily, the traffic island was located right outside a tyre repair shop – 'That's convenient – did they have that put there so they could get custom?'

It would take one more similarly embarrassing onstage experience to bring me to my senses. I'd been starting to think seriously about trying to get a solo career off the ground, and Phil King from Lush – who had also been in some of the later versions of the Mary Chain, so he couldn't say he wasn't warned – helped get me a solo show in London. It had sold well in advance and there were going to be loads of reviews. True to form I decided to calm my nerves before this big occasion by getting totally fucked up and had scored a gram of coke as insurance. Unfortunately my coke consumption had fallen off a little at that point – I was prioritising alcohol due to financial constraints – so I'd lost my grip of the old balancing act between booze and cocaine that I'd previously been able to manage quite successfully (or at least to my own satisfaction).

I started drinking and snorting in the afternoon, and when Phil was telling me 'You've got a gig, you've got to keep it together' I just waved him away, airily insisting 'Don't worry, I've been doing this for years.' What I'd not taken into account was that I was some way short of match fitness after a few years out of the spotlight, so by the time I got onstage I could hardly stand. I kept thinking my guitar was out of tune so I was trying to tune it up, but I was too wasted to do it and I just ended up standing there bashing my guitar without the first idea of what was going on. I can vaguely remember people in the audience were laughing at me – it was like something in a nightmare, but sadly others who were in attendance will tell you that it did actually happen.

The morning after that total public humiliation I woke up and went to start drinking again, before I realised that my drinking was out of control. I decided more or less there and then not to have another drink, and embarked on what turned out to be a five-year-long experiment with sobriety. I also moved to Devon – which meant I had to learn to drive, because you need to if you want to see the bright lights of Exeter without waiting three hours for a bus – and had two kids. I'd only just passed my test when Candice was born (we just liked that name, nobody calls her Candy), so in my early forties I became a dad with a driving licence and therefore a responsible member of society. I was a late developer but I got there in the end.

Obviously weaning myself off booze and cocaine at the level of dependence on them that I had achieved was a more complex process than what I've just said suggests, but there was a certain simplicity to it. There was no rehab, no therapy and (initially at least) no AA. It was just a decision I made. The way things panned out over the following two decades suggests that I have a pattern. I can stop drinking for about five years, then I hit the wall and fall off the wagon for a bit. At that point it usually takes me about six months to wean myself back off the booze.

The first time I fell off the wagon, a year or two after I'd moved to Sidmouth in Devon, where I still live, there was an AA meeting around the corner so I went there for a few sessions, but I couldn't get into it at all. There'd be all these people whining on, telling these terrible stories about how drink ruined their lives, and I'd be sitting there thinking 'Well, yes but what about the good times?' I suppose this went back to my formative childhood experiences at family parties in Glasgow, but when people would share their traumatic memories of the terrible things they did at their sister's wedding, my response would be 'Wow, fucking great. Wish I'd have been there.' Obviously I've got my share of depressing stories too, and I've told a few, but I have to say that if it wasn't for my health I would probably keep drinking forever, because I love drinking, and I only don't drink because I know that if I drink the way that I like to drink I'm going to die prematurely and I've got two kids and I don't want to do that to them. That said, I have been back on the bottle at the time of writing – the pressure of making a new Jesus and Mary Chain album can do that to a person – but once I get a few months of sobriety under my belt, I know I can keep it going for at least a few years.

Giving up the cocaine, in a funny way, was easier. First, because it tended to go hand in hand with the drinking anyway, and second, because I'd had so many of those horrible bad nights where I was wired and sick and ill and didn't know what to do about it, that those fucking awful experiences were kind of seared into my memory, so once I was away from it, it was easier not to go back.

I've always been pretty straight up about what I've done in these terms – it's just shit that happened and I'm neither proud nor ashamed of it. I don't like people that glorify drugs, and I hope no one could see this book as doing that. I hate the way that loads of people became junkies because of Johnny Thunders or even Charlie Parker, and in my experience there's nothing particularly glamorous about drugs. Quite the opposite in fact, because you find yourself in really horrible seedy situations and you feel like shit much more than you feel good. The bit where you feel like a god wears off almost immediately and the rest of the time is trying to chase that feeling . . . that's what happened with me anyway. The insanity of it is that once you come down and crash and get yourself together for a couple of days, then you're back out doing it again. There's definitely some research to be done into why people put themselves through that.

My problem when I was younger was that as soon as I started drinking, everything was a good idea. If someone came up to me in a party environment and said try something, I always would – 'Try this arsenic, it's new.' 'What does it do?' 'It kills you.' 'Great, give me some of that then.' If you name a drug, I've probably done it, but even though some people thought a lot of our songs were about heroin, that was never a big thing with the Mary Chain. I did dabble with it for about a year in the nineties but I think with heroin I realised that with my somewhat addictive personality it was probably something to be wary of.

The thing that clicked with me was coke. I think one of the reasons coke is so prevalent in the music industry is that any music sounds good when you're on it. That's one of the reasons I used to love doing it – because sometimes you go through a period where music just doesn't do it for you any more, but if you take drugs, music sounds great again.

I remember when I first used to listen to the Velvets, I used to say to people 'This music is like being on drugs', because it made me feel something physical which, when it wore off, was something I was always trying to recreate – you take drugs to get things back up to the level that they used to be without them. Obviously now I'm in my sixties I don't feel music in my body the way that I used to when I was seventeen, but I've learnt to be OK with that because it's part of life, so I no longer need to make up the deficit with cocaine.

William

Did you ever get your ma or da stoned? I got my ma stoned one night when we played Glasgow with My Bloody Valentine, and she was so happy. I was smoking a joint and she was asking 'What's it like? What's it like?' And so I just put it in her mouth and said 'Here ma, smoke it', and she did and when she got stoned she was giggly and hungry – all the clichés like if it happened in a sitcom.

In another life my ma could've been an actress – she was always showing off and being funny – but It's kind of weird when your ma is on the same weird drug high as you, in fact because you're stoned yourself it's quite overwhelming. It's like you went to the swingers club and found your parents there. Have you ever seen the episode of *Seinfeld* were George is single and he goes into the dating world and it turns out that his mother is doing that too? Well that's what I felt like when I saw my ma smoking dope – it brought out my inner George Costanza: 'I'm a rock 'n' roller but you're in my world and you shouldn't be here.'

Did my ma miss the sixties? Everything has many angles. She lived through the real sixties, where she had two children and we were poor as fuck, and then maybe later on some of the more easy-going side of it trickled through to her. I'd be proud to think that we helped with that, because as she grew older she became what you could call a late young person. She got very liberated. I remember going back to East Kilbride once and she was watching this show on TV called *Two Pints of Lager and a Packet of Crisps*. Oh my God it was so fucking filthy, it shocked me, but she was absolutely fine with it. She gave up smoking in her fifties too, which I was really proud of her for.

My ma never thought me and Jim had a problem with alcohol, even though I told her we were alcoholics. She said 'You're not', and I said 'We are, ma, we are.' She thought an alcoholic was someone begging on the street in rags, so she wouldn't accept that my da had been one either. Her reasoning was my da was not an alcoholic because he was not drunk all the time. I would say 'Well, I'm not drunk all the time, but when I have one drink I can't fucking stop till I've had thirty and I'm the most drunk person on the night.'

For people of my mother's generation – not so much for the women, who would just drink to get buzzed, but definitely for the men – that was thought of as par for the course. I had plenty of uncles I never saw sober, in fact pretty much every adult male in my childhood would now be thought of as an alcoholic, and I think that's a very specific culture. It's not just a Scottish thing, it's a British thing. That's why British soap operas were nearly always set around a pub – *Coronation Street* was the Rovers Return, *EastEnders* was the Queen Vic and *Emmerdale* was The Woolpack. I guess it's a lazy way of giving your characters somewhere to meet, but there's more to it than that, it's also about signalling an acceptance of alcohol dependency as something that is perceived as normal.

I was in an AA meeting once and a woman gave an amazing speech about all the terrible things that had happened to her while she was drunk. You hear a lot of harrowing stories in those meetings – everyone's invited to stand up, you're not really going to be there unless alcohol has taken you to some dark places, and a lot of those people are born storytellers. But even in that context this woman was exceptional. She was telling us how she'd hide all these little bottles of vodka at work and then she'd wake up in the street and she'd done this and she'd done that and it was all just awful. But then she started talking about how she wasn't really an alcoholic and everyone was just looking at her in amazement. Isn't that extraordinary, that someone could tell you all those things and then insist that they weren't an alcoholic?

The other side of it when you admit that you are one is that if you tell someone something that's happened to you, the first thing that will come into their head is that perhaps you've been drinking, as if that invalidates every other aspect of your perception. Let's say you went to the Chinese takeaway and the man that serves there, who usually likes you, spat in your face, but when you tell people they just say 'You were drunk', and then three weeks later he's in the newspapers because he was spitting in people's faces. Well, that sort of thing happens to me with my family all the time. When they tell me 'But you'd had a beer',

I'll say 'I'd had a beer, not a fucking tab of acid.' Yet pretty much everything I tell my sister, she'll still ask 'William, have you been drinking?' If I sent her a text message saying 'I've been half-eaten by a bunch of cannibals and here are my coordinates', she'd still ask me the same question. On reflection I suppose she'd have a point with that one.

When I told a psychotherapist about 'pretending to be confident because women like that', they seemed to think that was fair enough as a teenager but wondered why, years later, as an adult, I still felt the need to do it. Surely, they said, I'd have reached a point where I no longer needed to pretend and could actually just *be* confident? After all, I'd been in a band who were a wee bit popular in the eighties . . . On the face of it this seemed a reasonable suggestion, but looking at the way my relationships with therapists themselves developed probably shows you why it was not consistent with my reality.

From the beginning I found it completely impossible to talk to a male therapist. The first time I was assigned one was through the NHS in the late nineties. Me and Jim weren't wealthy at the point where the band broke up, but we had a bit of money. Still, we wouldn't have liked the idea of ourselves resorting to BUPA, so when I felt I needed to talk to someone quickly it was always going to be done through a referral from my GP. It was a personal thing I was dealing with – I had split up with a girlfriend and I wasn't handling it very well. I was trying to be musical and play solo shows and make records, but I just kept crying all the time and I knew I had to go and talk to someone to get over it. Not get over the woman herself – if someone's not going to love you any more, what can you do, apart from kill yourself? You just have to move forward – but get over the fact of the loss.

It was a traumatic point in my life and I didn't feel good about being alone and I needed to talk to someone quickly about my mental health. I don't know if I was gonna top myself but I was feeling pretty fuckin' desperate. So I went to this psychiatrist, and

I don't know why but I thought it was going to be a nice woman in a long flowery dress. Instead it was a fucking bloke and he was dressed like a Smiths fan – in black denims and Doc Martens. He wasn't quite wearing a Jesus and Mary Chain t-shirt but he might as well have been, and I knew this cunt knew who I was because he was startled when I walked in. I remember thinking 'What the fuck? I can't tell him what's going on – he'll just send it straight to *Melody Maker*.' I just said 'I can't talk to you, I can't tell you things', and when he said 'Why – what's your problem?', I didn't really have an answer so I just said 'OK, I'm going to go.'

When I went back to my GP they looked at me like I really was insane – 'You walked out of your session? Don't you know how lucky you were to even get one?' If it had been a hundred years ago they would've put me in an asylum at that point. They probably thought I was homophobic. But what I couldn't explain was a fear which was actually quite rational, which was that if the therapist never let on he knew who I was, then how could I trust him while I did what you've got to do with a psychiatrist, which is say your innermost everything? How can you pour your heart out to someone who only really wants to ask you 'What was it like when you were on that tour with Sonic Youth?' Or 'Did you ever actually meet J. Mascis?' I guess maybe I could've put up with a male therapist if he didn't look like he was in The Housemartins.

Apart from the fact that the North Circular was driving me crazy, one of the reasons I left London for America was all these gangs of little teenage idiots who give you shit at bus stops. You know if they came at you in a fair fight you could just kick their fucking head right off their body, but you also know the chances are they've got a knife, so when they say 'Oh, you've got funny hair, why don't you get your hair cut, mate?' – which is something that has been happening to me for decades – you've kind of got to watch what you say back.

Usually I'd ignore it, but every now and then I got pissed off and there was one time when we were at The Drugstore when this kid who thought he was so fucking witty with four or five of his mates said 'Oi, who cut your hair, mate?' Without really thinking about it, I replied 'Who cut yours? The same guy who cut everyone else's hair in the world.' Then I looked up and saw them looking at me like they were actually going to kill me. Part of you is thinking you could just swat them away, but another part is thinking, 'Am I going to die for these little fucking idiots?'

So that was one reason I moved to America – because I didn't want to be a hair martyr. Someone looking at the situation from outside might've also thought I was trying to get as far away from Jim as possible, but that wasn't actually what it was. Yes I was fed up with Britain in general and Muswell Hill in particular, but ever since I was a child America had always been a beautiful thing in my mind – shiny and attractive and exciting. And luckily because of my job I'd been able to go there often, sometimes as many as three times a year, and I'd kind of got to know it as a real place and not just as the fantasy of my childhood.

I'd started to talk about maybe moving to America as early as the late-eighties, when I was still with Rona. She was all gung-ho about it until I got serious enough to present her with some forms to fill in and then she backed out, which I was disappointed by at the time. So after the band broke up I felt like there wasn't really anything keeping me in Britain and I might as well give it a go.

I had met and married my first wife Dawn by then, who was American (from Seattle), so that was another factor in finally making the move. She already had an eight-year-old daughter, and we had a son in January 2000, so when we first went out there we moved to a family house in Redondo Beach, California. Part of the attraction being that it was mentioned in The Beach Boys' 'Surfin' USA'. But once I got to this mythical sun-kissed location, I hated it – it was a terrible judgemental suburban place full of Martha Stewart types who didn't like my wife because she had tattoos and a nose ring (I suppose I must've looked pretty weird to them as well). Everyone had this smug thing going on and by the time we realised we'd been given bad information and a house in Redondo Beach wasn't really much less expensive than a house in the Hollywood Hills, it was too late to do anything about it.

I guess it's funny that The Jesus and Mary Chain had to break up before Jim and I could have children – maybe because it meant we didn't have to look after each other any more. But I wasn't turning my back on every aspect of British culture. I had a gadget called a Slingbox which enabled me to watch British TV over the internet. Although this seemed like something from the world of science fiction at the time, it wasn't really high technology in that the people who ran it just rented a warehouse in Wembley and filled it with a hundred and fifty video or DVR recorders. Obviously in the modern world the idea of having all those different bits of hardware seems ridiculous, but at the time it was a good way of keeping up with *Coronation Street* or the British news, and one of the Slingboxes connected up to my ma's cable, which enabled me to switch channels on her sometimes during her favourite shows so she knew she wasn't watching alone.

When it went wrong – which it did quite often, just like our first four-track tape recorder before it (that's what you get with new-frontier technology) – you'd have to call this guy in Washington. He was a flamboyant ex-pat, a real Noël Coward type, who smoked cigarettes in a cigarette holder so they didn't have to touch his mouth. I'd ring him up to complain when things hadn't recorded properly and he'd argue with me in an accent I couldn't even begin to approximate.

I'd get quite irate if I missed certain shows, especially *Coronation Street*. To me the theme tune is like that poet that always gets mentioned with the cakes – Marcel Proust and his madeleines. That 'dah, da da da da dah' has been there all my life, from when I was crawling around on the carpet in Glasgow in 1962, to living in California forty years later, and you could make a case for it being one of the best pieces of music ever recorded, because people have heard it hundreds and even thousands of times and yet there's no petition to change it.

When you think about the theme for a soap, it's a tune you're going to hear several times a week for years on end, so it's got to be somehow not offensive and yet not too bland. I doff my cap to Tony Hatch for writing not only 'Downtown', which was one of the greatest songs of the sixties, but also the theme tunes for *Neighbours* and *Crossroads*. They had two versions of the latter, with the sentimental one Wings played for the times when someone died. Tony might've been a bit of a bastard on *New Faces* but that was pretty good going. I wish I could make a piece of music with those powers of endurance. The best Beach Boys singles are a bit like that – how many times have I heard 'Wouldn't It Be Nice' and I'm still not sick of it.

For some reason *Coronation Street* is something, like fish and chips, that always has the power to make me feel part of Scotland and part of Britain. Do I watch it for entertainment? No, I watch it to criticise everything about it – the dialogue, the acting. I just love to sit there and mock it. I remember reading a few years ago that Nick Cave had done this European tour and for every one of about ten gigs in four different countries this same guy was there at the front, shouting 'You're shit! You're shit!' Cave said he admired the dedication involved – all the hotels and planes just to do that – and I'm like that with *Coronation Street*. I boo it, but I'm still there to boo it.

When the band broke up, my ma and sister couldn't stand it. I think women feel emotional pain a lot more than men, or maybe they feel it better. I hope I'm not being sexist here, but I think the fact that women have babies shows they have a higher tolerance for physical pain than men, and maybe they experience emotions more directly.

I know I'm generalising because obviously plenty of men feel plenty of emotion – that's why *The Guardian* exists – but I think the reason me and Jim falling out hurt my ma and sister so much was because we'd all grown up together as a family, and in working-class families especially it's a given that you should stay together because you're so poor you've got nothing else to fall back on. So when two of your family start a band and they're quite successful, but then they have a big fight in Tokyo over some macadamia nuts and another even bigger fight in Los Angeles and everything has got too fucked up for them to even talk to each other, of course that's going to be incredibly distressing to you. And I feel bad for putting them through that.

ii. Sister Vanilla to the Rescue

William

Linda was always into music, and me and Jim had promised to make a record with her for ages, then somehow in 2002–03, it just happened. I guess from the outside this might look like an unexpected thing for us to have done at that point, but next to overcoming all the reasons for not being in a band with my little brother, making an album with my little sister was a breeze. We'd nicknamed her Sister Vanilla as a kid, because her skin was as pale as ice cream.

Jim and I still weren't really talking, so we did nearly all of it separately. I recorded my parts in LA and Linda, Jim and Ben did theirs in north London. I didn't really know what they were doing – Linda just asked me for a couple of songs so I gave them to her, then she wanted to be a bit more involved in co-writing, so I gave her a couple of tunes that she wrote the lyrics for. As some of Linda's lyrics were about her listening to our songs, I suppose you could see this whole project as an experiment with trying to feel more positive about the band again – even if we couldn't quite manage to yet, we knew that she could. And it was nice to be working on something with Jim again, even if we did still need the Atlantic between us as a safety barrier.

Since I went to America, I'd experienced a complete lack of confidence about making music on my own. Things between me and Jim had got so bad creatively by the time the band broke up that you'd think I'd have been happy to plough on without him afterwards, but instead I was hit by this strange feeling that if I did solo stuff – either under my own name or as Lazycame – it wasn't just me that was gonna be judged, it was the Mary Chain. I'm not sure why, but this became something of a mental block for me.

There'd been a couple of times where Jim and I working together again had been suggested – when I was still living in
Redondo Beach and a greatest hits was coming out, someone
said maybe we should do an EP of new songs to go with it. I
thought that was a brilliant idea and we should totally do it,
but Jim was really negative about it and I was very frustrated
and upset by that. I still thought Jim was a fucking prick and he
probably thought the same of me, so collaborating again – even
at a distance – on Linda's album was definitely an important step
forward for us. Even though the record didn't actually come out
for a few more years, it was the start of a bridge being built.

Jim

That was definitely the beginning of the healing process. There'd
been a period of time – I'm not sure how long, but it was definitely
years rather than months – where there was very little contact between me and William whatsoever. I'd been best man at his wedding, which was less than a year after the band broke up, but I
don't remember us talking much. Then our mum started to engineer
situations where we would both be back in East Kilbride at the
same time – especially at Christmas, when she would brazenly
manipulate things so we'd have to be in the same house and even
sometimes in the same room. Linda was in on that, too. When our
dad died in 2005 we were together and close again at his funeral.

Collaborating on the album had moved the reconciliation process forward. Us working together on that record, even though we
were mostly on different continents while we did it, was something
that would've been unthinkable a couple of years before. There was
a song on the album called 'JAMColas' where William suggested
we should all do a verse, so I went to LA to visit him and did a
vocal and that was where we started to come back together to
the point where we could be in the same room at the same time

without feeling totally uncomfortable. It helped that there was no pressure on us of any kind in terms of commercial expectations for the album. There was no deadline, no record company breathing down our neck, and it felt like we were just making music for the hell of it in the way that we probably hadn't since we made *Psychocandy*. You can almost hear us falling back in love with our own sound again – it was pure fun, and I think the fact that it was something we were doing for our sister enabled us to be less competitive and up our own arses about it.

We didn't have those long painful conversations about what had happened between us, we just kind of tolerated each other. It seemed like 'Well, this is obviously as good as it can get at the moment, and since we're not in a band any more, it's kind of work-able.' It wasn't like we were being falsely nice to each other – petty arguments would still flare up about one thing or another – but the geographical distance definitely helped with the emotional distance. The fact that we weren't bumping into each other on the high street, because one of us was in Devon and one of us was in America, was a definite plus.

Another thing that helped was that before we were even really talking properly, a load of money came through from one of our songs being used in a car advert in America. I can't even remember what kind of car it was. This happened totally out of the blue. Writing a song can be like buying a lottery ticket, and while it wasn't quite on the level of the Anti-Nowhere League getting rich overnight after Metallica covered them, it was still very well timed. I paid off my mortgage and William bought a fancy car. I can't remember what kind that was either – I've never owned a fancy car in my life.

William

'Happy When It Rains' was in a Chevrolet ad, and I didn't buy a car, I bought a house – 6938 Camrose Drive in Hollywood, baby.

Jim

It was around this time that there began to be a sense of some kind of enthusiasm out there – at least among promoters – for The Jesus and Mary Chain to get back together to play some shows. A few offers started to come in from people who had maybe grown up on our music and were now in a position to pay us quite substantial amounts of money to play it again, but we still never imagined it would happen, because I thought William would never be up for it and he thought the same about me.

William

The reason we finally got back together was probably because of my ma. She was with me at Christmas 2006, staying in my horrible divorce apartment in Hollywood. I slept on the couch, my ma got my lovely big Ikea bed and we were having a good Christmas when the first offer came through for us to play Coachella.

I said 'I still don't like Jim, ma. I don't know if I can even be in a room with him if we've got to be in the band again', and she said 'Well, he says the same thing about you', and there was a couple of full days of her reassuring both of us that no matter how much I hated Jim, he hated me just as much. This might seem an unorthodox strategy, but ultimately, it worked.

It would be a few more months before the gig finally happened – in April 2007 – and they upped their offer a bit in-between times. Good things come to those who wait, and the fact that they felt we were worth pursuing helped build our confidence.

Jim

There was definitely a bit of a dance involved as to whether me and/or William were up for it. I remember thinking 'We at least need to discuss this', while in the back of my mind feeling like it was still probably never going to happen. I was kind of into it, but I didn't want to lay my cards on the table and say I was, in case William said 'Well I'm not', because then I'd have had to pretend that I wasn't either. We were kind of feeling our way around each other, but when it became apparent that he wasn't wholly against it and neither was I, we could both start to relax a bit. Maybe we both had to go out and try other things that amounted to absolutely nothing to find out how much we needed each other, I don't know. Either way, we chewed it over for a while and then decided 'Fuck, let's do it.' That was that – the Mary Chain were back.

I did think it would be good to get on a stage with William again, but was also concerned that we might just pick up where we left off. By that time we had kind of gotten to the point where we could converse with each other and get along to a degree, but without really dissecting what had happened between us or going into the details of who slung what custard pie at who. So if we could still argue when we were on different continents, there had to be a danger that old wounds might open up again once we were in the confined spaces of tour vans and rehearsal rooms.

And the rehearsals were a bit spiky if I'm honest – there were a few points where we were screaming at each other, but it was more that we irritated each other the way normal people would. It wasn't like 1997–98, when we just argued about everything because we disagreed on principle with everything the other person was going to say. Now it was much less intense – it felt like we were no longer those weird Siamese twins who finished off each other's sentences, we were just different people who had evolved in different directions.

Even the fact that William was willing to accept that the band we came back with should basically be the band I had started doing some solo gigs with, plus him, was an illustration of the way things had changed. It obviously made sense to have him coming into a band that already knew each other and were playing together quite tightly, but before we broke up he would've had a problem with them being 'my people', and now he didn't. It helped that one of them was Phil King who William knew and liked, then there was Loz from Ride on drums – William had always liked his drumming so that was OK too – and the only one he didn't know was Mark Crozer. The fact that Mark is still in the band today (at least at the time of writing) shows you that worked out OK.

We didn't really have any idea who we'd be playing for, beyond a vague hope that we'd slipped out of the 'Where are they now?' bin and into the 'Now legendary and yet still alive' category. If someone cared enough to pay us loads of money on the assumption that there were people out there who wanted to see and hear our band play, then that was good enough for us. It felt great to be wanted after all those years in the wilderness.

For a long time after we split up I hadn't really been able to think about the band because it was just too painful, but when I did start to be able to go over what had happened, I began to wonder if maybe we'd split up when it wasn't really necessary. Readers of this book will no doubt have formed their own view on that question, but I felt like maybe if we'd just had the chance to go off and lick our wounds for a bit, then come back and bury the hatchet, we might have found a world that was more kindly disposed towards us. As it was, that's pretty much exactly what did happen, it just took nine years instead of six months, but I was still pleased with the idea of getting a second chance, and if those nine years had given people the chance to appreciate what the Mary Chain were about a bit more, then maybe that time hadn't been wasted.

The Sister Vanilla album *Little Pop Rock* finally came out in early 2007, a couple of months before we played Coachella. It was released on the Scottish indie label Chemikal Underground, which was a nice way of coming full circle. We might not have wanted to stay an indie band in 1984, but that wasn't because we were too big for our boots – we just favoured Marc Bolan's stack heels over whatever was the early-eighties equivalent of macrobiotic Birkenstocks. We had stayed friendly with The Pastels, who were probably our leading contemporaries from that time on the purely indie side of things, and not only does Linda duet with Stephen Pastel on the last song on the album, there's another track where the lyrics describe a car crash caused by being lost in their music, an experience I could certainly relate to.

Both our bands built camps in The Velvet Underground's garden – most of the good bands from the eighties and nineties were the Velvets' bastard children – but time passing gives you a different perspective on the choices you make. I guess whatever course you take, there's always going to be some cause for regret. We signed to a major and suffered for it, while The Pastels retained a reputation for being pillars of moral purity, which in the long run caused them to be almost as misunderstood as we were. I know that all the stuff about anoraks used to drive them mental, but so long as a band has made music that's good enough to stand there and shout at the world to fuck off, then that's all that matters. There's no arguing that The Pastels have done that, and hopefully The Mary Chain have done it too.

iii. Coachella and the Eternal Now

Jim

Before we played Coachella I was getting Lollapalooza flashbacks that we were going to be standing on a stage in front of tens of thousands of people at a massive festival in California and the crowd were going to go: 'Uh, The Mary and Jesus Chain? I don't know who that is – let me go and buy a hotdog.' I was also fucking terrified of the idea of doing my first ever sober Mary Chain gig.

And as if the thought of getting through a ninety-minute comeback set in front of a huge crowd without a drink wasn't daunting enough, I was going to be singing 'Just Like Honey' with Hollywood's own Scarlett Johansson. That was William's idea, as he was Mr Showbiz, and it was a good idea because she was doing a record at the time with a label who were reissuing our back catalogue, so we had a line of communication, and that song had recently featured on the soundtrack of her film *Lost In Translation*.

Of course, when the big day came, every fibre of my being was screaming 'Drink!' 'Drink!' 'Drugs!' 'More Drugs!' But on this occasion, I managed to ignore that siren call. I stood on the stage telling myself not to think about all the things that could possibly go wrong or how desperate I was to get wasted and just try to lock into the gig, and I did and it was OK. Did I enjoy it? I don't know because I was too busy concentrating on getting from one end of the show to the other, but I did appreciate the fact that we had a prime evening slot rather than the graveyard shift in early afternoon, so even though our lights weren't really working at the start of the show because the sun hadn't fully gone down yet, by the end the stage looked amazing.

Scarlett rebooted a 'Just Like Honey' tradition that went back to Bobby's girlfriend Karen singing on the original version. Nowadays when we're out on the festival circuit, we'll always try and find someone on the premises. At Glastonbury in 2023, when Phoebe Bridgers did it, that happened more or less on the day, and it's nice to feel that there are still people coming through who have listened to our music and are happy to be asked to sing it. I'm sure there've been a few people hiding under a table in the dressing room to avoid the call, too, but we're all right with that.

Once I'd found out that it was possible for me to do a show without being falling over drunk I started to enjoy subsequent live performances much more. Obviously I don't look like I'm enjoying it, because that's not really my style, but I have grown to appreciate how much easier it is to understand and correct mistakes when you've not had one over the eight. When you're drunk, your thought processes are very slow, so as you realise a mistake's been made – and whether it's you or someone else who made it doesn't really matter, but let's say someone starts playing a chorus when it should be a verse – you just think 'Oh, a mistake, I wonder if that was me?' And another eight bars have gone past before you can do anything about it. That's when you end up smashing equipment, because it's so frustrating not to be in control of what's going on. But when you're sober you can work out what's happened much quicker and adjust what you're doing to take account of the mistake, often before the audience have even noticed it.

Adjusting my performance settings to new-found sobriety was probably the hardest transition of those early gigs after we reformed. I learnt to shut my eyes and try to forget there was an audience when I could feel my energy dipping, and then before I knew it I'd be back in the room. It took me two or three years to work out what to do with my hands when I wasn't singing, because I just felt so unrelaxed, but maybe it was good that I had something new to think about as it stopped me falling into old routines. I don't know how William managed it!

There was one factory setting I couldn't manage to reset, though, and that was social anxiety. The next year after Coachella we did a South American tour with R.E.M., and on the night Obama got elected in 2008 we were playing in Chile. As usual, things had already been a bit awkward backstage with the two of us sitting in silence staring at the walls, so when we were invited to go and watch the election results come in with Michael Stipe and co, I wanted to because it was such a big moment but I just couldn't do it. Subsequently when people have asked 'Where were you on the night of Obama's victory?', I've always been able to answer, 'Back in my hotel room on my own, when I could've been watching history unfold with one of the biggest and best bands in the world.' I'd only been sober for a few years at that point and the thought of sitting around with all these famous people I didn't know was just too much for me. William had a different set of priorities but they directed him to the same conclusion. We could've watched Barack Obama become America's first black president with the band who sang 'Shiny Happy People', but we were too shy.

William

We weren't quite living the high life that first year after Coachella, but we did make some money. What I should've done was buy property with it, but instead I just thought 'I'm going to be a big shot for a year' and spent the lot on clouds and fluff. I went a bit nuts and leased a Jaguar XJ10. I'm not really a Jag type of guy, but I was newly divorced and living in Hollywood at the time, so I thought 'I'll show these Hollywood people.' It was great for maybe ten minutes, but then I went off it because all these women who weren't my type – surgically enhanced wanna-be actresses looking for a rock 'n' roll sugar daddy – kept trying to get off with me. I know some guys would've just said 'Yeah, OK baby', but if we've got to put everything into little boxes, I

like 'indie girls' not 'rock chicks', and when I had that Jaguar
I was not attracting indie girls, because that's not what they're
looking for.

Fifteen years on and hundreds of thousands of fucking dollars down the drain, I'm not as well off as I should be because
I've now been through two California divorces (which are the
expensive kind, because you have to give your wife of possibly
quite a short period of time half of everything you've ever had,
not just half the money you've made while you were together),
but I had a good time and I've got my memories.

I rented a place in Glendale for so long that houses which
cost three hundred grand when I first moved there in 2012 cost
nearly a million by the time I left. That's why I live in a Bruce
Springsteen song these days, in the desert on the edge of town
near Tucson, Arizona, because I wanted a house that could take
me to the end of my life – with a swimming pool and a studio
and a wee bit of space so my wife can still hear the TV while I'm
making a racket – but without a huge mortgage so I could maybe
pay it off with couple of big tours and a few festivals. I wasn't
the only one who had an idea like that – it's California liberals as
far as the eye can see in Arizona now, since they legalised weed.
That's why the Democrats won it for Biden against Trump in the
2020 presidential election.

Also, I love the dry desert heat where you never really sweat
much, unlike New Orleans or New York in the summer where
your balls are sticking together two minutes after you've left the
house. They should make more of that in the estate agents' bro-
chure – 'You won't have to use talcum powder for the chafing.'
The wildlife is another big asset. I'll look out my window and
see a huge desert wolf walk by. I don't know if it's a coyote or
a wolf but I wouldn't like to fight one. I feed them, that's why
they come around – I throw out things like apple cores and old
eggs and every now and then I'll chuck them a horrible wee
steak thing. I don't like to touch the steak – it's disgusting – so

I'll have to wash my hands for about ten minutes after, but the desert wolves are ungrateful bastards. They don't come by after to thank me saying 'I know you don't like to touch the steak, but you did it for me and my kids.'

I still love Britain – I love it so much that I've lived in America for twenty-two years. I was just on a green card for ages at first and it seemed like that was solid until Donald Trump and Stephen Miller came along with their hatred of all foreign people and anyone that travels. I thought 'Oh fuck, they're gonna kick me out.' As a rule you don't see ICE rounding up white guys in rock bands, but I'd got arrested in 2012 for disorderly conduct and when they said 'Not only are we gonna get rid of illegal immigrants, we're gonna get rid of green card holders who have had an arrest', I knew I'd have to do the Patriot test. I passed with flying colours and I could probably still pass the British one as well because I still know what happened in 1066. As shit as it was at the time, the way things went afterwards suggests that Jim and I probably had the best education that was ever available in Britain without paying for it.

It is strange watching historic events unfold from across the Atlantic in what I call 'Brireland', which is Britain and Ireland together (because Bernadette is Irish and when I mention something being the case in Britain she'll often say 'that happens in Ireland too' – although I didn't make that phrase up myself and I do recognise that there are pubs in Dublin, and Glasgow come to that, where this coinage would not be acceptable). Like the queen dying, for instance – obviously she'd been there for all mine and Jim's lives, but I think the way the monarchy was in Britain probably needed to die with her. It would be better if we adopted something more like what they have in Sweden or Holland – 'OK, you can still be monarch, because you had relatives in the Middle Ages who killed everyone else to gain their fortune, but let's do this on a smaller scale.' It's basically like the Kray twins had kids, and then their kids had kids, and then eight centuries later they own half the country, but if anyone asks how that happened they just say 'Oh that was all so long ago.'

Jim

From the moment we got back together, it wasn't just about getting back together to play the greatest hits set, we knew there was more music to make and it was always about making a new album. It was nice not to have the Armani suit guys breathing down our neck any more, but the release of that pressure combined with me living in England and William being in LA to make that process a long haul. We had to be careful not to push anything too hard – this also applied to our touring schedule – because we aware of how deep the fault lines between us still were. I guess it was like a divorced couple going on holiday together – maybe start with a week and don't book the full fortnight until you know you can do it. Also at times where one of us was trying to be sober and the other one wasn't, it was important to leave plenty of breathing space.

William

One reason everything takes us so long is that The Jesus and Mary Chain is a band with two songwriters. That's why it took a full decade from Coachella to the point where *Damage and Joy* finally came out. Because I write so many more songs than Jim does I find that very frustrating, but it is what it is and I'm reconciled to it now.

Jim

The technology might have changed but the process of recording *Damage and Joy* – which in the end we did with Youth from Killing Joke – was pretty similar to what it always had been. It was just me and William stuck in a windowless room trying to make sense together of these songs that we had written individually. I'd got no more self-assurance about what we were doing than I'd had the first time we went in a studio thirty years before.

It feels like everything's up for grabs and you're not sure if it's going well – one minute you're thinking it's great and five minutes later it's shite, then another five minutes on it's not bad again. The shite-ometer was fluctuating wildly on that album, but by the time we got to mixing, it was like the shite-ometer had finally exploded and I started to feel confident that we were pulling it off. And 'All Things Pass' is just one of several songs from that album which people tend to think are lost hits from our golden era – whatever that was – when we play them in the live set now.

William

You never know which are the records which are going to stay with people. I always thought *Darklands* would be the one for us, but when we played it in full on the anniversary tour, nobody seemed that bothered, where *Munki* and *Stoned & Dethroned* – which are two of my favourites that nobody was that into when they first came out – seem to be having a moment now.

Jim

One old favourite who couldn't be written out of our story was Alan McGee. We decided the time was right for a third entanglement with him in 2014. I'd always found it easy to be pals with him, though there was an undercurrent of tension between him and William which maybe got a little stronger with time, and some of the things Alan had said in his book didn't help.

William

'Chalk and cheese' would be one phrase you could use about me and Alan. Jim thinks maybe he was a bit frightened of me, and yes, Alan was someone who could often shout at people and dominate them and he could never do that with me – not at all, he just couldn't. But I thought we were friendly enough, until my wife Bernadette saw this documentary where Alan was saying I was a dislikeable person, and I just thought 'Why the fuck would he say that?' So when he became our manager again about a year or so later I asked him 'What was that all about?' And he said 'Oh, that was just for the cameras – I was talking shite.' I can't ever imagine a situation in which I would back down like that.

Jim

I've thought about this a lot and the conclusion I've come to is that 'Alan' is the person and 'McGee' is the character, and I kind of get that. He's created this cartoon superhero in his own mind which is the one he wants everyone to talk about and I'm not sure he knows any more where that fantasy self ends and the real Alan begins.

William

Drinking alone started in my thirties and I wish I could stop it. I had a bit of a crash in 2016 – I was just all over the place, mentally, and going through a pretty horrible time in my head. I think a lot of people say they're suicidal without maybe really knowing what it means to take yourself off the planet. Even when I've felt lower than dirt and that urge has been there, it's still a small thing which I hope I'm not ever going to explore. I think what happens is people get a little urge and they explore it and then it gets bigger and bigger, and they might end up killing themselves over a problem they could actually have solved. Like with Kurt Cobain, I don't know what his problem was but it looks like he couldn't handle fame, but with all the money he made couldn't he just have sat on a private island and played his guitar – were there not other options?

I hear about artists or writers or musicians who create things when they're depressed and I think 'Well, I must have a different kind of depression to them', because when I'm depressed I can do nothing, never mind pick up a guitar and a pen and paper and write a little tune – that's what I do when I'm happy. Melancholy and depression are different things – with the first, you might feel miserable and a bit shit but you're still above ground. With the second, you're fully down there under the surface. To me depression is like a full shutting down – sometimes you feel like that for a few days or even a few weeks, but a true depression is when you can't see any possibility of a way out.

At that time of crisis in my life I will tell you Jim was there for me. I knew he would be, but when it happened it was just amazing to see him showing an interest, because Jim shows an interest in nothing. He's the most blasé, 'Don't give a fuck' guy in

277

Never Understood

the world, but he's also got the most beautiful heart – he really has. You should see him with his children, he's just amazing. Everybody thinks he's a dark character but inside he's not, he's this beautiful character of light.

We're very close but we're not really guys that sit and talk about our feelings. Sometimes we do, but it doesn't get too deep and we kind of like it like that – we're more comfortable talking about music or films or books, and it's been like that with us our whole lives. But me and Jim do talk about each other's current mental state and we do worry for each other because we know how bad things can get. I've seen him at his lowest and he's seen me at my lowest and I don't want to see him feeling pain all the time and I think he feels that for me too.

I would say that with Jim's help – and Bernadette's, and David McBride's (he's the new manager we took on after the inevitable third parting of the ways with Alan) – I haven't been properly depressed for four or five years now. And I'm hoping I never get depressed again. That's one reason we managed to get our most recent album, *Glasgow Eyes,* finished and released in slightly better time than the previous one, despite a few arguments and an engineer losing all the recordings so we had to start again along the way. If we can carry on picking up speed at this rate, the next record will be done in three and a half years instead of six, but don't hold your breath.

A couple of months before *Damage and Joy* was released in 2017, the *NME* asked me and Jim to come and pick up a prize at their Brat Awards. We asked what it was for. 'Oh, we can't tell you till you get there.' But surely 'What is the award for?' is a perfectly reasonable question. 'Oh we can't tell you until you turn up' – can you imagine them saying that to any other band? I thought it was suspicious the way they wouldn't tell us. What was it – 'Dopes of the century' or 'The world's biggest idiots'? If it was 'Heroes', surely they could have given us a hint?

Luckily, we could survive without an *NME* award – we'd

managed pretty well up to then – because the whole thing just seemed weird. And then my suspicions were confirmed (or someone at the *NME* took their revenge for us snubbing their awards, depending on which way you look at it) when our album came out – the first new one we'd released for nineteen years – and they wouldn't even review it. I'm not talking about a bad review, I'm talking about no review, for a band that had been on their cover any number of times. That could only be down to either professional incompetence or a personal vendetta.

Jim still did an interview with them and the guy phoned him from a pub so there was too much background noise to hear what he was saying, then halfway through the interview he said he had to leave. Doesn't that sound like an insult to you? I said 'Did you tell him to go fuck himself?' And Jim was like 'No, why would I do that? We need to do interviews otherwise no one will know we have a new record.' And I suppose that's fair enough, but I personally will never talk to those cunts again. Most music journalists are incredibly pretentious and needy anyway – they're like groupies, only the transaction has less dignity.

When I've mentioned to people in my life that there is an aspect of having a little bit of fame that I don't like, their response tends to be 'But you're not famous.' Fair enough, I'm not John Lennon, but once you enter into that universe of someone that you've never met in another town knows you, then to me that's fame basically – if you're in Canada and you're trying to pump gas into your car and your hands are freezing and someone comes up to you and says 'Hey, William, you do it this way.'

What I've realised about the higher level of fame is that the people who get it want it a lot. A little baby was born called David Jones and all it wanted was for somebody to shine a torch on it and when it was one week old it was trying to shout 'Hi everyone, I'm David Bowie . . .' And then thinking 'Hang on, that hasn't worked, I'll try a new image.' He was always going

'Look at me! Look at me!' Whereas me and Jim were always going 'Look over there.' That's the kind of fame we want, and are lucky enough to have . . .

Jim

When I meet people who class me as some sort of celebrity, I can sense their disappointment at my cheery greeting of 'Oh, right – did you see *Midsomer Murders* the other night, pal?' As they look me up and down I know they're thinking 'Fuck me, this is not how it's supposed to be', because I've felt exactly the same thing when I've met people who did things that I admired. The fact that you're lucky enough to make music for a living doesn't make you special, and I don't have that need to hang out with the kind of people who would fan the flames of the vain hope that it might do.

This is what makes the life we have now my ideal rock 'n' roll existence. I know music is very important to people, because it's very important to me, and the fact that we can play songs we wrote forty years ago to audiences in Brighton or Tokyo and they'll mean something to people our age, but for some reason – probably to do with TikTok – there will be loads of teenagers there who are into it as well, completely blows my mind. Knowing that the pain of dealing with Warners for all those years helped facilitate this happy state of affairs even softens up some of those scars slightly, and being able to zip off to Portugal for a couple of days to be adored at a festival and then zip back to south Devon reality and buy a tin of beans in a Tesco Express where nobody knows who the fuck I am totally suits me.

Touring when the band started was rather gruelling – it was big ten-week slogs sleeping on buses that the 25-year-old off-my-tits-on-cocaine-and-booze version of me found strangely unenjoyable. This new weekend festival version seems like a much more civilised way to do what we do and I wish I could send my younger self a message to say that this was how things were going to turn out, as it would really have taken the pressure off.

If you compare the happy crowds in the photos our drummer Justin takes at the end of every show we do these days with the footage of the North London Poly or Electric Ballroom situations, something's definitely changed for the better. The painful levels of self-consciousness which are evident in my youthful filmed inter-views have definitely eased off a bit. And the funny thing about this happy ending is that it's not something anyone would have predicted, except maybe me and William, because we understood ourselves, even if nobody else did.

William

It's great that we can still draw a crowd, but I don't think it's really a happy ending until we can make more new records that fully re-establish us. I tell you what I want to do one day – just forget The Jesus and Mary Chain and go and stay on a nice island with a nice recording studio with air conditioning and just sit there all stoned and beautiful and make records. Jim has got a very distinctive vocal style, so of course I will fly him out there to sing on them, and not just at Musicians' Union session rates either – I'll give him extra for being family.

Picture Credits

All images belong to William Reid and/or Jim Reid, except for the following which belong to:

Stuart Cassidy: plate 6 (*bottom right*); plate 8 (*bottom right*)
Linda Fox: plate 6 (*bottom left*)
Rona McIntosh: plate 15 (*bottom*)
Bernadette Reid: plate 16

Acknowledgements

William:

Thanks to my wife, Bernadette, for her infinite love and patience, and to my wee sister, Linda, and the rest of my family for a lifetime of adventures.

Thanks to David McBride and Ben Thompson for making the book happen.

And thanks to everyone else I know for being in my life – you know who you are.

Jim:

The drink and drugs is the old Jim – these days I spend my time walking around the cliff-tops of Devon with my partner, Rachel Conti, without whom I'm not sure where I'd be . . .

Ben:

Thanks first (because this is the positioning she insisted on) to the light of my life, Vicki Duffey, for telling me to get off my arse and do some real work for once when everyone else was being very patient about how late this book was getting. Thanks also to William Reid and Jim Reid for being a joy to collaborate with; to David McBride for being the most helpful band or artist manager I have ever experienced and for making the considerable mental effort needed to get his head round the arcane analogue complexities of the proofing process; to Lee Brackstone for picking

Acknowledgements

me for the job in the first place and keeping the faith when the going got tough; to Keith Cameron for not pulling Caledonian rank in the course of a deft and gracious copy edit; to the White Rabbit/Orion Books A-team of Georgia Goodall, Sophie Nevrkla, Natalie Dawkins and Tom Noble for being entirely on the ball; to Kasimiira Kontio for managing the media scrum in a much less obtrusive manner than Wayne Barnes would; to Lesley Thorne for injecting a note of realism into the production schedule; to Richard King and Wesley Stace for being quick and meticulous first readers; to Jon Savage, Sean O'Hagan and Matt Thorne for being supportive shadows in the gloaming; to Steve Underwood of the excellent Pressing Matters record shop in Hastings for picking me up those hard to find *Munki* singles at competitive prices; and, last but not least, to Bernadette Reid for her sterling work as a volunteer picture editor, as well as tireless chronology checking and unravelling of gnomic utterance, in which last endeavour she supplied my favourite editorial note: 'I don't understand why William would have said this . . . Is it possible he and Jim had just had an argument?'

Credits

White Rabbit would like to thank everyone who worked on the publication of *Never Understood*.

Agent
David McBride
Lesley Thorne

Editor
Lee Brackstone

Copy-editor
Keith Cameron

Proofreader
Seán Costello

Editorial Management
Georgia Goodall
Sophie Nevrkla
Jane Hughes
Charlie Panayiotou
Lucy Bilton
Claire Boyle

Audio
Paul Stark
Louise Richardson
Georgina Cutler

Contracts
Dan Herron
Ellie Bowker
Oliver Chacón

Design
Nick Shah
Liam Relph
Joanna Ridley
Helen Ewing

Photo Shoots & Image Research
Natalie Dawkins

Finance
Nick Gibson
Jasdip Nandra
Sue Baker
Tom Costello

Inventory
Jo Jacobs
Dan Stevens

Production
Sarah Cook
Katie Horrocks

Marketing
Tom Noble

Publicity
Kasimiira Kontio
Aoife Datta

Sales
Catherine Worsley
Victoria Laws
Esther Waters
Tolu Ayo-Ajala
Group Sales teams across
    Digital, Field, International
    and Non-Trade

Operations
Group Sales Operations team

Rights
Rebecca Folland
Tara Hiatt
Ben Fowler
Alice Cottrell
Ruth Blakemore
Marie Henckel